Princess in the Land of Snows

D0725636

Princess in the Land of Snows

The Life of Jamyang Sakya in Tibet

Jamyang Sakya & Julie Emery

Foreword by the Dalai Lama
Introduction by B. Alan Wallace

SHAMBHALA
Boston & Shaftesbury
1990

Shambhala Publications, Inc.
Horticultural Hall
300 Massachusetts Avenue
Boston, Massachusetts 02115

Shambhala Publications, Inc.
The Old School House
The Courtyard, Bell Street
Shaftesbury, Dorset SP7 8BP

© 1990 by Jamyang Sakya and Julie Emery

9 8 7 6 5 4 3 2 1
First Edition

Printed in the United States of America on acid-free paper

Distributed in the United States by Random House
and in Canada by Random House of Canada Ltd.
Distributed in the United Kingdom by Element Books Ltd.

Library of Congress Cataloging-in-Publication Data

Sakya, Jamyang, 1934–
Princess in the land of snows: the life of Jamyang Sakya in Tibet/
Jamyang Sakya and Julie Emery.—1st ed. p.   cm.
ISBN 0-87773-521-2 (alk. paper)
1. Sakya, Jamyang, 1934–   . 2. Buddhists—China—Tibet—
Biography. 3. Priests, Buddhist—China—Tibet—Wives—Biography.
I. Emery, Julie. II. Title.
B984.A482A3   1990   951'.505'092—dc20 [B]   89-43320   CIP

This book is dedicated to my five sons with love and the hope that it will keep alive the memory of their heritage.

Contents

Foreword by the Dalai Lama   ix

Acknowledgments   xi

Introduction by B. Alan Wallace   xiii

  1   Growing up a Khampa   1

  2   Family Bonds   16

  3   Time for Dancing   28

  4   The Pilgrimage   43

  5   Romance and Strife   64

  6   The Wedding   89

  7   Palace Life   98

  8   On to Kham   122

  9   Home to Thalung   147

 10   Nomads and Monasteries   159

 11   Confronting the Chinese   178

 12   Peril on the Road   202

 13   Homecoming and Decision   224

 14   Lhasa Politics and Revolt   248

 15   Flight to Freedom   283

 16   Life in India   316

 17   Path to the West   335

Epilogue   347

Foreword

I am pleased to learn that Jamyang Sakya (Dagmo of Sakya Phuntsok Phodrang) has written her life story. This will certainly help in providing more information on Tibet and Tibetan Buddhism, especially the Sakya tradition, to interested people.

Tenzin Gyatso
The Fourteenth Dalai Lama
28 November 1988

Acknowledgments

The authors are deeply grateful to those who urged that this biography be written to help preserve a unique Himalayan culture in light of the near destruction of Tibetan civilization by the People's Republic of China.

We are greatly indebted to our families and others who encouraged and supported us in chronicling this multi-faceted portrait. Two prominent lamas enhanced our memories of factual events—Dagchen Rinpoche, husband of Jamyang Sakya, and the late Dezhung Rinpoche, her uncle.

We owe gratitude to the late Professor Turrell V. Wylie, who brought the Sakya family to Seattle under a Rockefeller Foundation grant to the University of Washington, and to Hugh E. Richardson, author and scholar.

We are immensely appreciative of the late Edna Georgeson, tutor to Jamyang Sakya and mentor to both authors.

Our warmest thanks go to Ani Kunga Zangmo, whose technical skills in this literary production greatly eased our burdens. Her willingness to share her knowledge on a variety of topics inspired both writers.

*   *   *

This biography is written primarily for Western readers. Therefore we have not identified the high-ranking lamas and those in the Tibetan nobility with their formal titles. Please accept our apologies.

Introduction

This autobiographical account of Lady Jamyang of Tibet exudes a charm and endearing quality that its author embodies in everyday life. Lady Jamyang, known to her friends as "Dagmo-la," begins her story by describing her childhood in eastern Tibet. Raised in a loving family of moderate affluence, she enjoyed frequent contact with monks and nuns, and her way of life and education were pervaded by the spirit of Buddhism. Her childhood was one of good cheer, of innocence and—by Western standards—of naiveté. In a society in which most education was of a religious nature, available chiefly to monks, she had the unusual good fortune to receive a fine education from an early age. From her childhood account we witness the vivacious and at times mischievous qualities that have remained with her to the present.

Jamyang's childhood came to a swift end. As a very young woman she went on pilgrimage from Kham, her homeland, to Sakya, the headquarters of one of the four major orders of Tibetan Buddhism. In her account of her pilgrimage she vividly describes the awesome beauty of the rugged, mountainous land of Tibet and the profound piety of the people who made it their home. In Sakya she is introduced to the politics of the Sakya ecclesiastical hierarchy, and she finds herself eagerly courted by a young religious nobleman of the Phuntsok Palace who was being prepared to become the Head Lama of the Sakya Order. Their romance led to Jamyang's engagement to the dashing young Jigdal Rinpoche. With her marriage she accepted the heavy burden of entering the ranks of Tibetan nobility and of representing the ancient tradition of this spiritual lineage.

While the young Lady Jamyang accustomed herself to her new way of life and to the political intrigues of the two ruling houses of the Sakya tradition, the freedom of the Tibetan people began to be eroded by the infiltration of Chinese Communists into eastern Tibet. Thus, when she visited Kham with her husband not long after their marriage, her delight at returning to her homeland was tinged with anxiety at the threatening changes she saw taking place. For some time, however, the native population was allowed to continue in its traditional ways, and Lady Jamyang enjoyed a colorful life meeting high lamas, visiting monasteries and continuing her own studies. But before long, open hostilities between the communists and the Tibetans became more prevalent, and the Chinese responded with increased oppression and flagrant disrespect for the native culture.

As the traditional ways of the Tibetans were broken up, moral decay became increasingly evident among the native population. The communists displayed great ingenuity at manipulating the Tibetans, making them more and more dependent upon Chinese transportation, food, lodging, and medicine. Using scare tactics and rewards, the communists skillfully created schisms among the Tibetans. While offering valuable services to the Tibetans, these invariably came with provisos designed to undermine their way of life. The carefree days of Jamyang's youth had now vanished.

Upon returning to Central Tibet, Lady Jamyang witnessed the severe oppression, deceit, and manipulation the communists perpetrated upon her people. As violence erupted in Lhasa, where she and her family were visiting, they were forced to flee for their lives. Optimistic, like many other Tibetans, that they would return home once hostilities had subsided, they fled south, but as they received reports of the growing violence in the Tibetan capital, these hopes vanished. Their only wish now was to escape from the unbearable oppression of the communist invaders of their homeland. Enduring extreme hardship and fear in their flight from Tibet, her family frequently relied on prayer for their safety and looked to divinations and omens to guide them to freedom.

Once uprooted from her beloved homeland, Lady Jamyang's relief at the safety of her family was sobered with her awareness of the continuing plight of her loved ones, her mother and many other relatives, and the loss of much that she held dear. Yet even in such dire circumstances her family displayed a resilience and courage common among the Tibetan refugees. With an abiding faith in the Buddha, they opened themselves in trust to an unknown future which presented itself in an offer to Jigdal Rinpoche to come to the United States to collaborate in research at the University of Washington. Jamyang's narration ends with her emigration to the quasi-mythical land of America.

During the years since their arrival in the United States, the author and her husband, widely known as H. H. Dagchen Rinpoche, have established a thriving Tibetan cultural center and a monastery in Seattle, Washington. In the meantime, Lady Jamyang has quietly devoted herself inwardly to her spiritual practice under the guidance of her revered uncle, the late Venerable Dezhung Rinpoche. Outwardly she has selflessly devoted herself to bringing up her five sons and assisting her husband in his many religious activities.

It was my delight and privilege to meet Lady Jamyang in the spring of 1982, while I was serving as interpreter for a Tibetan lama who had been invited to lecture at the Sakya Cultural Center in Seattle. I was immediately struck by her graciousness in the role of hostess and by her cheerful, unassuming purity as a human being. Clearly here was someone who had experienced the depths of Buddhist practice and set a heart-warming example for others seeking an integration of spiritual and worldly life. Several years later, I learned that the Venerable Dezhung Rinpoche had encouraged Jamyang to begin teaching Buddhism and granting initiations. She had been authorized to accept the role of lama by one of the foremost Tibetan Buddhist masters of the Sakya Order. Since then, I have come to look upon her as one of my most cherished spiritual mentors. Like many other western Buddhists, I continue to seek a balance and integration of contemplative and active life—of meditation and service—and Dagmo-la's guidance and example have been invaluable. I hope that many readers will enjoy this account of her early life and that an increasing number of spiritual seekers will take advantage of her qualities as a guide on the path.

B. Alan Wallace

Princess in the Land of Snows

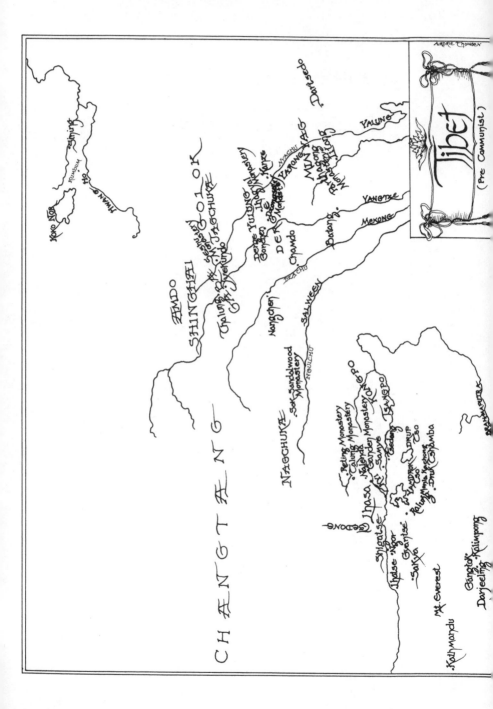

AIRDRIE THOMSEN

Tibet
(Pre Communist)

1

Growing up a Khampa

Our monk-teacher, Tenzin, gave us reading assignments and then stepped outside the classroom to his quarters across the hall of Thalung Monastery. We children sat cross-legged, facing one another on two long rugs, but out of each others' reach. We read from our block-printed loose-leaf religious books and then chanted the memorizations at the tops of our voices. Uncannily, Tenzin always knew if one of us had stopped reciting, immediately sensing a missing voice, even though we were out of his sight.

Tenzin, about thirty, was a distant relative. Slim and of average height, he wore an ankle-length maroon wool robe. His head was shaved, as were those of his fellow monks. Their hair was cut when it was longer than the thickness of one's finger. Taking his teaching duties seriously, Tenzin seldom smiled in class. But he was an inspiring teacher, and our attention was riveted upon his words. We minded him and respected him as a scholar who had spent years in the disciplined religious life. In Tibet there is a saying that parents must be respected because they give precious human life and teachers because they are the source of knowledge, imparting sacred words to their students.

1

Religion was inseparable from much of our daily life and central to our formal learning. The books we read at school were the scriptures of Buddhism translated from the original Sanskrit, many containing the words of the Buddha. We studied from the five volumes of the *Monlam*, the prayer books of mahāyāna Buddhism. Some of the memorizations we chanted were in Sanskrit. These incantations were not translated from Sanskrit, the language used by the Buddha, because that was how he and his followers spoke. Once I learned to recite a passage of about one hundred words of Sanskrit, without any knowledge of the meaning. But the sentiment and reverence attached to the incantations were clearly understood and accepted as beneficial to all other sentient beings. Perfect accuracy was required or the blessings would not be granted by the deities, and no benefit would result from our efforts. Learning to write came much later in my education.

The books were loose-leafed volumes that rested on small, low tables and sometimes on small folding stools. When not in use, each one was wrapped in bright-colored cloth and tied with a light cloth strap. Books were never placed on the floor, but if by accident one fell there, I quickly would bring it gently to the top of my head in a gesture of respect.

We looked up at wall hangings, known as *tankas*, which contained detailed paintings of the Buddha and Buddhist deities, framed in colorful brocades. One wall contained books stored on carved wooden shelves. Large butter lamps in metal pots burned constantly. A brazier, fueled by charcoal, stood in the center of the room. There was little dozing in class, as the large room was never too warm. When chanting, I often kept my hands inside the sleeves of my ankle-length *chuba* (the belted, wraparound garment worn by both men and women in my country), which had a lambskin lining. We children wore boots called *lham*, with leather soles and woolen tops to the knee. They were held up below the knee with long woven ties, the color of which identified the wearer as a monk, nun, or layperson. Traditionally, neither children nor adults wore garments with holes or that were ragged. Tibetan psychology dictates that food and clothing are important, reflecting upon the family and individual merit.

The boy who sat next to me was a mischief-maker who sometimes pulled my hair when Tenzin wasn't around, but I never tried to repel him. I wore my hair in as many as thirty small, long braids, brought together at the end with three red tassels. Marrow from musk-deer bone made my black hair look shinier, a goal of all women and girls in my culture.

It was important for women and girls to have strong hair, as they wore jewels in it—in our case both sewn and tied in. Beautiful hair was the background for these varied gems, which were always genuine and had cultural meaning, such as one's marital status. As a schoolgirl, I wore amber, coral, and turquoise in the style of someone single. Except in times of mourning, it was considered bad luck to go without one's hair ornaments.

My hair had not always been pretty. When I was younger, I had brown, rather than the more desirable black locks. My uncle, Dezhung Rinpoche, whom I called Uncle Tülku-la, had teasingly called me "Rango," meaning "blonde head," a name I detested. When I was six, a lama, Nawang Legpa Rinpoche, head of Thalung Monastery, had snipped off a bit of my hair and placed it on an altar as an offering to the Buddha for long life and good health for me. This snipping ritual was common procedure for many Tibetan children, and some also received a special name at that time. This particular ceremony was especially significant for me because Nawang Legpa Rinpoche was a very holy lama who was a reincarnation of Mañjushrī, the Bodhisattva of Wisdom. After the lock of hair was snipped off, my head was shaved so that healthier hair would grow in. When it did, I reminded Uncle Tülku-la that he no longer could call me "Rango"—but sometimes he did, lovingly.

Classes were held from about eight o'clock to noon, seven days a week. Exceptions were the first two weeks of the New Year and on various festival days at the monastery. Although the boys went to classes in summer, I did not, because that was when I went with my family into the lush pastures of the upper valleys several miles from Thalung where our yaks grazed.

Our first chore upon arriving at school was to clean, polish, and fill with water the one hundred brass cups used as offerings in Tenzin's chapel. This polishing, done with a soft white handwoven wool cloth, warmed our hands on chilly days and was our "good deed." When dismissed from classes, we would empty the bowls, sometimes drinking part of the water from our cupped hands. Sometimes the water had frozen, which afforded us the delightful opportunity of eating ice. At other times it was poured on windowsill flower beds or put to some useful purpose, never merely thrown out where it would be stepped on, as it was considered blessed water. The brass cups then were returned to a windowsill outside Tenzin's quarters, placed upside down in a line.

My Great-Uncle Nawang Nyima had taught me this ritual of the brass cups, which I performed better than the boys. The bowls must not be too full. When pouring reverently into the bowls, we had to keep both hands on the copper offering pitcher and could not touch each other. At home we had twenty-one such bowls, which were filled each morning with fresh water from the Tha River.

We students treated Tenzin with great respect as he conducted the lessons, often walking between the two rugs on which we sat. When Tenzin's servant served us butter tea at mid-morning, we clasped the handleless wooden cups to keep the chill from our fingers. The tea was strong, nourishing, and very welcome. It refreshed our minds and was our morning recess.

Tenzin was not liberal in his praise of any of us. "You can do better," he would implore. When Tenzin pinched the boys for misbehaving, or used his switch lightly, I too sometimes shed a tear. He also pulled the boys' ears when they had not prepared for their lessons. Although strict, he seldom reprimanded me, his lone girl student. On special occasions, Tenzin gave us gifts of sweet rice, dried fruits, and dried yak meat. A piece of candy or other sweet was rare and, when I got one for superior classwork, I ran home thrilled. Once when I memorized five lengthy pages of the *Tungshag*, one of the prayer books of mahāyāna Buddhism, he was surprised. That day I went home with my pocket filled with dried fruits and cookies. Nonetheless, two days later I could not repeat my performance.

For relaxation at school we played *lhomo*, a game using sheep knucklebones in a manner similar to the Western game of jacks. But for sheer joy, nothing could surpass jumping in the hay stored near our classroom. This area of the monastery was a repository for the grain, hay, and other products with which many families paid their taxes. I learned to jump as far as the boys—at least twelve to fifteen feet. My mother repeatedly warned me about getting my clothes dirty during these hay-jumping sessions. Consequently, I wanted to wear old clothes to school but was overruled. "You must be well-dressed and clean when you go to the monastery," she admonished.

After school was dismissed, I would walk slowly about a block and a half to the monastery gate. There was a small stream that I crossed, jumping from rock to rock. It was a rule that no one could run or shout inside any monastery. If someone greeted you from a distance, you simply would wave and give a "ssshhh" in acknowledgment. If I happened to see one of the two monk leaders who kept order in the monastery, I would avoid them. Each carried a large whip that was made of a strip of knotted leather. The whip handles were of wood decorated with silver. Although I didn't fear these high monks, by custom I kept my distance. If by chance we came near each other, I kept my head down as a gesture of respect to them and to the monastery.

For this block and a half I was bareheaded, even though it might be snowing, as it was not permissible for laypeople to wear hats inside the monastery. Then, when I had reached the gate, I put on my warm fox-fur-trimmed hat. There I often was joined by some of the regular monks who received religious instruction in the main monastery school. Most of them lived in Thalung. As we made our way, we skipped, jumped, and sang merrily, cutting loose after hours of class-work. I did just what the boys did. If I spotted a girl friend from Thalung, she would not join me until I had left my young male companions. Often these girls and my family members said I acted like a tomboy. But I didn't consider my position unusual, and I never felt guilty about being a girl, as some of my friends did. Besides, it was less confining and more fun being with the boys.

Ours was the best private school in Thalung, but it was separate from the strict section of the monastery where the regular boy monks were instructed. My classmates were eight boys from well-to-do families, ranging in age from seven to eleven. Some planned eventually to work for the government. Some wanted specialized instruction and later would go into the religious life. Some were already wearing monk's garb. In Thalung, a town of some thirty-five families, I was the only girl to attend school. No other girl chose to go. Indeed, it was through my Uncle Tülku-la—Dezhung Rinpoche—my moth-er's eldest brother and titular head of our family, that I was afforded the privilege of formal education. A high lama with the title of *tülku*—or reincarnation—he then was head of one of the two labrangs, or lama's residences, at Thalung Monas-tery. While away several years at a monastery in Minyag, to the southeast, he wrote that I was to be sent to Tenzin's classes.

I was then eight. My classmates had started at age six, two years ahead of me. But I soon caught up scholastically and was a bright student. I had already learned the thirty letters of the alphabet from my Great-Uncle Nawang Nyima. How-ever, I felt the keen competition of the boys. One row of the class was reserved for the brighter students, but being a girl, I never could have sat there. Nevertheless, it was not long before I was proud to be in school. Sometimes the boys were jealous when I chanted my recitations. "We don't like the girl's voice too loud," they remarked. And if I made a mistake, most of the time they would catch me and tease me for days. But I never corrected them.

Not everyone thought extending education to a Thalung girl was a good idea. Some of the older monks remarked that I got into the classroom because of my uncle Tülku-la's influence and position. Puzzled, they would ask, "Why are you here going to school? Are you going to be a nun?" or "How are you going to use a boy's education?" Embarrassing as these questions were, I usually replied vaguely that my family wanted me to learn and let it go at that. There was resentment, too, because of the access I had to the monastery, taking my girl friends there to visit my uncles, who sometimes were very busy with other monastery officials.

These girl friends thought me an unlucky child, burdened by both the studies customarily reserved for boys as well as the chores of girls, leaving me little time for play. But my mother insisted that I learn household work, dairying, and field tasks. After school and later in my girlhood, many days I went home to spin my quota of yarn, often working with my grandmother. My mother also saw to it that I had errands and chores in the fields. There seemed to be few idle moments. Mother stressed that I might not use all this knowledge, but on occasion I might need to instruct servants and others. There were no written procedures for any of the work of cooking, sewing, weaving, or outdoor chores, and so one learned by direct instruction from another person or by simply observing. Thus from early childhood I had a wealth of practical experience.

I enjoyed learning these tasks. Especially during my first year of school, I would have preferred to be out in the fields with the other girls, since at times the customary attitude that girls were inferior brought unpleasantness to my life at school. When treats were passed out, for example, the boys gave me small portions or leftovers because I sat at the end of one row—and I was a girl. If the monastery received gifts of food or money for a special religious occasion, they were shared with the little boy monks in our class. But I was not included.

Often I had to stand by and watch as they ate and drank in my presence. Now and then there were taunts of how wonderful it was to be a boy. Sometimes I almost cried as they devoured rice, raisins, and other delicacies. On rare occasions they gave me a taste, or, if Tenzin were present, he would share his portion with me.

My Great-Uncle Nawang comforted me when I arrived home, saying it was better not to be included in these gifts. Sometimes when I did receive a portion, he reminded me that I must say special prayers, since the gifts were presented to the monks with the understanding that prayers would be said on behalf of the donor or for his family, or sometimes for the ailing or deceased. This explanation comforted me greatly.

Always Great-Uncle Nawang was my savior, praising me in front of visitors. He said I was precious—one who had brought happiness and good luck to the family. He saw my special respect and love of older people and warmed to this. He somehow foresaw that I would have an eventful life. He gave me love, encouragement, and protection. "You're not going to be like other Thalung girls," he said. "You're going to be something special—not like any other housewife." This led me to wonder what I would be in the future. I knew I didn't want to be a nun. I loved to wear jewels and planned to spend my life with my friends in Thalung.

Often I was on his lap, telling him my night dreams, which he interpreted. He listened very carefully and sometimes took notes. Several times I dreamed that I was flying through the sky in a small house with wings. I had never seen airplanes, and believed, like my classmates, that the world was flat, according to the traditional descriptions. My world was bordered by Dartsedo to the east, India to the southwest, and Nepal to the west. In my dreams, I would meet many strange new people in big cities with tall buildings—things I never thought existed. Years later, my airplane trips and international travel seemed to make these dreams reality. Sometimes, Great-Uncle Nawang would interpret my dreams negatively and urge me to recite certain mantras. He also said prayers, not always for me, but for others in my dream.

When anyone suggested that Great-Uncle Nawang might die before I was married, I was terribly distressed. My solution was that I would hold him tight. That way I was positive that he would not get away. I recognized his unique spiritual powers, especially his gift of prophecy. When he made a prediction, it would all come true. Never did he lose his temper or scold in my presence. I followed his advice, keeping his words fresh in my mind.

Although my formal schooling at the monastery ended after four years, my informal education in a world of adults was one that no other girl in Thalung could dream of. Great-Uncle Nawang taught me much in the way of literature and religion. We spent many happy hours singing from *The Hundred Thousand Songs of Milarepa*, a classic work of Tibet's greatest poet, who was also a hermit and ascetic. The work was Great-Uncle Nawang's favorite.

There was about a mile between our house in the town of Thalung and the monastery, home to about three hundred monks of the Sakya religious group, one of the so-called Red Hat schools of Buddhism in my country. Thalung Monastery was a very strict one, which set the pace of life for our town. We lived under the five basic precepts of Buddhism: not to take life, steal, tell untruths, engage in illicit sexual practices, or use intoxicants or narcotics. The rules of dress for monks and others were rigidly observed. No offensive smells, such as burning leather or bones, were permitted in the vicinity of the monastery. Such offensive odors would anger our mountain deities, bringing hail on the crops or disease to the town. Thalung residents were very respectful of this religious atmosphere. But visitors from nearby Tindu and Zindah, where some of our relatives lived, found our way of life too binding. I knew no other and was blissfully happy.

On the way to the monastery each morning, the pleasant sight of the red-painted main temples greeted me, along with

the cheery red, white, and blue vertical stripes on the labrangs, or monks' residences. These distinctive stripes identified the structures for miles as being Sakya buildings. The
three colors represent three auspicious Buddhas: red for Mañjushrī, the Bodhisattva of Wisdom; white for Chenrezi, the
Bodhisattva of Mercy; and blue for Vajrapāṇi, the thunderbolt
bearer who is the deity of protection from evil forces. Thalung
Monastery served about eight small towns in Kham, the name
of our section of eastern Tibet.

Each building of the monastery was painted once yearly. If
the refurbishing was not completed by a certain date in late
fall after the harvest was in, the monks responsible had to pay
a fine to the monastery. Townspeople sometimes joined the
workforce in order to meet the deadline. This deadline was
the fourteenth day of the ninth month on the lunar calendar,
a memorial day for Sachen Kunga Nyingpo, the founder of
the Sakya religious group. This refurbishing was done at
every Sakya monastery in Tibet.

One fall when I was about seven, as my family and servants
were helping with the painting on the residence of Great-
Uncle Nawang Nyima, we made a startling discovery on the
roof. Tibetan roofs are flat, covered with a sprinkling of small
stones and hardened earth. The painting was executed from
the roof down, using a long-handled cloth mop. The painter
first dipped the mop in a huge bucket of thick paint and then
reached down as far as possible, pounding against the wall
and drawing the brush upward. Sometimes it took two coats
to cover the walls with these paints, which were made from
mountain soils near the monastery.

As the painting chores got underway that day, one of our
young women servants, Dezong, who had carried paint buckets to the third floor ahead of us, suddenly called loudly,
excitement in her voice, "Come look! There's a horse's hoofprint here." At first we thought she was joking. But as voices
were traditionally kept low at the monastery and she repeatedly called out to us, we rushed up the stairs to the roof. Last
up, I arrived in time to see everyone gathered around in the

center of the roof. I wasn't very excited, but I looked at the hoofprint anyway. Since I saw such prints daily almost everywhere on the roads, I wasn't very impressed. "So what," I thought. But my relatives gasped, wondering how the print got there. Work was resumed, everyone carefully avoiding the area of the hoofprint.

Caught up in their excitement, I desperately wanted to discuss this phenomenon with Great-Uncle Nawang Nyima. But, as usual, he was meditating in his room and could not be disturbed. Great-Uncle Nawang Nyima, who was more like a grandfather to me, was a tall and slim monk, widely respected as a yoga teacher and for his religious work and leadership in the general community. An amateur horticulturalist, he was the only one who had flowers in winter in Thalung Monastery. He always listened very carefully to my exploits, paying great attention to me and defending me.When a bell sounded, ending his meditation, I ran to his room. Now I was almost shaking with excitement at this seemingly impossible discovery. But Great-Uncle Nawang Nyima was not surprised, calmly uttering a phrase roughly equivalent to "Oh, really." Then he asked, "Did you really see it?" "Oh, yes. Oh, yes," I replied. He said that since a horse had four feet, then probably there was more than one print.

With that observation, I ran back and told the others what Great-Uncle Nawang Nyima had said. They halted their painting to search for more prints, even though they had already walked over much of the roof. But a little way away from the first print were several other indistinct parts of hoofprints, indicating that a horse had indeed been there. Great-Uncle Nawang concluded that the hooves belonged to the mule ridden by Palden Lhamo, a protective deity of mahāyāna Buddhism and one whom our family had worshipped for generations. Palden Lhamo sits on her red mule, her legs dangling, with the scalp of the enemy of religion tied to her saddle. It was good fortune for us to have seen this clear evidence of her visit to my great-uncle's house. He was a devout man, and this new revelation lent credence to his powers as a lama. Later, townspeople said that he had spiritual power to summon such deities to his presence. We automatically accepted her miraculous spiritual powers and that she can be anywhere. But she did not always leave evidence of her presence. Visitors to Great-Uncle Nawang Nyima's labrang many times had reported hearing the tinkling of the mule's bell and ornaments, the clicking of hoofbeats, and snorting sounds.

I loved my pretty little town nestled between two mountain ranges in this section of northeastern Tibet, accompanied by the sounds of the passing waters of the Tha River and the barking of the mastiffs that guarded our homes. One of the ranges was snow-covered the year round, providing us with majestic vistas and constant reminders of the deities we believed dwelled there. Sometimes early in the morning as the sun rose, the topmost peak was capped with beautiful clouds, rising like white smoke. We interpreted this as the sign of an auspicious day, on which the mountain deities were burning incense. We believed that these deities had celebrations much as humans do. When a high lama was born or passed away, for example, we viewed phenomena such as rainbows, thunder, and earthquakes as the deities marking the event.

In the early morning, and occasionally in the evenings, we heard the trumpets, drums, and conch shells being sounded from the monastery, ever reminding us of the way of good Buddhists. There were few clocks in Thalung, and those in evidence were used largely for decorative purposes, so the monastery sounds served as our timepieces. When the older laypeople heard the sounds, they often began to pray. Trumpets sounded from Thalung Monastery to mark the special memorial days of great lamas and other important days of the Buddhist calendar. A certain special conch shell was blown to alert us of an emergency such as serious illness. My grandmother had taught me the meaning of these sounds at an early age. When the emergency conch shell signal reached our ears, she would begin prayers on behalf of the victims, even though she was unaware of their identity or problem.

Whenever my grandmother and other Thalung residents

went on *kora*, we children accompanied them. Kora is the circumambulation of a temple or image, during which it is always kept to one's right. This worship was customarily done before breakfast, and sometimes also in the early evening. It adds merit and purifies sins and defilements, we believe. It adds to our *karma*, the net effect of actions in one life as transmitted to and exemplified in the next. During kora, the adults spun their prayer wheels and used their prayer beads, or *mālās*. By custom, eastern Tibetans favored ornate prayer beads. The one hundred eight beads represent the bodhisatt-vas of mahāyāna Buddhism. The string symbolizes immortal-ity. The central bead, the head of the mālā, represents the Buddha and is usually made of ivory and decorated with special gems. This head bead is larger than the others and has three holes or, as we call them, eyes.

Besides the one hundred eight required beads, there were beads of coral, onyx, amber, and turquoise. Counters of several kinds of metals, including gold, were added. Lamas and other high-ranking religious persons used different kinds of mālās to pray to specific deities. Some of these special prayer beads were made of human skull bones, but the most common type was of wood from Nepal or the Kongpo area of my country. Mine was of red sandalwood and well decorated with jewels. Prayer beads are treated with respect, much in the same way that one would treat a statue of the Buddha.

From the time I was three or four, I had used prayer beads daily. My tutelary deity is White Tārā, a female deity of mahāyāna Buddhism, with seven eyes. The extra eyes of mercy enable her to see and save suffering beings from misery. I had selected the White Tārā when I was about three and old enough to pray with some understanding. I learned the pray-ers of this deity of wisdom and long life. Upon rising each morning, I prayed and prostrated three times to her.

Kora was a happy time of routine. As we circled Thalung Monastery, our immediate group often consisted of six or seven persons. Many older monks were among the groups making the rounds. We children went on ahead, but were not permitted to run or sing; generally, we held to reverent behavior. One complete kora took a half hour, and generally we made at least two or three rounds before I went off to school. Many times the weather was very cold, and we children would tuck our hands inside our wraps close to our bodies to keep warm. Walking along the hillside in the cold and frost, bundled up as we were, it wasn't easy to keep one's balance.

On one such kora when I was about six, I fell on a narrow slippery road around a steep incline, rolling like a ball some ten feet downhill. Grandmother and other elderly ladies rushed to my side, as did some monks. I had facial cuts, a cut knee, and bumps on my head. During the course of a two-week recovery, herbs and other medicines were administered, and the pain was eased with a face pack of special herbs. All were fearful of writing Uncle Tülku-la, who was away, about this misfortune. When informed, he was upset, for if I were scarred, my beauty would be marred, a fate for a girl to avoid at all costs. For a boy, such matters were much less important.

Great-Uncle Nawang, who was in retreat at the time of the accident, interrupted his meditation period upon learning of my mishap. I spent part of my recuperation at his section of the monastery. The rules allowed girls under ten to visit the monastery, but they could sleep there only with special permission. Mother came every day to see me.

About a year after the kora accident, Uncle Tülku-la's fears about my disfigurement became a reality. One spring day during the plowing season, my Aunt Chacha and I took lunch out to two of the field workers. We also carried hay to feed the two yaks during their midday rest. These were gentle, hardworking yaks that were used to children. I had petted them many times before. Today they were tired, but I rode one of them anyway. After dismounting, I went up to him, grasped his left horn, and tried to move his head toward the hay he was eating. He shook his head in anger, throwing me to the ground several feet away. I screamed in pain. His horn had gored my face, leaving a gash to the right of my mouth. The blood streamed down my neck, and it appeared that it too was cut. I still recall the horrified looks and cries of, "The only daughter finished!" Then I thought, "I'm dying now." I heard one very strict monk official point and say, "You treat her like a Tülku but she's not. This is what you get." That made me feel even more pain.

Uncle Kunsang Nyima, a doctor and younger brother of Uncle Tülku-la, was summoned, and I was carried to the monastery. First he cleansed the cut and then dressed it with musk, the traditional medicine we used to stop infection. No stitches were given. Once again I was housed in Great-Uncle Nawang's quarters in the monastery for more than a week. This time my activity was very limited; for fear of reopening the cut, I wasn't even supposed to laugh. The wound healed slowly, but I was left with a scar for life.

Great-Uncle Nawang ordered several inches of the yak's horns to be cut off so it could not harm other people. The animal was then turned loose in the hills, and henceforth was said to belong to the mountain deities. It was now to be known as a *lhayak*. The animal, previously gentle, was believed to have been possessed by an evil deity when he harmed me. In his new status, he was placed under the protection of a new, beneficial deity and freed from the workaday world. Small strips of brightly colored cloth were sewn into his ears and tied into his long shoulder hair. Thus identified, he would not be killed by a hunter or again taken into domesticity. Soon his hair would grow long, dragging on the ground and giving him a nearly square appearance. He would probably join the wild deer and other such yaks that roamed in the general area of the monastery. It was considered a good deed for our family to place the yak in the hands of the deities and thus save the beast's life.

2

Family Bonds

Uncle Tülku-la and I had a special bond. I was born in Thalung on March 3, 1934—the Wood Dog year on the Tibetan lunar calendar. March 3 also was his birth date, but he was born in 1906—the year of the Fire Horse. My birth was on a Monday—thought by Uncle Tülku-la to be an auspicious day—in the first month of the new year. He named me Sonam Tshe Dzom, meaning "the uniting of good deeds into a long life." This name-giving was a privilege reserved for the lamas.

Initially, much of my family was disappointed that the new infant was not a boy, who would have received a monastic education. Nevertheless, as I was the first born on my mother's side of the family, there was great rejoicing and celebrating, including gifts to the monks of money, scarfs, food, and tea. Although my father's work required his presence in Jyekundo, he came for a short visit upon being notified of my birth.

My father, then thirty-five, was an official of the Chinese government at Jyekundo, the administrative headquarters of Gaba province and a day's walk from Thalung. He had held his office of *sago*, consul, for three years in the government

16

building in Jyekundo when he and my mother were married. My father sent imported foodstuffs and other supplies to her family yearly, including bolts of silk and clothing from China. There were elaborate embroidered silk quilts in Chinese designs and embroidered silk house-slippers. Once when I was older, he sent a Chinese silk and fox-fur-lined hat designed to resemble a cat's head, complete with amber-colored eyes, whiskers and big ears. When it arrived, I couldn't wait to show it off to my girl friends.

My mother's name was Phuntsok Drolma, but she was called by her nickname, Phuya, by everyone in Thalung. A natural beauty, she generally was a conservative dresser, choosing clothes that were in good taste but never bright in color. Taller than the ordinary Tibetan young woman, she had especially thick, long black hair and a relatively high voice. Many of my girl friends wanted to be like her, as did I. They also envied her skill in cooking both Tibetan and Chinese dishes. She worked very hard, especially at harvest time. The field workers liked to have her around because of her cheery disposition.

Being extremely kind and generous with her goods, time, and efforts, she was much revered. She was a magnet for beggars and the other poor. The townspeople confided in her and sought her counsel. Upon running short of food or other supplies, they felt free to borrow from her. She shared everything, even the clothing off her back. Once I recall her tearing up a new blouse to bandage a girl who had been cut while working in a barley field. She held the belief that when you give generously, you accumulate greater merit for your future life.

Besides being pretty and intelligent, she was a social leader. In her youth she had danced considerably. It was she who helped teach my friends and me to dance, the primary recreation for young and old alike in Thalung.

Mother, at twenty, had returned to Thalung a few weeks before my birth. When I was seven months old, she returned with me to Jyekundo, where we resided in the government house until I was three. In Jyekundo, she had many servants at her disposal and enjoyed the social life of the government house residents. During that time, she and I traveled back and forth to Thalung every few weeks.

My father had been born of a noble and wealthy family in Amdo, in the Ching-hai province of China, the site of a large Tibetan settlement. In later years he had worked in Sining, the capital of the province. From there, he was assigned by the Chinese government to the post in Jyekundo. He was so well received that the people of Gaba province asked that he be permitted to stay for another term of three years. When my father's second term ended, he was reassigned to Sining and, of course, wanted my mother and me to accompany him. Uncle Tülku-la and other members of my family, however, refused to give their consent, in accordance with the original marriage agreement. For if we had gone to this city in China, it undoubtedly would have meant leaving our close-knit family forever.

It was an agonizing decision for all of the family to make, particularly my mother, for I believe she loved my father very much. But I felt secure in my close family circle and dreaded the thought that I might have to go to such a strange-sounding place as Sining. Even when I visited relatives in neighboring towns for a day or two, I was homesick for Thalung. How would I manage being away for such a long time?

Our area of Kham was under the jurisdiction of the Republic of China and had been so in previous Chinese dynasties since the 1700s. Although Chinese politically, it was culturally Tibetan. The border often was in dispute. Nevertheless, Thalung and other monasteries in the area had complete freedom to operate, and their activities were not interfered with in any way by the Chinese government headquarters in Jyekundo. Thalung was about four miles off the main road between Jyekundo and Sining, and directly on the route to the nomad areas in the Changthang, the great wasteland to the northwest.

Most of the higher officials in Jyekundo and other headquarters stations were respected and honest men. We had to accommodate them occasionally when they passed through Thalung needing horses or lodging. Many of the Chinese officials personally showed respect for the monastery, and sometimes gave it money when they stopped there for tea. They were expected to observe the rules, such as the one forbidding hunting deer within earshot of the monastery. Often, hundreds of graceful wild mountain goats and deer grazed here. They seemed to know they were protected. If a Tibetan violated the hunting code, monks would track him down, take his gun and return him to the monastery, where he would be required to pay a fine. If the violation were severe, the hunter might never get his weapon back. Instead, it would be placed in a special shrine room where such weapons were offered to protective deities.

We were wary, however, of some of the Chinese officials who passed through. Occasionally some of the lesser officers would demand special privileges, and they took our attractive young girls and women for a night or two. I remember our family once hiding Ani Chimi, my aunt who was a Buddhist nun, from the eyes of these Chinese travelers. People in Thalung and other towns dared not protest these violations of our women, who were usually freed in a day or so. Some of the townspeople felt we ought to report these infringements on human rights to the higher officials, but others feared reprisals. The next time around, they reasoned, the visitors might do even worse.

Generally, however, we just tolerated the Chinese and tried to avoid them whenever possible. Our sympathies and loyalties were with Tibet proper, and we certainly thought of ourselves as full Tibetans in every sense. We just happened to live in territory that was under Chinese jurisdiction.

A kind man, my father while in Jyekundo favored Tibetan customs and religion and gave perfect freedom in all such matters to mother and me. It was unlikely that he would have been able to show us these same deferences in Sining. He was a Buddhist, and in Jyekundo he had worshipped in the

Buddhist faith and given food offerings and other gifts to the monastery, monks, and townspeople. But if he returned to Sining, he would not enjoy this religious liberty. Buddhism was not strong there, and he would not have the same political powers.

So at five, I bade farewell to father. When he left for the new job in Sining, mother, friends, a number of servants and I went with him from Thalung to the Dri River, some five miles away, where he crossed on a ferry to begin the month-long journey. He carried me all the way to the ferry then sadly put me in my mother's arms. I still remember his waving goodbye to us from the ferry. I never saw him again. Mother said he would try to return to Jyekundo, but the future had changes in store for many in our peaceful section of the world. Before long my father fell into the hands of the Communists, and his estates and wealth were confiscated. He was put under house arrest and was never heard from again.

Consequently, I had no brothers or sisters. I was reared in a world of adults, which may account for an early love of old people that persists to this day. Tibetans are taught deep respect for age, and I was particularly blessed with favored senior loved ones. There is a strong tradition of honoring the experience of the elderly and following their good example. Besides my mother, Aunt Chacha and Uncle Kuyak, our immediate family included Uncle Tülku-la, his brother, Uncle Kunsang Nyima, the monk and doctor, their sister Ani Chimi, and my maternal grandmother.

When my maternal grandmother was a young widow with six children—one an infant born shortly after her husband's death—she had, according to custom, given money, jewelry, horses, yaks, and other animals to lamas, monasteries, and charities as a memorial. This greatly depleted her resources. Then at my great-grandmother's death, when I was about three, Uncle Tülku-la gave the monastery much of the remaining assets, keeping the house and land. However, he and my Uncle Kuyak, his brother-in-law and a trader, built up the household and its holdings extensively until ours was the most prosperous family in Thalung.

Uncle Kuyak also was an excellent appraiser. Townsmen as well as nomads from a day's journey away would call on him to appraise a gun, horse, jewels or other belongings. As a young man, he was an excellent goldsmith. He knew the value and purity of gold and the quality of workmanship. If someone asked him, for example, to estimate the value of a charm box, saying it took a month to make, Uncle Kuyak could tell if the work had, indeed, taken that long or it it had been completed in only ten days. When he grew older, his goldsmithing was done only for the family, as his heart was really in the trader's realm.

Uncle Kuyak became the one I regarded as father. He was the husband of my Aunt Chacha, my mother's eldest sister. The two sisters were very different and, although her senior, Aunt Chacha always stood somewhat in awe of my capable mother. While mother was busy caring for the household, Aunt Chacha was active socially and in demand for resolving property and financial disputes. Aunt Chacha was not well, frequently afflicted with back problems and migraine headaches. But she was an excellent seamstress, specializing in leatherwork design. She made appliqués for our chubas, belts, hats, and lham. Aunt Chacha wasn't one for field labor, but she was an excellent cook. She was also outspoken. With my mother often gone to work in the fields, I developed a strong and close relationship to Aunt Chacha. She taught me much about sewing, design, and the culinary arts.

Usually two or three girl servants helped with the housekeeping in our home. They worked and dined with us, eating the same food we did. Ours was a three-story, square-shaped residence with a nearly flat roof, constructed of mud and stone. It was named Khang Se Tsang, meaning the Yellow House Nest. Three rows of prayer flags flew from the roof. Flowers grew in a window box on a front balcony on the third floor, and the smell of incense filled our rooms. The ground or first floor included the stable for three or four of our best horses, who were kept there at night. These reddish brown horses with black manes and tails were from Sining and were similar to Arabian horses. Here also were kept small farm implements, the year's supply of foodstuffs, and countless boxes, baskets, leather bags, and other storage containers. The ground floor also was where Uncle Kuyak stored much of his trading goods, such as wool, silk, cotton, wire from China, and big boxes of tea, sugar, and cheese.

The second floor included the living room, a kitchen at the back, and a big pantry holding food brought up in small quantities from the ground floor. These included brick teas wrapped in woven bamboo or yakskins, noodles, grains, dried fruit, and large pottery containers of soy sauce and vinegar.

The eastern Tibetan kitchen is the center of family life. At New Year it is the most decorated room and the place for entertaining guests. This large room had a central supporting post, wrapped from floor to ceiling with small knucklebones from sheep and goats, knotted together in long garlands. These garlands were wound around the post so closely that it was entirely hidden. It required thousands of these small bones, uniform in size, to cover one post. These bones were very white and shiny where they had been brushed by our clothing for so many decades. Objects such as these knuckle garlands had a strong influence on the family, as we believed the garlands brought prosperity and wealth to one's household. And, in fact, only old wealthy families had them.

On built-in wall shelves there were many ivory curios which, although small and toylike, were not playthings. There also were small china cups and other decorative objects, some of which bore religious inscriptions. Some were very old. They included a monkey, frog, bird, and other representatives of the animal world, and some vases.

The most important object of our household—one which had a certain sacredness—was our big cookstove. The stove had its own protective deity. We believed it bestowed certain blessings upon the household and that people owed it some form of gratitude. When, for instance, we made New Year cookies, the first one was given to the fire. The cookstove was not touched by visitors. It was the special domain and responsibility of the householder. Even a new servant in the home steered clear of the stove, tending to other chores instead.

Made from rock and clay and blue-black in color, the stove was about three-and-a-half feet high and about six feet long, with only one end attached to the wall. Underneath in the back was a hollow space where our two cats slept. The stove was constructed so that it could be fueled from two sides. In it we burned dried yak dung and occasionally wood. During much of the year, the stove burned all day. Two goatskin bellows were used simultaneously, one in each hand, to start the fire. The bellows were attached on either side at the back of the stove. A servant sat on a low bench, facing the fire, so as to operate the bellows. One side of the stove was decorated with small bits of broken china, pieces of broken colored glass, conch shells, and Buddhist signs. On the opposite side there was an opening for removing coals and ashes. These live coals were raked out into a boxlike projection and mixed with ashes to form a bed in which we placed a special covered pot. One kind of bread was baked in this covered pot two or three times a week. On the top there were five holes arranged in a row the length of the stove, which held our various sized cooking pots. The center hole was huge, to accommodate even the largest kettles.

Our kitchen also had several floor cushions made of colorful woolen fabric and stuffed with deer fur. There were traditional Tibetan rugs on top of the long cushions. We ate, seated cross-legged on these, at long, low narrow tables. On them at all times were three carved boxes filled with *tsampa*, barley flour, of varying degrees of coarseness. My mother liked the brown, more coarse variety. We helped ourselves from these boxes at mealtime, and my mother checked daily to see that they were filled. Three round, covered butter containers made of hardwood and decorated with silver sat adjacent to the tsampa. Traditionally, these were kept side by side because they are eaten together. Butter was made every day except in winter when fewer animals were giving milk. Yogurt and milk were kept in wooden buckets. Water was carried from the Tha River and kept in a huge wooden-covered container from which we dipped. We washed dishes in a large wooden bucket in one corner of the kitchen.

A master batch of very strong tea was made once a week from two tea bricks, two gallons of water, and one cup of strong soda, the latter to cut the tannic acid and so spare the lining of one's stomach. The soda also helped to bring out the color and flavor from the tea leaves more rapidly. Portions of this master batch were mixed as needed, in a ratio of one-tenth tea to nine-tenths water, and heated for the day. Breakfast tea, with generous portions of butter, milk, and salt, was strong, while tea drunk during the day was much weaker. This rich breakfast tea was mixed in a narrow wooden churn about three feet high. First hot water was swished around and then poured out of the churn to warm it. Next the boiling hot tea, butter, milk, and salt were stirred continuously for five or six minutes. Then this mixture was transferred to one of two large clay teapots which rested on a charcoal-fueled warmer kept on the floor beside our dining table. The churn, which had rings of brass, was hung up on the wall after breakfast. The remainder of the day we drank from the clay pot. On each of the teapots was a bright-colored woolen tea cozy, which I mischievously liked to use as a hat when the family was gathered, providing a convenient audience. When we were thirsty in summer, there was plenty of cool buttermilk, also kept in the kitchen. We seldom drank water at home.

One large three-legged brazier, in which we burned charcoal, furnished extra warmth in the large kitchen. My grandmother spent many hours in winter sitting around this warming stove. She was a fine weaver and taught many other townspeople this art. Most of the yarn, first dyed yellow, using wild rhubarb roots, was easily dyed into other colors. The softest wool was finely woven for use as monks' robes and ladies' aprons. The shaggy leftover wool was woven into one thickness, to be used as blankets. Most blankets were white with red, green, or black designs. There were other coverlets, matted and stuffed with natural wool. Grandmother was very skilled in spinning the yarns and weaving the soft material for the monks' robes.

The third floor had a shrine room, three bedrooms, and a central open area. Family clothing was kept in a big bedroom near the shrine room. Garments were thrown over a rope, clothesline style, hanging inside out to catch the air. Our finest clothes were kept in labeled boxes. During the winters Ani Chimi lived at the Dronda Nunnery. During the rest of the year we shared a third-floor bedroom. After dinner and during our evening prayers, I became sleepy. Then it was bedtime for all of us. I made my way upstairs to bed with a little lamp that burned animal fat. I slept in a wooden bunk nailed to the wall. The "bedspring" was woven leather strips, over which was a mattress stuffed with deer fur. Sometimes the mattress padding was yak wool covered with cloth. Our bedroom had benches and a small table with a single drawer, in which we kept candy, toys, and snacks.

During one period that lasted about six months, Ani Chimi and I kept dates, figs, raisins, and rock candy in our room for snacks at night. This was forbidden, but Ani Chimi preferred to think that she couldn't get to sleep without such nourishment. These dried fruits came from a locked pantry adjacent to the kitchen, which was opened several times a day. I followed mother into the pantry, and when she wasn't looking, I would hide some of the fruits away in the front of my chuba. These were expensive fruits from Sining, a treat served primarily to guests. The average family had such delicacies only on rare occasions; we had this fruit because Uncle Kuyak made an annual trip to Sining. A young servant girl who cleaned up after us each day and saw the seeds and remains of the fruits kept the secret from my mother, as Ani Chimi and I bribed her by giving her a share.

One day when the girl was unable to come to work because of illness in the family, our plot backfired. Instead came a man servant who disclosed the seeds, first to my grandmother and then my mother. She came and surveyed the scene, spotting additional uneaten fruits under our table. She put them under lock and key. That evening the two of us couldn't sleep—we thought—because of our hunger for sweets. So we went up to the roof where some dried turnips were stored and ate them. This was food for horses and other livestock. Stomach aches and swelled abdomens resulted. Uncle Kuyak heard us crying. "Where is the key?" he asked. "I'm going to get them some fruit." Which he did. He continued this several nights following, but after that a close watch was kept on my pantry trips.

Nearly every Tibetan home has a shrine room or some type of altar. Our shrine room contained an altar with a series of graduated shelves above it, the highest of which held a seated figure of the historical Buddha, Sakyamuni, three feet high and cast in copper with a gold overlay. The wider shelves below held butter lamps and the family's twenty-one brass water bowls. The butter lamps were kept burning day and night. On the altar there was also a variety of religious objects and silver bowls holding offerings of uncooked rice, dried flowers, incense, and choice foods. Elsewhere in the room were tankas and shelves of religious books, the latter wrapped in brocades. These included twelve volumes of the *Teachings of Transcendental Wisdom*, the fundamental philosophical system of Tibetan Buddhism.

A traveling monk from Thubten Monastery came and stayed at our home for three winter months, aiding in my education. He came nearly every year, reading aloud in the shrine room from the 130 scriptures. We paid him, and other families who could afford it engaged him after he left our house. He was an excellent reader, and I liked reciting prayers with him. It was from him that I also learned about vowels, pronunciation, and grammar.

Some four *dzomos*, sheep, goats, and cattle were kept in the barn adjacent to our house. The dzomo is the female in a cross between the *dri*, the female yak, and the cattle bull. This group of animals was taken out to pasture daily by teenage herdsgirls. The animals provided some of our daily food, but they were not slaughtered for meat. We bought all of our meat from traders and others. We had not taken the life of any of our domestic animals since the death of my great-grandfather some years back.

Besides Gyado, my pony, I had a most unusual pet, a four-horned sheep named Yang Rashi, who was a familiar figure to the neighborhood. He had been given to me by a nomad friend of Uncle Kuyak. It was good fortune indeed to have such an animal, and Yang Rashi clearly liked his home. He scaled the stairs easily and whipped about my bedroom. Almost daily, I combed his soft white wool, which never was sheared. His brown eyes seemed to glow out from the wool. I kept Yang Rashi well decorated with braided, colored wool tassels and small jewels that hung from his neck. When I called his name, he came from afar. Besides barley, he accepted sweets and leftovers. His sleeping quarters were in a special room on the first floor. At night, I wrapped him in a blanket.

3

Time for Dancing

When I was about eleven, Uncle Tülku-la returned from several years of studying and teaching in Minyag and Derge to head Thalung Monastery. Uncle Tülku-la, who had entered the monastery at age four, was serious and studious by nature, progressing rapidly. He had studied in celebrated monasteries under some of the famous lama-scholars of his time. Now he had attained the rank of head lama and planned to remain in his post the remainder of his life.

Visitors from many parts of eastern Tibet called at Thalung Monastery to study under him. Over his labrang flew the victory flag of Buddhism, a yellow banner some six feet tall, resembling a closed umbrella, which had been earned by his great-great-uncle, a highly respected lama. It was a time of great pride in our family. Now that I was growing up, I quickly gained a new respect for uncle Tülku-la. Whereas in the past I had preferred to go out and work in the fields, I now found it much more interesting to visit the labrang. As I was his only niece, visiting monks showed me more attention than before. It was a new phase of my education, listening to the dialect of the visiting Minyag monks. I learned much about my country—about distances, markets, and what one

28

could buy where. Two of these Minyag monks particularly sparked my attention. They were tailors by trade, but also excelled in producing beautiful embroidered religious items and colored paper flowers. When I told my girl friends of these new discoveries, some thought them very exciting indeed; others concluded that these exploits were just stories.

Uncle Tülku-la had brought two parrots with green feathers and red claws and beaks from Minyag for Great-Uncle Nawang, and they were a great attraction for me. When I called one, he would answer "la," the Tibetan word for "yes" and repeat his name. The birds soon had flourishing vocabularies, and officials learned not to say anything in their presence that would not bear repeating.

My close friend from early childhood was a distant cousin, Lhayag, two years my elder. She also was the lead dancer in Thalung's dance group. Dancing was the highlight of my young life, and the focal point of entertainment for all young people. It built character, performed a service to the community, and it was fun. Our group had fifteen girls and seventeen boys, who not only danced but also sang and chanted religious music. Two middle-aged women taught us to dance. Sometimes my mother, who as a girl had been excellent in her footwork, filled in as a teacher. An older man played the *dranyen*, a stringed instrument resembling a guitar, and a young woman played the flute. Frequently older people joined in and sang together as a chorus.

The boys' costumes featured short necklaces, loose white shirts with brocade on the collar and large fancy buttons, and bright-colored long pants. Their three-quarter length belted chubas had sleeves, one of which was worn hanging empty. I wore a full-length chuba and often three blouses of different colors with sleeves of varying lengths, all covering my hands. When I waved my arms gracefully, a rainbow of colors appeared. My chuba was lined in lambskin and trimmed with otter fur and brocade of gold and silver design. I wore three or four necklaces of varying lengths, strung with turquoise, onyx, and coral jewels. In my hair I wore pieces of amber, coral, and turquoise, indicating I was single. My elaborate leather belt was also decorated with jewels.

In good weather we often practiced outdoors in the early evening in the courtyards of homes. Usually we went to Lhayag's, but people generally loved to have us come and never refused permission to use their courtyards, some of which were covered. In winter often it was bitterly cold and our fur-lined garments were none too warm. We had to keep standing and moving about to be warm enough. Sometimes in the winter we would dance around a huge bonfire. The colors of our best blouses flickered in the firelight.

It seemed that nearly everyone in town came to watch us as we practiced our heel-clicks and side-kicks. The boys, of course, jumped higher than the girls in executing this foot-work. They danced on one side and the girls on the other occasionally they joined us in a circle. When we danced, often with our hands raised high above our heads, we slipped our right arms out of our sleeves for comfort and ease of motion. Each dance was repeated two or three times, the final one being performed the fastest, with the boys and girls singing together.

Often these dances paid tribute to Tibet's beautiful mountains and streams and the deities that dwell there. In Kham, and especially in the Gaba province, the young people's dance groups were a source of great community pride. Competition between towns was fierce, both in the dance routines and costumes. When we visited other towns in Gaba, we watched their dancers closely and came home hoping to choreograph a new routine. We knew more than thirty dances.

Besides dancing at homes, we appeared at weddings and festive celebrations such as the visit of an important lama. On such occasions the people for whom we were dancing gave us gifts of scarfs and food. These were basic foodstuffs, such as brick tea, meat, and tsampa, which we often saved for camping and other parties. The gifts also might include a whole dried lamb or two. When these payments were bestowed, we continued dancing, politely pretending not to notice, but as soon as our audience departed, we rushed to see what they had left.

Sometimes between dances, we had a little *chang*, or barley beer. In summer, buttermilk quenched our thirst. I had to be home exactly when my mother indicated. I was sad when I had to leave before the games and dances were over.

During these formative years of my life, I regarded Lhayag, my best friend, as a sister. I looked up to her in matters of dress and in all things generally. When Lhayag was sixteen, she was married in a big ceremony in Thalung, and I was a wedding attendant.

The bridegroom was the son of a Jyekundo trader. The marriage had been arranged several months earlier by the parents, and Lhayag by custom had no choice. When the parents had reached an agreement, they would exchange scarfs and sign a written contract. Lhayag's parents then paid the young man's parents a small amount of silver money wrapped in a white scarf as an official symbol of the couple's betrothal.

The traditional Tibetan white scarf, or *khata*, which is long and narrow, conveys many messages. Primarily, it is used for greeting, but it is also given as a symbol of respect, friendship, and good fortune. Strangely enough, these scarfs were not made in Tibet but imported from China and India. Only the silk ones with special Buddhist symbols were expensive. We never washed our scarfs; after long use, they would be discarded.

It was the custom for a woman to go to the home of her husband after their marriage, but if the bride were the only child in her family, the husband would live in her home and take her family name, and thus carry on her family line. Since Lhayag had no brothers and only one sister, a nun, the bridegroom would come to live with her family.

I went to Lhayag's house the evening before the wedding, assisting her whenever possible. The next morning, the bridegroom, Tsegya, and some fifteen men in his party rode into town. They were an impressive sight, dressed in finery and jewels and carrying guns and decorated swords. Even their horses were decorated.

Lhayag and I were on the third floor. Lhayag was not to look, as it would be bad luck, so I reported events to her. Lhayag's mother repeatedly warned her not to peek out, but that didn't stop Lhayag from asking, "What does he look like?" She had never seen the young man, who was five years older than she.

The bridegroom's party was met in the courtyard by several young girls carrying a large cup, beautifully decorated and filled with chang. One man sang about the significance of the day, and Tsegya made the traditional offering by dipping his finger into the chang and flicking it into the air. When they entered the house, I could see Tsegya clearly and judged him to be handsome, not too tall and lighter skinned than his brother.

Once Tsegya and his party had entered the house, it was proper for Lhayag to don her wedding outfit, a brocade chuba with the hem outlined in otter fur. She joined him on the third floor where the ceremony was performed by a lama, assisted by two monks. The couple was blessed and prayers were repeated. Tea and auspicious food, including sweet or long-life rice, were then served downstairs. The young boys and girls of Thalung's dance group performed outside around a bonfire. I was among them, dancing for at least an hour. The couple sat nearby on cushions, while townspeople stood and watched. Two women beer servers sang to the couple, who then took the traditional sips of chang from an elaborate silver cup—acts symbolizing their unity and good health.

Gifts to the bride brought by the bridegroom's parents were placed outside in the yard for all to see. A long list of these worldly goods was read by a man in the wedding party, who also told something about Tsegya's life and good character. The roster enumerated horses and other animals, saddles, guns, and necklaces. It was read with great pride, with the guests listening intently.

The wedding party continued for the next three days. I helped prepare pastries and special cuts of lamb for Tsegya's attendants to take home. With Lhayag no longer available as the lead dancer, I took over her duties. As events unfolded, I took mental notes of the social customs, manners, and procedures of this traditional Khampa-style wedding.

After the wedding, I was lonesome. Lhayag and I had been very close, frequently staying overnight at each other's homes. Many people told me that I probably would be the next one in Thalung to be married, and this was the type of ceremony I hoped to have.

During the summer, I helped my friend Khando with paper making, which I greatly enjoyed. Paper was made by poor people who did not own land but needed income. On our best days we made some fifteen sheets a day. The process began by digging up the roots of the *rechapa*, a plant similar to the Daphne shrub, that grew wild in the Thalung area. Khando's mother would put the roots in a cool place for a few days, after which we removed the fibers from under the root skin. These fibers were placed on a flat stone and beaten with a deer horn until fine. This material was rolled in balls. Three or four balls were placed in a churn, water was added, and the mixture was worked until it had a consistency like bread dough. Then we went to a pond or slow stream and placed the mixture on a screen laid on the surface of the water. Slowly and gently, we pressed the mixture into the screen, and then dried it in the sun for fifteen or twenty minutes. The dried sheets of paper were white and smooth, good enough for books.

Khando's mother would take the paper to Jyekundo to sell. When I was little, I'd ask my mother, "Why can't we do this?" But commercial paper making was below my family's status. Happily, my mother had no objection to my helping Khando, who was two years younger than I.

Summer to us also meant nomading, the happy but very busy time when the family spent two to three months up in the higher mountains with our yak herds, preparing supplies for winter. Four servants accompanied us for this season of tenting, recreation, and labor, One of the reasons I looked forward to this time was that Khando came along.

About fifteen Thalung families had yaks and dris which were kept in designated areas belonging to the Gaba provincial government. Each family was assigned spring, winter, and summer areas for grazing their herds. Names of the families were written on pieces of paper, placed in a bowl, and drawn. Thus, one received his plot by chance. I became so adept at drawing the best grazing areas that a rule was made that no one under a certain age could make the draw.

We had about three hundred yaks and dris. In winter the animals were left to graze at lower elevations, with herdsmen keeping watch in a pasture area about three hours' walk from Thalung. At night these valuable animals were led further down into sheltered valleys. These herds were kept separately from the farm animals which herdsgirls took from our back-yard to pasture twice each day. Sometimes Lhayag, Khando, and I would ride our horses back to Thalung on a family errand. Then we would stop and talk and have tea with the herdsgirls, who were always eager for our companionship, sharing with them the food we were supposed to be deliver-ing to our family homes. But I never gave away anything destined for Great-Uncle Nawang Nyima or offerings for the monastery.

Some ten or twelve families hired these herdsgirls for daily care of dzomo, sheep, goats, and cows. The animals were not tied together as they moved out to the grazing areas, but they always somehow knew where they were headed. The herds-girls had plenty of spare time, which they used for naps, dancing, singing, and water fights in the meadows ringed by mountains.

Out in the nomad area, I arose early and often helped with milking the dris. There were usually about fifty dris with calves. All of them had names, and I knew exactly which calf went with which mother. The calves were kept separately and tied in a line until it was their mother's turn for milking. We first took the calf to its mother and let it nurse briefly. We then tied the calf close enough for the mother to lick it while we milked the mother. Then the calf was untied and brought back to nurse the remaining milk. My job was to untie the calves at the proper time. I often directed the women milkers to "please leave more milk for the calves." Sometimes the calves, when their stomachs were full, would lick my hand affectionately and play.

We made two churns of butter a day. After being kneaded until hard, the butter was either placed into wooden buckets or wrapped in yak skin. Unlike some families, we did not have to buy any butter or cheese. We even shipped some of our dairy products for sale in central and western Tibet. This was also the season for cutting wool from the yaks with an especially sharp knife. Some of the yak wool was sold and some kept for clothing for the family and servants and for making other household items. This cutting was a specialized skill, as certain areas of the animal's body was left uncut for aesthetic reasons.

It was in the nomad area that two experts in leathercraft cured the sheep and yak skins from animals that had died throughout the year. The skins were hung up to dry in the summer sun. At one stage, the preservation process involved stomping the already softened leather with bare feet for many hours. I loved to watch the men as they sang to lighten the burden of this tedious work. It was a friendly, if busy, season, characterized by its neighborliness and willingness to share in the tasks of earning a livelihood.

In late summer, we returned to Thalung for Song Cho, a week-long festival in which incense and fragrant wood smoke was offered to Thalung's mountain deity in an area some four miles west of town. There was a statue of our deity on the mountain. It was believed this mountain deity, known as the Lord of the Soils, protected us, watched over our animals, warded off disease, and provided rain. All of Thalung went to Song Cho, pitching fifty or sixty tents on reserved sites. If there had been a death in the family in the past year, the

survivors attended Song Cho only for a day. Earlier, the
Thalung lamas and monks conducted their separate Song Cho
higher up on the mountain.

Song Cho was our most important summer festival and
much more informal than the leading winter event, New Year's
Day. It was in many ways a time for showing off. Many
families had new white tents with black or blue designs, and
many rugs were displayed. Even the trip from Thalung for
the Song Cho was impressive, with the townspeople riding in
single file, dressed in their colorful summer clothing—a bright
contrast to the heavy woolens of the cold weather. The
prosperous, especially the young, would change outfits up to
three times daily. Rich and fancy foods were cooked. It was
rumored that many of the food boxes displayed so ostentatiously by some families were empty. There was horseback
riding, archery, singing, and dancing, and the inevitable
pranks the boys and girls played on each other. The Tha
River flowed nearby, and the boys were not above dipping the
girls in the cold water. When water fights ensued and the girls
were losing, women came to their aid. And when the boys
were taking a beating, the men stepped in.

A lama and two monks were in attendance, and each
morning they made ceremonial smoke offerings to the mountain deity on our behalf. This special smoke was made of a
combination of forest woods, with twigs and leaves added.
Juniper and pine lent a pleasing aroma. The mixture was
burned in a small clay and rock receptacle to the accompaniment of hand drums and horns.

The fourth day of Song Cho marked the Lha Gyalo ceremony. This event was in honor of Gesar, whom we regard as
our national protector against war. On this day, men and boys
went to the top of the mountain, riding horses with beautiful
saddles ornamented with gold and silver. Dressed in fine
clothes, they wore fancy hats and carried guns and swords
along with family and personal prayer flags on poles. Women
were not permitted at this ceremony, as traditionally they did
not handle weapons. We watched from below with the chil-

dren as the figures of the climbing men became smaller and smaller. At the top of the mountain, the men made a pile of stones to hold up the flagpoles. Each man and boy put his hat on the end of his rifle barrel and held it high in his left hand, while raising his sword high in his right hand. Then sweeping the sword up and back, he would cry, "Lha gyalo!" This swordstroke and victory cry were repeated three times.

Later in the summer, Uncle Kunsang Nyima and I, together with Ani Chimi and sometimes a monk or two, went up into the nearby mountains to gather medicinal plants. We took several horses and tents and camped at a lower elevation, trekking higher during the day. Uncle Kunsang Nyima gathered these plants, not only for medicine for his own patients, but also for two other doctors in Thalung and for his teacher-doctor in Jyekundo with whom he had studied for seven years. I became skilled at recognizing and naming several hundred plants. Some I tied in bunches and others I placed in big bamboo baskets. Afterwards, when the plants were dried, I helped Uncle Kunsang Nyima grind and measure them out in a big medicine room in the monastery. I knew many combinations of medicines for a number of ailments and how the medicine was to be administered.

In winter, one of my favorite diversions was to visit Dronda Nunnery where Ani Chimi was assigned. Although she lived there in winter, she, like many of the nuns, came out in summer to help with harvesting and to work with dairy animals. The town of Dronda, in a farming area, was about four miles away, and was larger than Thalung. The nunnery, also of the Sakya school, was home to about eighteen to twenty nuns every winter.

Food was pooled at the nunnery. One wealthy family from the Dronda area delivered milk to the nuns each morning and also furnished fresh yogurt when needed. Often when mother and Aunt Chacha delivered food, I went along and stayed a few days. It was a delightful respite for me, and I was never lacking for attention there.

The abbess, in her forties, was a distant relative. She and

the other nuns, who had shaved heads, wore maroon chubas. Their three-story structure, which looked like a dormitory, was mainly white, making it stand out on the mountainside. The front door was kept locked from the inside, but the mountainous area drew few visitors other than the townspeople who came out looking for firewood. When visiting lamas taught in the town of Dronda, the nuns went there; lamas seldom went to the nunnery.

While the abbess sat on a high cushion in the shrine room, the nuns, seated cross-legged in lotus position, recited prayers and sang and chanted. Butter lamps and incense burned night and day. The nuns also practiced meditation three times daily, focusing their prayers on Chenrezi, the Bodhisattva of Compassion. Girls entered the nunnery in their late teens. To enter one had to know how to read and to have one's parents' permission. Like Thalung Monastery, Dronda Nunnery was considered strict. Many of the nuns ate meat only once a week or so, and, as with the general citizenry, never before noon. Two or three nuns lived together in a single room.

I loved the singing, chanting, and praying of the nuns. When I ran or made too much noise, Ani Chimi or one of the other nuns would correct me. I listened intently as they told me stories of the Enlightened One and explained the content of their songs. I also helped clean the brass offering bowls for the shrine room. These visits to the nunnery were mentally stimulating, and I applied what I learned there in my classes at school.

I went out in the morning and evening with the nuns who brought in water in wooden buckets strapped to their backs. Water was seldom taken in midday because as the temperature rose, melting snow and ice from the higher elevations muddied the water. In the late afternoon I watched as the herds from Dronda returned from the hills, past the nunnery and into town, the herdsgirls singing happy tunes about the countryside.

Although the nunnery did not command the spectacular view of the Gaba countryside that could be had from Thalung

Monastery, it overlooked a main crossing point of the Dri River. From the nunnery, I could see the wooden ferry, replicas of horseheads on its bow and stern, making the diagonal crossing of the swift waters. Some people crossed in yakskin boats. It was a dangerous river, and many people died during the flood seasons. At times in winter, large chunks of ice came floating downstream.

For just over a month in winter, when the Dri River froze over, we could see the travelers walking across. The ice then functioned as something like a prayer flag: on special Buddhist celebration days or when someone was sick, townspeople would carve in the ice "Oṃ Maṇi Padme Hūṃ," which means "Hail to the Jewel in the Lotus." This is a blessing for whoever utters it or for whom it is said or written.

The lunar New Year, occurring in late February or early March of the Western calendar, was our most sacred holiday. On the first day of the New Year, one practiced the exemplary behavior one wished to continue throughout the remainder of the year. Good deeds—and bad ones—were magnified during this time, it was thought. Thus, for example, the poor who came to the door asking for food must not be refused, as giving away food was a positive symbol of generosity. Our conversations and attitudes also were positive.

As for the New Year festivities, my girl friends and I looked forward to the last five days of the old year, which marked the observance of Gutor at Thalung Monastery, featuring sacred dancing. The highly ritualized footwork was performed by costumed and masked monks, with a different program each day. Since we knew the monks, part of the fun was trying to guess who was behind what masks as they danced, sometimes inside the monastery and sometimes in the courtyard. The purpose of these five days of festivity was to drive out all the evils of the old year and prepare for the new. Townspeople dressed up for Gutor. The monastery courtyard was crowded with people from throughout Gaba and booths selling prayer flag material, candies, scarfs, small mirrors, and bright-colored tassels. The last day was the most impressive, for it included the ceremonial burning of the *torma*, a figure made of tsampa and decorated with colored butter. This burning symbolized driving away evil forces and prepared for a new year of good influences.

The Tibetan lunar calendar consists of sixty-year cycles made up of twelve five-year cycles. Each year in the twelve is represented by a specific animal and one of five elements. The first day of the New Year was reserved for family. There had been much housecleaning and other preparations for the event, and the house had been decorated the night before. The shrine room was first, with butter lamps and fruits and many other kinds of foods bedecking the altar. Because it was winter, dried barley and wheat and paper flowers were used. Very impressive were the large fancy pastries, formed by lacing narrow strips of dough in complicated patterns resembling the interwoven Knot of Life, one of the eight auspicious symbols of Buddhism. We did not make any pastry figures in the shapes of animals or humans because eating them would symbolize the destruction of life.

Our best rugs made their appearance in the shrine room and upstairs bedrooms. Good-fortune signs were placed on the kitchen walls and specially made rugs lined the bench seats. Our best silver cups and plates were used for entertaining. Now the heavy brass pots and other cooking utensils decorating the kitchen shelves were put into use.

We arose at about three and washed in water to which milk had been added, always facing east, as that direction symbolizes peace and purity. It was necessary to have at least one new garment to wear at New Year, but when possible we would each have a complete new outfit. Next we prayed and chanted in the shrine room, where each of us put a ceremonial white scarf in front of a statue of the Buddha. Upon entering the shrine room we performed the *chatsa*, or prostration, three times. Then each of us placed his scarf on the altar and with hands folded to the heart, bowed very low. Before leaving, we poured a little of the blessed water into our palm; as we went out the door, we drank it and then wiped our palm on the top of our head.

The shrine room also contained a good luck offering in a decorated, divided wooden box. On one side was tsampa, topped with five butter figures. The other side contained wheat, on which rested a large piece of rock salt. Adjacent to the box was a pitcher of chang, topped with a butter decoration. Each person took a pinch of tsampa and butter, tossed part of it into the air, and ate the remainder. Progressing into the kitchen, we ate a special cookie for good luck, followed by a soup containing *droma*, a vegetable resembling a sweet potato. Then came a regular meal.

New Year also meant going on kora, during which we presented white scarfs at the monastery shrine rooms. From the monastery, one could sense it was New Year merely by watching the smoke that curled skyward from the houses in Thalung, where festive meals were being prepared. It was cold, usually with snow, at the New Year, and a day of little work. Lhomo, knucklebones, and other games were played indoors by all members of the family.

With the formality of the first day over, we turned to the outdoors for community singing, lhomo, and snowball fights. The men concentrated on archery. Chang flowed freely and hard liquor was imbibed by many. Our family's official New Year season lasted for two weeks. On the second and ensuing days other Thalung families were invited to our home, staying for a half hour or so and always being entertained in the kitchen. Upon leaving, the guests took some of the food home. It was customary to attend many of these open houses during the New Year's season and sometimes we would go to six or seven parties a day, as it was not polite to refuse such an invitation.

On my last New Year's in Thalung as a young girl, we celebrated without Uncle Tülku-la. He had departed about a year before for Ngor and Sakya monasteries in western Tibet. At Ngor, he was to receive three months of special advanced religious instruction that would enable him to teach Buddhist doctrine brought from India to Tibet in the eleventh century. It is the Sakyas' main teaching, focusing on the Buddha's path to enlightenment. It is passed from generation to generation. It was mandatory for Khampa lamas to receive this instruction from the Ngor abbot. Then Uncle Tülku-la would have the rank of the highest order of an ordained lama-monk. Because of him, a trip was in the offing for us. I knew that the next New Year would find me participating in festivities with new flavors and customs exciting beyond words to a teenager from Kham.

I was only vaguely aware of the great revolution that was now taking place in 1948 in China proper. I was absorbed in my dancing and other activities and unaware of the grave danger facing my peaceful countryside. Certainly I knew the Communists were bent on destroying our religion, which was deeply basic to our lives. I envisioned communism as something evil and was convinced that those who advocated it were subhuman, perhaps some kind of furry men.

Undoubtedly all of us would have been far more concerned had we not been in such an isolated sector of the world and so removed from mass communications. With no radio or newspaper, we heard news only by word of mouth. Town meetings were held during which word of the possible fall of the Nationalist Chinese government was discussed. Prayers were said not only for our lives but also for the survival of Buddhism and all beings. Daily, monks at monasteries throughout Gaba prayed with more fervor in hopes of warding off this enemy.

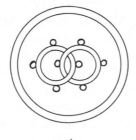

4

The Pilgrimage

A pilgrimage to the capital city of Lhasa and other holy places of western Tibet was to be mine. This is a trip that almost every Tibetan dreams of taking sometime in his life. We would go as far west as Sakya, seat of the Sakya religious school and home of the powerful rulers of my country in the thirteenth and fourteenth centuries. There we would rendezvous with my grandmother and Ani Chimi, who had left Kham the previous year with Uncle Tülku-la. Thus our journey also held the happy prospect of a reunion with the rest of the family. At fifteen (though by the Western calendar, I was still fourteen), I was the youngest member of the pilgrimage, fortunate indeed to be party to such a venture. Since most of my countrymen make pilgrimages much later in life, I was the envy of Lhayag and my other girl friends. It would be a full year before I would see them again. This was also the first such pilgrimage for my mother. Uncle Tülku-la's group and the rest of the family planned to make the return trip home together.

Permission to leave the area was granted by the Drawu-pon, hereditary governor of Gaba. A cousin was left to be caretaker of our home and other properties. We felt no danger in leaving our property, as the Nationalist Chinese were still firmly in control at the government headquarters in Jyekundo. Forty people, including seventeen in our family group accompanied by our huge watchdog Gyadrup, were to make the first lap of the trip to Nakchuka, a major trading center inside Tibet proper. There the actual pilgrimage, undertaken on foot, was to begin. The party had some three hundred yaks, about one-third of them belonging to us. We were to leave some of the animals at Nakchuka, boarding them until our return home. The other yaks carried brick tea, wool, butter, cheese, money, and other supplies to be offered to the main Sakya Monastery and the Ngor Monastery, and their lamas. Uncle Kuyak, with the help of some hired men, would take these goods to western Tibet by a different route.

One of the most difficult of my farewells was to Great-Uncle Nawang. Although he had many grandnieces and grandnephews, he often confessed to me that I was his favorite. Over the years he had told me stories of places I now was to see with my own eyes. Although as a young monk he had traveled to these same monasteries in the West, he had not left Thalung Monastery in forty-eight years, except for family emergencies; then he always managed to return in time to sleep inside the monastery. Three times each day he went into meditation; after his meditation a bell would ring and towns-people would line up outside his window, waiting their turn for consultation and advice about family and other affairs.

In 1948 we set out on a day chosen by monastery astrologers as auspicious for our departure. One began such a trip in the fall, avoiding the extreme cold of winter and the high river waters of the late spring. Lhayag and some of my other girl friends had stayed with me the previous night, none of us getting much sleep. Lhayag cried as I did. That morning we went to the monastery to offer money and ceremonial scarfs to the monks and then dropped by to say goodbye to Great-Uncle Nawang. I kissed him goodbye after he had given much advice, saying, "Be careful when you cross the rivers, and at night." He again told me of things I would see on the pilgrimage—tidbits I was to remember as the trip progressed. He requested that I bring him plenty of flower seeds and good-smelling incense. He was to be the only immediate family member left behind, and we both wept at parting.

My mount was a large white horse with a gray mane and tail, brought from Sining especially for the pilgrimage. He was gentle and sturdy. Each of our horses had a decorated leather carrying case, in which were a cup, snacks, and other travel essentials needed in the course of a day. Having made the trip west many times on trading missions, Uncle Kuyak would be the party leader until we reached Nakchuka, about a two-month journey.

About three days from Thalung we stopped to visit with friends, a wealthy nomad family who had a son about my age and whose company I enjoyed. The father, Ruyag, was the trader and long-time friend of Uncle Kuyak who several years earlier had given me my beloved pet sheep, Yang Rashi. Uncle Kuyak had arranged to remain here about four days, as it was beautiful flat country with lush grazing land for the animals. It was also a nomadic trading center where we could obtain fresh supplies for our trip. But there was another reason for the stop. Unbeknownst to me, Uncle Kuyak and Ruyag had made a loose arrangement for me to marry Ruyag's son, Phuntsok. This was to be a formal meeting of the families. But there was no definite marriage arrangement for the reason that each of us was the only child in our respective families. As such we were expected to inherit the property and carry on the family line, he here in the Gyesang area and I in Thalung. Some in my family, especially Great-Uncle Nawang Nyima, were opposed to such a union. He envisioned me marrying a lineage-holding lama or into a family deeply devoted to Buddhism. My mother realized the security that marriage into this wealthy nomad family would provide; nevertheless, she sided with Great-Uncle Nawang.

Phuntsok and I raced his horses, accompanied by several servants and family members. He seemed surprised at my skill in riding and in handling the horses. It was great fun, and I longed to tell my girl friends about this. Part of the terrain was swampy and inhabited by huge white cranes. From a distance, we watched transfixed as they moved their long necks and wings, almost in unison, like ballet dancers on a stage. One would sound a signal, and they all seemed to follow. My companion and his servants said they had seen much better performances by the birds. But I was fascinated. The scene reminded me of the fairy tales I had heard about the prideful long-legged dancing cranes. We Tibetans believed that witnessing such an event was auspicious and would surely bring us good luck.

Phuntsok was about two years older than I, neat, nicely dressed, and well mannered. Undoubtedly, he knew about the tentative plans for our betrothal and was behaving in an exemplary manner. The day before we left, he was helping me onto my horse when suddenly he removed one of the brightly colored ties at the top of my boot. It was a symbol of affection—a sign that he wanted to keep something that belonged to me. But I didn't attach any particular significance to his action.

The families parted, planning to meet again after I returned from western Tibet. Our servants teased me about my "future partner," but I didn't take their comments seriously. Months later I learned about the would-be marriage arrangement during a discussion with my grandmother. I didn't like the idea for many reasons, but had no animosity towards the young man. When Uncle Kuyak returned a year later without me, by custom they had to pay his family for the brief but broken agreement.

Travel with the yaks was slow, covering from eight to ten miles in four or five hours a day depending on the weather conditions. We arose early and started without breakfast, subsisting on snacks instead. In the late morning, we stopped for the day. The remainder of the day the yaks grazed and rested. This was the daily routine as we made our way through the great northern wasteland, the Changthang. This is a remote area in which the sparse population still holds to Bön, the animistic religion of early Tibet, in contrast to most of the more settled areas, which had long since adopted Buddhism.

We came across treacherous rivers and, occasionally, nomad families. There were no ferries or yakskin boats in the Changthang, and we forded these cold waters on horseback either in the morning or in late afternoon, when waters were considerably lower and less swift. Had it been summer, to make the crossings we would have had to swing much farther north where the rivers were narrower and not yet swelled by melting snows. Since there were no trees there was little firewood, and we did not see permanent dwellings for almost two months. Although it was cold, we had only two days of snow.

At Nakchuka we camped about a half-mile out of town. A crossroads town and important trading center, Nakchuka had shops and bazaars full of things I had never seen before, such as fresh oranges and colorful fabrics from India. For the first time in two months we enjoyed the luxury of fresh radishes and turnips and a dish made of fermented cabbage. On the way from Thalung our food had been mainly meat, wheat, rice, tsampa, soups, and stews. Residences here were of a type built by nomads—lower and more modestly constructed and furnished than ours at home. It was here in Nakchuka that I first became acquainted with restaurants. We found a favorite which served tasty *momos* and Lhasa-style food. Momos are steamed dumplings stuffed with seasoned, finely-chopped meat, eaten throughout Tibet. We hadn't tasted them since leaving Thalung.

As Nakchuka was the border-point for entering Tibet proper, taxes were paid to the Tibetan government on our tea and other goods. We paid no money. Instead, we turned over a percentage of our goods—as tea, butter, cheese, and silk from China. Uncle Kuyak requested a lower tax because many of the goods were going to lamas at the Ngor and Sakya monasteries, but the collector was not persuaded. We were assured that the tax fees would go to finance the big New Year Monlam Festival in Lhasa. I thought these tolls were rather unfairly collected. I was appalled as the nobleman collector strutted around pointing to specific boxes and directing our servants to "show me that." The painful process took several hours. We had one hundred boxes of tea, and they took about ten of the best ones.

Our party then broke up, with Uncle Kuyak and the hired men taking the supplies, goods, and all but one of our horses to Ngor Monastery on a more northerly route via Shigatse. Thus our pilgrimage began, with eight women and two men heading south on the ten-day walk to Lhasa. The women included mother, Aunt Chacha, two nuns, and myself.

The way of a pilgrim is not an easy one, I soon learned. My feet became so swollen that I could barely get into my boots; once that was accomplished, it was nearly impossible to walk. Several times on this leg of the journey my mother insisted I mount our one horse when the pain in my feet became intolerable. I also rode my horse when crossing shallow rivers because the rocks hurt my feet. In hopes of relief, I had tried borrowing boots from my mother and aunt, but they were too large. Our bootsoles were one thickness of yak leather, and when one wore out we removed it and stitched on another. Inside we stuffed yak hair and hay, which helped keep our feet warm and dry.

We covered some twelve to fifteen miles a day, the horse carrying our food and supplies. We passed through many meadows, after which we passed Samten Gangsang, a famous mountain whose beauty had been visible for about a week. On it, we believed, dwelled a rich mountain deity who had been the patron of Padmasambhava, the Indian master of tantric Buddhism. Known as the Lotus-born, Padmasambhava built the first monastery in Tibet at Samye. He was endowed with miracle powers by which he subdued all heathen demons, including the Samten Gangsang deity. Passing this mountain and the plain around it gave us a spirit of calmness and joy.

There followed rocky roads and steep hills that made my feet even more sore. At the village of Chado we left our horses to visit Reting Monastery, home then to a depleted population of about two hundred monks. A familiar song told of this and other famous monasteries: "Lhasa was built on a lake; Samye Monastery rests in the sand; Reting rises amid juniper trees; Chamdo is built between two large rivers; and Ganden is located on the top of a mountain." I feasted on my first sight of these famous places of which Lhayag, Khando, and my other girl friends and I had sung so many times. Many of their priceless historical artifacts were not on display as the monastery had not yet returned to normal after the three-week conspiracy that shook the government in 1947. Monks, many looking sad, graciously showed us what was left inside the temple. To me, this history-laden center, founded in 1057, was a beautiful sight. It was the first monastery I had seen situated in a forest. Many kinds of birds sang out from the juniper trees; some of their songs reminded me of Thalung. When we went on kora the smell of juniper lifted our spirits. Reting's Yellow Hat, or Gelug school, monks also looked out on a river that flowed into a picturesque valley.

We called on the head lama at another old monastery, Taglung, founded in 1180. Its community of five hundred was of the Kagyü school. Just before the town of Phongdo we crossed a 500-year-old suspension bridge built over the Taglung River by Thangtong Gyalbo, a lama who gave himself the name "King of the Empty Wasteland." An especially holy person, he attained buddhahood and lived to be 125. Instead of dying, he vanished much in the way a rainbow disappears. When he was about to die, Thangtong Gyalbo's disciples supplicated him to remain and not leave them. He instructed them to make a statue of himself, which I was to see much later in eastern Tibet. He was said to have built, by magical means, 108 wooden bridges throughout Tibet. One could always identify them, for their iron chains bore the design of the *dorje*, or thunderbolt. I was so frightened going across the bridge over the Taglung River that I was unable to look for these symbols. The bridge swung back and forth as we crossed, single file, grasping the side rails of chains with both hands. It was constructed of wooden ties placed several inches

apart, forcing one to see at every step the swift waters far
below.

After a brief stay at Nālandā, another Sakya monastery, we
began our way up the Phenpo Pass, the northeastern gateway
to Lhasa. We left Nālandā about four in the morning and
three hours later, at the top of the pass, we beheld the Holy
City, whose name means "Place of the Gods." Glistening in
the sun were the golden roofs of the majestic Potala, the
winter palace of the Dalai Lama. In the distance I saw the
Chagpori. One could see smoke rising from the city rooftops,
a friendly sign that the residents were awake and at their
breakfast routine. Now I knew the meaning of the saying,
"One who does not get to Lhasa has only half a human life."
It looked exactly like the descriptions of it that I had heard so
many times. "Now really I'm here," I thought. "It's no longer
a dream."

We arrived in the city in the late afternoon, and spent the
night at a friend's home. The next day we rented a house for
the remainder of our brief stay. That day we went to the
Jokhang, the main temple of Lhasa and the most holy place in
Tibet, open to the public three times a day. During our week
in Lhasa, we visited it daily. Each morning, we made a kora
around the Barkho, or central square, where the Jokhang is
situated. In this temple is housed the statue of Jo Rinpoche,
Yizhin Norbu, "Lord of the Wish-Fulfilling Gem." This
statue had been brought to Tibet in the seventh century by
the Chinese wife of Songsten Gampo, the first of the great
religious kings of Tibet. Pure gold butter lamps burned in
front of the gold-encrusted, heavily jeweled image, which by
tradition was the size of a sixteen-year-old boy.

There were so many wares new to my eyes that I was
mainly content to look, buying little. One could easily get
lost, and I was fearful of this as we made our way around this
city of 25,000. I saw no Caucasians, but there were many
Indians and Nepalese and some Moslem merchants.

It was the start of the pilgrimage season as we set out on
what is the most common of religious tours of temples,

shrines, and other holy places of Tibet. First we would swing south to Samye, and then travel in a clockwise direction around to Gyantse and north to Shigatse. Then our family group would go west on a side trip to Sakya before returning to Lhasa. While visiting the temples of Lhasa, we had made inquiries and found others planning the same side trip to Samye and the Lhokha areas. Our final tour count was twenty-nine, larger than most groups. All were Khampas and women, except for two monks from Amdo, who walked ahead and whom we gladly followed on the two-month journey. Women often made this circle tour while their husbands were conducting business in the Lhasa area. Yet, for the sake of protection, it was not wise to have an all-female pilgrimage.

It was imperative that we travel on foot as our family had only one horse to carry supplies. Near the pilgrimage sites, there were caves and other places for us to camp. We bought supplies as needed en route, and sometimes were given them by the generous laity. These donors, who considered it their duty and privilege to help pilgrims, also were generous with food for horses. When we stopped at the end of the day, however, we had to collect firewood and sometimes fresh milk. If we stopped in towns, people often offered us what we needed, or if a large group of us were camped in a field near a town, people would bring firewood and hay for the horses, and they always asked if we needed anything else. They would direct us to a supply of what they didn't have.

One of the first stops as we moved east from Lhasa was Ganden Monastery, home to some thirty-three hundred monks of the Yellow Hat school. Ganden (the Joyous) was founded in 1409 by Je Tsongkhapa, the great religious leader whose efforts to reform Tibetan Buddhism resulted in the rule of the Yellow Hats. The anniversary of Je Tsongkhapa's death is celebrated widely in Tibet. After being granted special permission, we visited a golden stupa containing his body at the main temple of Ganden. At most of the pilgrimage temples and monasteries, a monk conducted the tours. It was customary to place on a shrine a khata containing some money. We also offered the monk a small monetary gift. If he refused it, we usually insisted he take it, asking him to pray for us.

Although those who band together for a pilgrimage do so informally, lasting ties are formed among those who make this commitment. It was believed that pilgrims had a bond of brotherhood in this life and that they would surely meet again in the next one. Many persons along the route remarked that I was very young to be on a pilgrimage.

Pilgrims were distinguishable immediately. On a holy trek one did not dress ostentatiously or display signs of affluence. On the pilgrim's back was a pack, built around a bamboo frame, in which food and clothing were carried.

We arrived at Samye, Tibet's first Buddhist monastery, founded in C.E. 779 during the vanguard of transplanting Buddhism into my homeland. Samye was believed to be unique in that while humans built the structure in daylight, deities and other creatures contributed labor during the night. Architecturally, this early seat of learning is unlike any other Tibetan monastery in that its temple has three stories, each with a different architectural style—Indian, Tibetan, and Chinese. As we approached this cherished structure on the banks of the Tsangpo (Brahmaputra River), I could see its other distinguishing feature—the varicolored heads of the *chötens* dotting the top of the wall surrounding the monastery. The chöten, or stupa, is a structure that symbolizes the mind of the Buddha. Often used as a reliquary for deceased high lamas, some were built as memorials to Tibet's early religious kings. The word *chöten* means a "symbol of offering."

We headed east out of Samye, walking for three days along the Tsangpo. My feet were tired and the sand blew in my face. My feet were swelling and sinking into the dusty sand. Often I wrestled and played with Gyadrup and now, because I was walking so slowly, he again thought it was playtime.

"Stop it, Gyadrup," I scolded. "Don't bother me. I'm too tired to play. I have to catch up with the rest."

I didn't know whether he sensed my exhaustion or if he just

wanted to cheer me up. During this ordeal, I was reminded of the true purpose of my pilgrimage. "These hardships will cleanse me of defilements," I thought. It gave me courage to keep going. I was greatly relieved when we arrived at a ferry crossing. When it was possible to do so, we, by pilgrimage custom, were supposed to wade across rivers. But here the water was far too deep. The ferry boat had a horse's head carved on either end. We had to wait through several crossings as the ferry boat took on a few animals at a time. As he rowed, the oarsman sang about a peaceful and happy ride. From the ferry we could see Tsethang Monastery silhouetted against a high mountainside. This was the site about which I had heard so much. We visited the monastery temples, then stayed overnight at a nearby guest house.

Everyone in my country knew this place as the birthplace of human civilization in Tibet. According to religious belief, the name *Tsethang* means "playground," stemming from the story of a monkey that was a compassionate emanation of Chenrezi, the Bodhisattva of Mercy. This monkey married a demon-woman who had threatened to kill herself if they weren't wed. Their offspring, six baby monkeys, symbolized the six forms of sentient beings. The generations of monkeys increased rapidly, bringing about poverty and starvation. In despair the original monkey went to Chenrezi, telling of their plight. Chenrezi told him not to worry, and gave the monkey five seeds, each from different grains—barley, wheat, peas, millet, and *sowa* (unhusked paddy). The monkey planted these with Chenrezi's blessing, and the following year they yielded a bountiful crop. Soon after, the monkeys began to lose their tails and fur and became human. I lingered to view the paintings depicting these monkeys' playground on the inside walls of the temple. Shyly I asked the monk conducting our tour, "Where is the monkey's playground?" He smiled, looking as though he had never fielded such a question before and said, "There is no such playground anymore." He assured me that all the structures in the area had been built on a playground.

In my excitement, that night I dreamed that we were visiting a temple filled with numerous Tārās. Tārā is a female deity, the mother of all beings, who cares for them as though each was her own child. One Tārā gave me friendly advice. I felt uplifted and blessed that she was speaking to me. I told my mother and Aunt Chacha about this phenomenon, but they didn't take me seriously. The next morning we arose at about five o'clock and went up the mountain on kora. We visited a nunnery and stopped there for refreshments. Descending into the Tadrug vicinity, we visited a town that had a big temple in its center containing many Tārās. As we entered to pay our respects, I gasped, as the temple was exactly as I had dreamed. There were twenty-one life-sized Tārās, and a central gold-encrusted bigger one. A nun in our party observed in her guidebook that one of the Tārās spoke. She very humbly pointed to the central Tārā, asking our monk tour guide, "Is that the one who talks?" I interrupted excitedly, saying "No, no. That one!" pointing to a statue behind us near the entrance. The monk was shocked, knowing that I wasn't from the area, and asked, "Who told you?" The nun nudged me and told me to be quiet, but the monk said, "That's right. That is the one." We went over to the statue to pray and make an offering. To me, the talking Tārā behind the flickering butter lamps didn't look much different from the others. As I moved in front of her, her eyes seemed to follow me, and I felt that she was watching over me. I left Tadrug with a good feeling.

We headed into the Yarlung Valley, visiting the six holy places linked to the deeds of Padmasambhava. Our agenda included the famed castle of Yumbu Lagang, the oldest surviving dwelling in Tibet and reportedly the home of the early kings. The tall gray building contained a lookout tower used for defense purposes in olden times. I was disappointed that it was not more liveable. The keeper wasn't friendly. He showed us only two rooms on the first level. That was enough of this historic sight for me.

After a few days of walking for miles on a very cold barren

plateau and sleeping beside caves and rocks, I felt tired as I leaned against the biting winds. But this hardship would benefit me later in my life in overcoming obstacles. "This will accumulate good merit and remove all my sins," I thought. In contrast, in the Changthang we had camped more comfortably in tents surrounded by tea boxes and other supplies that warded off the cold winds. But here, there was no such luxury. We lit a fire in the evening to keep our feet warm, but when we awoke there was frost between our hats and our blankets. Gyadrup slept by my feet, warming my body. We finally descended into a warmer area and reached Lhokha Nowache. This town had been regarded as evil before Padmasambhava came and subdued their cannibalism and other harmful practices. At the small monastery I gathered a little bag of souvenirs, for here were the small bulletlike rocks which, we believed, the anti-Buddhist enemies of Padmasambhava attempted to hurl at him. But the stones did not harm this yogin-sage. Instead, he transformed them into protection against evil. We regarded these as holy rocks; I picked up enough to share with my girl friends.

I stared at the people here in their strange attire. They were dressed in sleeveless garments made of goat and monkey skins, with the fur on the outside. The dried feet of the animals were still attached to the skins. Some of the women had painted faces, their makeup resembling masks. They were friendly people, but I thought somehow they didn't belong in Tibet.

Now we were in Lhokha proper, the warm and sunny "breadbasket" of Tibet, just north of Bhutan. Here there were many new kinds of vegetation, including bamboo trees. Wild monkeys and bright-colored noisy birds inhabited these trees, and the air was sweet with refreshing fragrances. There were many pine trees here, and I braided sprigs of them into the ends of my hair. Pitchy boughs of pine were used as torches here. It was a new and exciting experience for me to have light furnished in this manner. We feasted on semi-dried apricots which were an inexpensive treat. Sometimes it was difficult to find fresh water, particularly as we were passing out of Nowache.

At Lhodraglhamo Khachu, a monastery of the Nyingma school, we visited Padmasambhava's cave. His footprint was in a rock there. Inside was a statue of him that was about twenty feet high. To reach this cave, one had to make a treacherous descent and then a tricky ascent. Many pilgrims didn't dare make the climb. Even some people who lived there had never seen the cave.

It was many miles later at Lhakang Dzong, an administrative headquarters, that we met with an unexpected delay at a toll bridge over the swift and dangerous Lhakang River. Tickets had to be bought from the *dzongpon*, the nobleman assigned there. Upon reaching the toll house on the opposite side, the ticket was stamped with a seal. Before we arrived at the *dzong* or fortress, however, Gyadrup, our dog, bit a nobleman's pig, causing much commotion. Gyadrup had never seen a pig before and clearly marked the animal as his enemy. I had to separate the two animals, the pig squealing and attracting attention. The pig sped away, scarcely scratched, but mother and Aunt Chacha offered to pay for the inconvenience, fearing Gyadrup would be confiscated or even destroyed by the estate administrators. He was a good watchdog and we needed him. Our offer of payment was refused.

Outside the dzong, a handsome, well-dressed youth in his late teens came around several times to make conversation with our group. He was the son of the dzongpon. They were a Lhasa family, but the father was engaged in the traditional term of government service in this area. We had arrived at the dzong in mid-morning, but there was hesitancy and delay about our ticket and soon it was afternoon. As we waited outside in the courtyard, I grew ever more fearful that Gyadrup's attack on the pig was the cause of our detention. The noble's son continued in his efforts to make conversation, and it soon became clear that it was my companionship he was seeking. He asked us many questions. The young man was intrigued—or pretended to be—by my Khampa dialect, frequently asking me to repeat what I had said. It was embarrassing to me. He offered chang to a number of pilgrims and gave gifts to my family. And he walked beside me as I moved about the courtyard area. He told Aunt Chacha and me that he liked my company and asked that we stay longer at the dzong.

Aunt Chacha stressed that I was "only a child" and that we were on our way to Sakya. He offered to escort us to our next stop if the other members of the pilgrimage wanted to go on ahead. We refused because we all wanted to stay together. By custom, we had to be polite to any noble, but there were no pilgrimage attractions in this area and we felt we couldn't delay any longer. By late afternoon, everyone had been issued tickets except four in our family group, and our horse and dog. The toll fees, we learned, primarily were donated to financing the Monlam, the great New Year Butter Festival in Lhasa. Despite our pleas, it was near sunset before the young man relented and we were finally given our tickets—free—and permitted to cross the bridge. But our problems were not over.

There was a small town on the other side of the river to which the noble's son followed us, asking if he could be of assistance in getting accommodations. He ordered the townspeople to bring firewood for us and hay for our horse. We accepted his assistance in a limited manner, settling in a large room in the lower level of a house, which he came to visit. It was a moonlit evening and the pine-bough torches flickered inside our quarters. Usually on pilgrimage we retired early, but he stayed late as we talked about our families and he chatted enthusiastically about the Butter Festival, which I had not seen. During the evening this young noble took me on a tour of the village, accompanied by Gyadrup on a leash. I was conscious of being observed with interest and curiosity by the townspeople.

The next morning, our breakfast visitor was the young man. He slipped a silver and turquoise ring made in the shape of a saddle off my finger and tried it on his. By custom, taking a personal item in this way is regarded as a mark of affection. I requested it back—with no results. I was apprehensive of what my mother would say. But when I explained, she recommended I not insist on getting the ring back. He also gave me a pen and asked that I write him a letter. I did not promise, and I never wrote a letter in return. The young man rode with us out about a mile, then sadly said farewell. As a final gesture, he gave me his handknitted scarf, saying it would keep me warm. He put it around my head and tied it under my chin. I was reluctant to take even that. Looking back now, I realize I didn't comprehend the depth of his feelings, for it was my first such experience. My thoughts were of the great excitement ahead—the visit to Sakya and seeing my grandmother again.

Some three days later we arrived at a highlight of the pilgrimage, Mila Sekarguthog. At our first sighting of this nine-story white structure, we performed prostrations. This monastery was built by Milarepa, the revered eleventh-century saint and poet, at the order of his teacher, Marpa. Known as the "suffering building," it had been started and razed three times before Marpa let Milarepa finish it. On each floor there was much to see—statues and shrine rooms relating to the greatest of my country's poets. Doors opened from each of the four sides of the top floor of the structure. Pilgrims circumambulated a ledge there. This ledge was only about a foot wide and one had to hang on to a chain above your head to keep from falling. As this footwork was too dangerous for youngsters, and I couldn't reach the chain, a monk was paid to go around several times on my behalf. The monk was also paid to go around for Great-Uncle Nawang and my grandmother. By making this circumambulation, one was kept from being reborn in the three lower realms of existence: the animal realm, the hungry ghost realm, and the hell realm. All of the stories that Great-Uncle Nawang had told me about Milarepa flashed back in my mind here. It was sad to be the only one not to circle the top floor, but I saw many of the personal effects of Mila—his tools, garments said to be his clothes, and the crude tools he used magically to construct the building.

We made a careful approach to our next stop, Druptsho Pemaling, a lake that was said to have been blessed by Padmasambhava. What distinguished this spot was the quiet. The only sounds were those of nature. It was feared that noise would disturb the powerful water deities that dwelled here. And it was advisable to keep voices low and other sounds to a minimum for fear of causing an avalanche, for snow-capped ranges ringed this lake and snow extended halfway down their sides. The sun rarely appeared here, and half of the lake was frozen over. By looking into this lake, it was believed, one could tell the future. I looked but didn't observe anything significant. Inside the little monastery at the lakeshore, there were famous statues that were said to be among Padmasambhava's hidden treasures. Only four monks lived here. It was not a desirable assignment and monks were given more generous supplies and privileges for remaining in this eerie atmosphere. A promotion was assured after such duty.

That evening, while we rested in camp, we could hear ice jostling in the lake and thought we heard the movement of the mountain snows. I was constantly alert; I thought that if I laughed or coughed, it would disturb the mountain deities. I feared the lake would rise up under us, or an avalanche would sweep down upon us. Gyadrup, too, seemed to sense the eerie feeling. I kept petting him and telling him in low tones to be quiet. I was all to happy to depart the next morning.

Crossing two mountains we arrived at Phurma Yutso, a large lake with an island in the center, on which was a small Nyingma monastery. It was the first island I had seen in my life. It was picturesque—the clear, blue waters, the white monastery with red and yellow markings, the ice on the banks of the lake, and waves that appeared to be several feet high. This monastery was open to visitors only three months of the year when there was a bridge of ice to the island. I gathered round white stones at the shoreline, disappointed that I found no shells. We were on lower terrain here and it was extremely cold. Despite the gift scarf I had received earlier from my would-be suitor, I was very uncomfortable. My breath quickly turned to ice on the scarf. Our horse had no problem; he was accustomed to cold. Happily, we moved on to warmer areas, where I was to have my first brush with the culture of the Western world.

We now swung northwest, taking the route from Ralung to Shigatse. At Ralung we joined the thoroughfare that for centuries had been the main route from India to Tibet. The weather was comfortable and we moved with ease on what was a freeway in comparison to many of the modest pathways of the Land of Snows. It was dusty and colorful. Bells on the horses and mules tinkled as the travelers moved along—some of them traders and farmers on their way to market with produce. By custom, even on this roadway they gave way to pilgrims on foot. The mules wore gaily decorated forehead caps made of wool. The lead mules sometimes had a small mirror or piece of tin can on these caps. Large bells and yak tails dyed red also hung from their necks, sometimes touching the ground. The freight carried by these pack animals was so well boxed and concealed that I often wondered what was inside and tried to guess. Overhead I saw wires and inquired of some girls nearby about these lines. "Very dangerous," they decreed. Later I learned they were telegraph lines to the Indian mission at Gyantse. My excitement grew at the thought of Gyantse, our next major stop and the third largest city in Tibet. It meant the distance was narrowing between us and Uncle Tülku-la and my grandmother.

At Gyantse, we spent the first night near the Indian trade mission. The mission had been under British control for decades and remained so for some years after India gained its independence. The two-story hospital here was staffed by British and Indian personnel. Medical treatment was free and there was a fine first-aid center used extensively by Tibetans, who frequently brought gifts such as fresh eggs to show their appreciation for these services. The mission had lovely gardens and a greenhouse, which we toured with a guide.

It was here that I saw a blond blue-eyed woman for the first time. I found myself staring at her light pink skin, delicate like that of a baby, I thought. I was impressed at how skilled this woman was as a knitter. She was extremely fast and seldom seemed to look at her hands. She was completely at ease, composed and smiling, as we watched her every move. I thought her to be very good natured and friendly, and I wondered how many more women there were like this. "How old is she?" I wondered. I had no idea, having no one with which to compare her. The woman was the wife of the Englishman who headed the mission. We were introduced to them, after which he took our photographs. Apparently we were interesting because we were a large group of Khampa women and were differently attired than the usual pilgrim.

Soldiers drilled each morning and evening, drawing spectators. I was intrigued by these khaki-clad men, who were larger than Tibetans and generally handsome. They wore caps and gloves, so only their faces and uniforms were visible. We saw only about twenty marching on the field, but it was said there were many more stationed here.

Our pilgrimage group broke up here, with only about fifteen of us going on to Shigatse. These included the two Amdo monks, who planned to study at Tashihunpo Monastery, home of the Panchen Lama, who is the second-ranked Yellow Hat religious leader, one having limited temporal power. The four-day trip through the flat country between Gyantse and Shigatse consisted mainly of dusty roads and a series of small towns. Along the roads there were grain mills, operated by water wheels, where barley was ground into tsampa. Usually older men worked in the mills, and they presented a strange picture, covered with barley-flour dust even to their eyebrows. We asked these millmen for samples of popped barley, which we ate like popcorn.

When we reached Shigatse, we had completed the main walking phase of our pilgrimage. Now we had the option of walking or riding while visiting monasteries and shrines. Two weeks in Shigatse gave us an opportunity to rest. Here we visited the temples at Tashihunpo, the great monastery of the Yellow Hat school, built in the fifteenth century, whose name means "heap of blessings." This city had markets, bazaars, and vegetable stands where I felt at home. While staying with Uncle Tülku-la's treasurer, we threw away our old pilgrimage clothes. We were only too happy to don the new clothes the treasurer had made for us.

We waited here for Uncle Tülku-la to arrive at Ngor Monastery from Sakya. When he finally did, four of us women set out for Ngor. Our subsequent joyous reunion at Ngor occurred in time for the lunar New Year observance. Uncle Tülku-la stayed at one of the labrangs, and we tented in a nearby garden. This educational religious institution was very strict, and no women were permitted in the monastery.

Next we made a trip from Ngor to Sakya through an area of farms, during which we stopped at a town called Shap, famous for its wheat bread. When residents offered us a basket of their tasty dark bread shaped in a large ring, we expressed our gratitude by placing a white khata in the basket; Tibetans never return containers empty. There was great competition among these breadmakers. We relished this flat and slightly salty bread, dipping it into tea before eating it. As we moved toward Sakya, I was overcome by homesickness, despite the fact that soon I was to see my grandmother and Ani Chimi. I was moving farther and farther away from Kham and felt sure I would never get home. Tears came as I rode along, looking out on treeless bare mountains and hills. I felt lonely and saddened. No wonder they called it Sakya, "the gray place." "Will I ever make it back home?" I thought.

But as we came to Ado Pass and I saw in the distance this town of several thousand people, my outlook abruptly changed. I could see the gold roofs and bright red, white and blue colors glistening from the monasteries, the Phuntsok and Drolma palaces, and the Gorum Temple. Founded in 1073, the temple held statues, war trophies, and cherished religious books, some centuries old. Many of these valuable items were from China, India, and Mongolia. And there was the Lhakhang Chenmo, the Great Temple, built in the thirteenth century and the seat of the Sakya school in which I was reared. It is the largest temple in Tibet. I was consumed by the scene before me.

From here, the once vastly powerful Sakya lamas had established relations with the Mongol Khans. This relationship was begun by one of the most famous lamas, Sakya Pandita, who lived from 1182 until 1251, and whose role was tantamount to king of much of Tibet. His work was carried on by a nephew, Chögyal Phagspa (1235–1280), who clearly established the priest–patron relationship between the Sakya lamas and the Khans. Under Phagspa's negotiations with the Kublai Khan, the lamas had precedence in spiritual and strictly Tibetan affairs, while the Kublai Khan was the supreme power in secular affairs of the Mongol empire.

With this history in mind and with reverent hearts, we approached Sakya. In the glow of the late afternoon sun, I felt a warmth and welcome here. There was an air of ease, a certain staidness that would be true of any great religious center, I thought.

5

Romance and Strife

Since we were carrying some supplies to a learned abbot who was a friend of Uncle Tülku-la, we stopped at the Great Temple of Sakya to deliver them. We moved toward the two main palaces, the Phuntsok and Drolma, magnificent structures with long and intriguing histories. These were the homes of the spiritual rulers of the Sakya school. At this time spiritual power was held by the Trichen, who was from the house of the Phuntsok Palace. The Trichen and his family were in residence in their winter quarters inside the monastery walls, where they were better protected from the cold and inclement weather.

My grandmother and Ani Chimi were residing in a summer palace of the Trichen near the Phuntsok Palace. When passing the Phuntsok Palace, as a gesture of respect one dismounted and went on foot. As we approached, my grandmother heard the bells on our mules and came running. More than a year and a half had elapsed since we had parted in Thalung. Grandmother had been worried about us, she confessed.

Our home on the second floor of the two-story summer palace was very comfortable indeed. I thought how fortunate we were to have such quarters, due to Uncle Tülku-la's respected position. He had spent a year in Sakya receiving instructions from the lamas and carrying out various commissions for the Trichen.

We talked until late that evening about relatives from home and my adventures on the pilgrimage. I slept that night in my grandmother's room, feeling relaxed at having reached my destination. But I was strangely restless in my sleep, awakening frequently. I dreamed I was seated on a high cushion looking out from the palace into a courtyard filled with a variety of people and creatures. Lovely women attired in Sakya clothing, with large headdresses and jewels, called out to me. They seemed to be saying, "We finally brought you here." I thought their words were peculiar, since I was only visiting Sakya and had firm plans to return to Thalung. I thought, "I don't belong to you." I awakened my grandmother, saying that I couldn't cope with all these people. She comforted me, observing that I was simply tired and excited. I climbed into her bed for the remainder of the night, but still awakened frequently.

Grandmother and Ani Chimi had bought wool from the supplies at the Phuntsok Palace. They had been weaving cloth with a hand loom and had made chubas and many aprons to take home to Thalung. They had also made many new acquaintances here, who now came to our quarters to visit.

We paid a formal visit to the Drolma Palace, home of the other branch of the Sakya family, whose head was the lama Drolma Kyagon Ngawang Rinchen. He gave us his blessing and we presented the traditional white scarf with offerings. While there, Uncle Tülku-la had a conversation with the Drolma Kyagon's wife, Drolma Dagmo Kusho. I listened as Uncle complimented her on the long hours she spent daily in religious practice. Her duties included the rearing of three children—a boy and two girls of the Sakya lineage borne by her sister. Unable to have children, Drolma Dagmo Kusho had given permission to have her younger sister marry her husband as a second wife. That marriage produced the three youngsters before the younger sister's death.

Drolma Dagmo Kusho told us that her spiritual teacher, or root lama, had stressed that while *dagmos* have all the privileges of high rank, unless they produced sons they would be reborn in a lower existence in the next life. Since she was barren, the teacher's words had struck deeply in her heart. She became very pious in order to escape this fate. I admired her diligence, openness, courage, and devotion to the religious life. Later in my life I would often remember our conversation.

Mother and I soon found ourselves busy visiting the temples and shrines of Sakya. When we had been there about three weeks, the laity began clearing the road for the Trichen to move back into the Phuntsok Palace now that a warmer season was beginning. One day I watched the ceremony and pomp as this high-ranking lama and his family, carrying out centuries-old tradition, made their way home to their main palace. The parents were carried in sedan chairs.

The Trichen and his wife had seven living children, the eldest son destined by tradition to be the next ruler of the Sakya school. My first acquaintances in the Trichen's family were two daughters, Tsegen-la, thirteen, and Chimi-la, about nine, both nuns. By custom, all male offspring of the Trichen are lamas and the females are nuns. The family's nuns were not supposed to marry—although they sometimes did—but all of the lamas in the family could take wives if they chose. The eldest son carried on the family title.

Our friendship grew as we spent afternoons outdoors around the palace grounds. They taught me western Tibetan songs, and I showed them our style of dancing at home. They studied in the morning. My Kham-style clothes and dialect were a novelty to the girls, who always were accompanied by a servant. I always kept my place, treating them with respect. When I was with the girls, I was always well dressed, feeling that in their company it would not be correct to be too casual. But my garb sometimes brought remarks from the sisters not to wear "those good clothes," for on meeting us, outsiders mistakenly took me for a member of the Sakya family and paid respects to me too, removing their hats and bowing.

Regardless of these new friendships, I was still very much in awe of the family. One day the girls took me to their rooms in the palace to show me their belongings. Their mother, the Gyayum Kusho, a very proper lady, gave me a package of dried fruit and wrapped candies, saying that I was to "come back anytime." The title *Gyayum Kusho*—meaning the mother of a prince—was given to the wife of the Trichen only if she bore a son. The Gyayum Kusho wore the traditional jewels and headdress at all times. A Lhasa girl before her marriage to the Trichen, she had given birth to a total of sixteen children.

Despite her invitation, I did not make another visit until Uncle Tülku-la returned to Sakya from Ngor Monastery. Soon after Uncle Tülku-la joined us, we heard some news of Kham. A traveler told Uncle that the Communist Chinese had taken over part of Chinghai province, including Sining. Strange things were occurring in our home province, although there was no word of the Communists coming to Thalung. However, some Chinese had come to the Jyekundo area from Sining and were confiscating animals and telling people about the changes Communism would bring. They said they were Communists, but it was believed that some were Nationalists who were fleeing the Communists. Many Tibetans were confused, the traveler said, as they didn't know with whom they were dealing. There were other odd occurrences—taxes weren't being collected on time, for example.

But there was nothing in the traveler's report that made us deeply concerned about our loved ones and possessions in Thalung. We were led to believe just a few Chinese were involved in these events. Sakya was very isolated from world events, so we were woefully ignorant of what was about to happen in our hometown.

It was shortly thereafter that our family paid its first formal visit to the Trichen's family. The Trichen was a very powerful lama with great responsibility for the Sakyapa monasteries throughout Tibet and in Mongolia, western China, Nepal, and Bhutan. For so long I had heard of this lama, and now I was visualizing what it would be like to tell my friends back home that I had met him and his family.

Uncle Tülku-la, my mother, grandmother, Ani Chimi, and I made the mid-morning call and were shown to a large reception room on the second floor of the palace. The Trichen sat in the lotus position high on a thronelike platform. With him, besides his wife, were the eldest son, Jigdal Rinpoche; a second son, Trinly Rinpoche; the two daughters who were my friends; and a third named Kunyang-la.

It was a ceremony similar to our visit to the Drolma Palace, but somewhat more impressive. We brought gifts in honor of the family that included money, huge boxes of brick tea, bolts of silk fabric, quantities of packed butter, and several horses and mules. These gifts were specified for individual members of the family on a list wrapped in a ceremonial khata presented on the throne table in front of the Trichen.

The Trichen, in his late forties, immediately gave me the impression of being a living Buddha, who, if I did something wrong, would know it without being told. He was attired in an embroidered robe worn atop a white skirtlike garment, over which was another robe. Only he wore these garments, which I had seen in photographs and in fleeting glances when the family had ceremoniously returned to the palace. He also wore coral prayer beads around his neck.

We drank tea with our heads slightly bowed and eyes down in a measure of reverence and respect. The Trichen was smiling, however, and had touched his hands to our heads during the course of the meeting, putting us somewhat at ease. We women sat in front of a table on a long rug. Uncle Tülku-la sat on a cushion higher than ours, and the Trichen had reached down to touch Uncle's forehead.

The Trichen and Gyayum Kusho asked us our ages and all about us, how long we were to stay, and if we needed anything. The Gyayum Kusho mentioned the importance of Uncle Tülku-la, reaffirming to me the wide respect with which he was held.

Although servants came by repeatedly with tea, cookies,

and rice, I found it difficult to eat in this atmosphere. The room contained some of the most elegant and inspiring decorations I had ever seen. When we left, the Gyayum Kusho politely asked us to make a return visit.

The next day the two daughters came outdoors to play after lunch and from that time on we saw one another almost daily. Tsegen-la and Chimi-la called me "little Kham girl." I didn't like it, but I couldn't correct a member of the Trichen's family. But I did tell servants my name was Sonam Tshe Dzom. They usually called me by my proper name or referred to me as "Dezhung Rinpoche's niece." For fun we made headdresses out of willows that grew around the palace. With these, we practiced bending and entering doorways as if we were Tsang women. They liked to try on my boots, hiding amid the trees so that no one could see them. Since I was a little older, it was to them a little like playing dress-up. Such an exchange of clothing, if discovered, would have been frowned upon greatly, since they always wore the Sakya family's nun's attire—a maroon chuba and red blouse. Their hair was short but not shaved.

Meanwhile, I was learning much of the Sakya dialect, customs, manners, history, religion, and even games. It was a new world that was opening up to me—an exciting education. Mornings I studied with Ani Chimi, mainly reading and memorizing prayers in Sanskrit. There was much to see in this busy palace, parts of which were strictly off limits to all but a very few. We also made the rounds of the stables. Because of so many special ceremonies in the palace, the women workers spent lots of time making cookies and barley popcorn. We girls took great delight in watching them make barley popcorn and sometimes even helped them. The cookies were in elaborate shapes, many of them Buddhist symbols. I liked to be on hand to listen to the women sing as they worked. The songs were different from those sung in eastern Tibet. In my country such chores are always done with the benefit of musical accompaniment, most of it religious. In the fall, the women made a year's supply of wheat flour noodles.

Great quantities of eggs were brought in from the Sakya estates during this time.

Several times while with Tsegen-la and Chimi-la, I went to the quarters of their eldest brother, Jigdal Rinpoche. He was busy in the morning studying with his private tutor, and his food was served to him in his room. Besides his prayers and study in the mornings, he was receiving instruction on the trumpet, flute, and other musical instruments for religious ceremonies. Several monks, all skilled musicians, came to his quarters in the afternoon, about three days a week, to practice with him. He, according to long history, would be the next Trichen. Although I felt a trifle strange and uneasy here—not being a family member—the sisters managed to pull me into the section of the palace that was his. Often they were on a "begging" mission to Jigdal Rinpoche, hoping they would get candy, money, or some other item wanted at the moment.

Jigdal Rinpoche, twenty, was very generous, fun, and indeed much more casual than I ever dreamed. He was carefree and had a sense of humor that I enjoyed. He got on well with people of all circles, it seemed. And he was powerful and was being prepared for his future role. After his classwork he would go on kora around the Phuntsok Palace. This immediately drew a group of beggars, who were all familiar with his generous nature. He had a bicycle—new to me—which he rode. Some of the older people didn't think this was quite proper, the making of the rounds on wheels. Bicycles were not traditional, they reasoned.

Jigdal Rinpoche's personal servant was Singtashi, a trusted member of the household. Singtashi's mother had been servant to the Gyayum Kusho, brought with her from Lhasa when she was married. When we girls went on picnics, Jigdal Rinpoche and Singtashi sometimes accompanied us.

One day my mother advised me that since I was seeing this high lama frequently, I should ask him how long I would live in this world. Especially with Khampas, this was a common request made to a trusted favorite high lama. So, shortly thereafter, I asked him. "I have to see your palm," he replied.

He took hold of both of my hands, throwing his head back. He wasn't even looking at my hands! I started to shake. "You almost died when you were seven years old," he said. "So your major obstacles are removed. You will live a long life, if you do certain mantras daily." He then recommended the mantras that I was to recite.

I took this message back to my mother, and she summoned the rest of the family to tell them the good news. She said he was indeed correct, that I had nearly died of measles at that age. Ani Chimi recalled that during my illness, she had served me boiled tsampa with a lot of butter in it to give me extra strength. Then my fever soared very high. Convinced that I was going to die, the family had requested the monks at Thalung Monastery to blow a conch shell for emergency prayers on my behalf.

It was essential that the patient hear the conch shell sounding. Ani Chimi swooped me up from the bed, wrapped me in a blanket, and took me upstairs to the flat roof of our home. In her haste, she bumped my head on the stairway. It hurt very badly. She implored, "Please don't cry, because the family will scold me." I agreed and kept our secret. But when I arrived on the roof, my head hurt so badly that I just faintly heard the conch shell. Once back in my bed, I called the family in to request that, if I died, Ani Chimi should not be blamed for my death. She had, after all, only served me the butter-laced tsampa because I was so weak. These and other memories surfaced in the light of Jigdal Rinpoche's prediction. We laughed as Ani Chimi revealed the long-kept secret of the fire in my head after it was whacked on the stairs.

Sometimes we played cards on a low table, with Jigdal Rinpoche sitting next to me on the floor. It was my first time, and he helped me with the rules of rummy and the other games we played with small Tibetan coins. The sisters thought he was teasing with the little displays of affection that were beginning to come my way. When I left, he often gave a parting remark, such as "We will see you soon."

Occasionally Jigdal Rinpoche would send me a note by

Singtashi, indicating he wanted to see me at some rendezvous point. Sometimes Singtashi would just inconspicuously put the note in my pocket because he knew I was afraid of accepting it. Then without saying anything, he would run back to the palace. Usually these meeting spots were in one of the four gardens near the Phuntsok Palace. Jigdal Rinpoche would pretend he was leaving to go on kora.

Upon meeting members of the Trichen's family one bowed and received their blessing. However, Jigdal Rinpoche began the practice of touching his forehead to mine, a custom usually reserved for high lamas, important officials, and relatives. I felt flushed, warm, and nervous when this occurred. Except for the sisters, no member of the Trichen's family knew of this, but the girls didn't read anything into it. Nor did any member of my family know, for such behavior would certainly have brought me a severe dressing-down.

When the Trichen's family planned to visit nearby Chökhor Lhunpo Monastery, the girls asked me to go along. Jigdal Rinpoche stayed home to watch over palace affairs. The Trichen, his family, monks, and Sakya officials formed a party of about sixty invited for a week-long celebration marking the birthday of Padmasambhava. I felt fortunate to view a thirty-foot high statue of him that rested inside the monastery's main temple.

While some of the ceremonies were taking place inside the temple, we walked with the Gyayum Kusho into a beautiful valley dotted with manmade irrigation ponds. I saw baby ducks swimming dutifully behind their mothers in the ponds and ditches. Peas were ready to eat, so we indulged. The field workers were delighted to offer the fresh, tasty abundance from their property. Barley and wheat also were plentiful. There were many wild flowers growing on the edges of the fields. It was another adventure I planned to relate to my girl friends at home in Thalung.

We slept in tents in a parklike area below the monastery. Monks served us all of our meals there. From the hillside, we could see the main Sakya monastery and town in the distance.

In the evening I was homesick. It was the first time since leaving Thalung that I had been separated from my family for this length of time.

I brought home sweet rice, dried fruit, a leg of lamb, cookies, and silver coins in a white scarf, all gifts from the Chökhor Lhunpo Monastery. I had a wonderful time that week, but upon returning I found that Jigdal Rinpoche was very disappointed that I had gone away without telling him. This alerted me that he cared for me in some special way.

When he came to our home to visit, he received a warm welcome and seemed to enjoy my family. The feeling was mutual. Mother, who knew nothing of the casual relationship between this lama and me, was impressed and said that surely he was a "Khampa lama," a high compliment from an eastern Tibetan.

Both Jigdal Rinpoche and I were beginning to care increasingly for each other. Although I knew he liked me and was trying his best to please me, it seemed impossible that we could ever marry, for we held very different stations in life. If his parents had known of this growing affection, they would not have approved, for they expected him to marry someone belonging to the nobility. Jigdal Rinpoche always was accompanied by Singtashi or another servant on these missions. Whatever romantic notions I was harboring, none of them included any thought of spending the rest of my life in western Tibet. Home to me was Kham.

Servants were beginning to suspect our association, but fortunately this information had not yet reached our families. When Jigdal Rinpoche came to our house, frequently it was on the pretense of business in the storage areas there. These storage areas for the Phuntsok Palace, while on the first floor, were accessible only through the second floor—our quarters. There were several secret rooms that could only be reached through trap doors from which ladders descended to the lower floor. The trap doors were kept locked and sealed with wax. A bed or other large piece of furniture was placed over each door. These secret rooms held valuables of many kinds—

ancient ceremonial objects of gold and silver, great supplies of silks, religious trappings used on special occasions, and other old costumes, as well as gold and jewels.

During this period, the star Karma Rishi shone on our world, providing blessed water and dew with its eight attributes: coolness, sweetness, digestive lightness, softness, clearness, freedom from impurities, being soothing to the stomach, and making the throat clear. We believed that for one week Karma Rishi purified our waters and for another week blessed our lands. During the purification, we not only bathed ourselves in rivers, streams, and lakes, but also put water on our animals. It was the perfect time to wash all of our clothing. This purification period was observed throughout Tibet, but especially in Kham. Not only was it appropriate to cleanse away one's sins and misdeeds, but it promoted good health both physically and spiritually.

During this festival a week-long garden party was staged in honor of government nobles and other officials, paid for by the Sakya government. About sixty persons attended, with the Trichen and his wife arriving about noon and staying until about nine o'clock daily. It was the first time for me to observe this type of party, peculiar to Sakya. It was a festive string of hours, with mostly Indian music from a hand-wound record player. People were dressed in their best and spent their time playing *mahjongg* and cards and rolling dice, and, of course, eating. There were no special religious events here. As they were leaving, each guest was given money, khatas, and food.

After his parents had left, Jigdal and I met in the garden near where some tents were pitched. When Singtashi had first told me Jigdal Rinpoche wanted to see me, I was hesitant. He had been busy with guests, but soon he came. We were alone, finally, in the bright moonlight, seated under a tree. We talked and he held my hand. Then he said, "If your mother and uncle give their consent, will you marry me?" I said nothing. He said he was not speaking in jest, but that he was serious. "I have checked in many ways and you are the one who has the qualifications to bear sons for the Sakya lineage," he said.

I was surprised that he brought up the subject so directly. In my country, marriages were arranged by families. But I knew he was serious. I recalled that earlier, during our card games, he had remarked to his sisters and servants, "This is my life partner." These words had frightened me, but I couldn't respond to them because of his rank. I knew that I personally loved him in certain ways and that I admired him. But I was not ready to give up all my adventures. I was still "collecting" culture and customs to bring home to Kham.

With some mixed emotions, I replied indirectly with all the seriousness that a fifteen-year-old, who indeed was marriageable, could muster. I said I wanted to return to Thalung to see my friends. "I am so far from home," I said. "I like you, but I want to go home."

At first Jigdal Rinpoche seemed shocked. I had, it seemed, the worst case of homesickness in my family. Knowing that my family would be returning to Kham, I envisioned how lonely it would be here without them, especially since we were so close. Life here, even the games, was so different. I felt like an outsider in this environment. I suddenly wanted to be home—to tell my friends all that I had seen and done.

In the moonlight, I could see that Jigdal Rinpoche was both hurt and surprised. After all, I was turning down a proposal from the future Trichen. Hundreds of girls and women would have snapped up the chance to say yes to his offer. Again I thought of this lama's distinguished family line.

Jigdal Rinpoche's ancestors were the historically and religiously important Khon, who, according to Tibetan tradition, were a family of three brothers who descended from heaven as representatives of the Great Teacher, the Buddha. Jigdal Rinpoche was from the unbroken lineage of Khon Kunchok Gyalpo, who founded the Sakya Monastery nearly nine hundred years ago.

The priest-patron relationship that began with Kublai Khan and Phagspa lasted almost a century. But the Sakya leaders continued to exert their influence in religious affairs long after their political support from the Khans ceased. The Sakya Trichen continued to be not only head of the school but also the leader of the local government of Sakya and its widespread holdings. Thus, it was natural for me to look at Jigdal Rinpoche with a sense of history, as well as admiration and affection.

Other guests drifted into our company. It was getting late. Jigdal Rinpoche urged me not to go yet, so we began playing cards. He was watching my hand and then said, "Keep this for me." He dropped something wrapped in his handkerchief into my chuba pocket, where I kept my money and keys, and then left. I didn't open the handkerchief, and in fact, paid it little attention. Later it felt heavy and I became curious as to what he had asked me to keep. Then I unwound the handkerchief and gasped in disbelief. There were his earrings! All Tibetan men wear at least one earring. Jigdal Rinpoche, as the Sakya heir, wore a leaf-shaped pair that were old and valuable. However, these were a formal pair, different from those he wore daily. They were extremely distinctive and easily recognizable as belonging to him, made of solid yellow gold with inlays of turquoise, emeralds, and diamonds. "What if I should be caught with these?" The thought horrified me. What would I do with them?

Meanwhile Jigdal Rinpoche was in one of the tents with some of the high government nobles. I couldn't go there to return the incriminating jewelry, and I dared not return them to Singtashi. If Singtashi lost the earrings, he would be blamed. I felt guilty and must have looked that way. The earrings were Jigdal Rinpoche's way of keeping me at the party, I surmised, when I had recovered from the shock of finding them. I felt I should go home, but knew I could not until I got rid of the earrings. Every moment I felt I would be found out.

Singtashi came later, saying that Jigdal Rinpoche wanted to talk to me. When we finally got together, I tried to return the earrings, but he refused. Finally, I insisted and made the return, unloading my conscience. It was a great relief.

A few days later, Jigdal Rinpoche gently removed my ring

and placed it on his finger. The ring actually belonged to my mother. It was of turquoise and a family heirloom, but I didn't feel that I could ask for its return because of his rank. And, further, by custom this gesture was a sign of affection. At the same time, he gave me the small onyx charm box that hung from his neck. "No, no, no," I protested, but he persisted. A charm box is an item of deep spiritual significance, for its purpose is to shelter the wearer from any harm. A charm box contains relics and mantras consecrated by an incarnate lama. "He must care for me," I thought, but I felt an uneasiness because of its great spiritual value. I feared I might contaminate it. He told me to remember what I dreamed that night and tell him the next day.

I was afraid to go home, but when I did, I hid both my hand and the charm box. I felt guilty deceiving my family, but reasoned that these tokens of affection were between Jigdal Rinpoche and me. I was admitting to myself that I cared for him and that we had a special private relationship.

That night I dreamed I was dressed in finery sitting on a high throne, holding five beautiful long-stemmed orange flowers. When I returned his charm box the next day and told him about the dream, he said it was an excellent one. He said that earlier he had experienced a similar dream that his father had interpreted for him.

This growing affection thrust great anxieties upon me. I liked Jigdal Rinpoche but, I told myself, in our case the geography was wrong. And I felt that under no circumstances would his parents accept me as part of their family. I didn't want to get into trouble. There was also the growing difficulty of secrecy and sneaking about, and the resultant guilty feelings. Yet each time I saw Jigdal Rinpoche I felt closer to him.

It was not long until Jigdal Rinpoche's two young sisters noticed that my familiar ring was on their brother's hand. But luckily, they didn't attach any particular significance to this. His older sister, Thubten Wangmo-la, lived separately in the main town of Sakya. One evening she invited me and many other guests to a lovely dinner party. I was invited because I was a playmate of her sisters. After dinner, servants—all girls—danced and sang for us.

That evening Jigdal Rinpoche and I had a rendezvous in one of the dark hallways. He wanted to know if I cared for him and sought an immediate answer. I had had a few sips of chang and was so tense and surprised by the question that my first impulse was to flee, to get away somewhere. Instead, I confessed that I did like him very much. That night we talked seriously about our possible future. This secluded hallway also was the scene of our first close affection. "You're still afraid of me," he observed, sensing my overall feeling.

After the party I thought of myself as shocked and changed. I wanted to go home, but earlier in the evening I had agreed to stay overnight at his sister's home together with Tsegen-la and Chimi-la. A servant already had been dispatched to notify my mother of this overnight stay, so I was stuck. I left after lunch the next day, perhaps a changed person after all. Later I reflected that perhaps had I not had the sips of chang I wouldn't have been so forthright in my expression of endearment. But that was only temporary doubt, for I found myself wanting to be with Jigdal Rinpoche. The feeling was mutual and we became inseparable.

Meanwhile, the inevitable occurred. Aunt Chacha told my mother and grandmother of the romance. Aunt Chacha had surmised the seriousness of the relationship from observing us together and after seeing Singtashi deliver Jigdal Rinpoche's notes to me. She always came to escort me home from those afternoons with Tsegen-la and Chimi-la at the Phuntsok Palace. Usually Jigdal Rinpoche and Singtashi came with us to our door at the summer palace on the pretense that they were going on a walk. I had had to confess to Aunt Chacha that the notes were from Jigdal Rinpoche. He had signed them "From my heart," followed by his name.

My mother was very confused by the news. She was also very happy because she knew that if her only daughter married Jigdal Rinpoche, she would be in good hands. However, our whole family depended on Uncle Tülku-la. We would abide by his decision in any family matter. My mother also was convinced that the Trichen and his wife would never approve the match. My grandmother was delighted. She adored Jigdal Rinpoche.

One day, Jigdal Rinpoche and I again met at a spot with which we had become familiar in a parklike site along the Da River, which runs through the center of Sakya. Few people visited here, but some of us came here to wash our clothes and hang them on a rock wall to dry. I was scrubbing my clothes when Jigdal Rinpoche joined me for another of our serious conversations. He asked that if he promised to take me to visit Kham in a year or two, would I marry him? It made much sense for Jigdal Rinpoche to go to eastern Tibet, for he was the reincarnation of a Khampa lama, Derge Gyalse Rinpoche. Jigdal Rinpoche also had many followers in Kham. There had been invitations for him to visit Lhagyal Monastery, home monastery of Derge Gyalse, since Jigdal Rinpoche was three. With his promise that there would not be a prolonged separation from my family, I said yes, I would marry him. But I quickly added that I had no idea what my family would say of the proposed union. What, indeed, would Uncle Tülku-la think? What embarrassing position might this put him in with the Trichen? Knowing that there would be powerful opposition to a proposed marriage between an ordinary Khampa and the son of the Sakya Trichen, we decided nonetheless to try.

We agreed to start with Uncle Tülku-la. He was in a period of special prayers in the Gorum Temple, a museum and library containing ancient treasures inside the main Sakya monastery. The Gorum was the most sacred spot in Sakya. Here was a hundred-year-old mask of the wrathful Buddha, Mahākāla, who had the power of protection against evil. Mahākāla is the militant aspect of Chenrezi, Bodhisattva of Mercy.

Thus Jigdal Rinpoche wrote requesting my hand, placing the message on a *samdra*, five sheets of thin wood edged in red and with a designed cover and bottom also in red. The message was written on a coating of powder. All this formed a kind of layered box, with each wood "sheet" separate, held together with a decorated band of leather and silk. It was very elegant. An auspicious day was selected and the message was delivered by a Sakya government secretary. The samdra, sealed and wrapped in a khata, arrived when Uncle Tülku-la was at lunch. He knew the message was from the Phuntsok Palace and thus automatically important, so he opened the letter in the presence of a number of monks. He was shocked when he read it and at the same time filled with questions.

The secretary waited outside for some time while Uncle Tülku-la drafted his reply. Jigdal Rinpoche had directed the secretary not to return without a reply. The secretary had no inkling of what the samdra message was. What could Uncle say? Here in this sacred place he was forced to consider the fate of a number of people. Had the Trichen and his wife asked permission for the marriage, he would have said yes, of course.

Uncle Tülku-la did not like giving a negative reply to their son, but feared more the consequences of a positive one. Basically, he replied that the marriage met the religious requirements for my bearing Sakya sons and that I came from a good family background. I was a virgin and had the qualities to serve the Sakya lineage, he believed. But in recent generations, Sakya dagmos had been selected from high-ranking families, preferably with close ties to the central government. There had been intense rivalry between the Phuntsok and Drolma Palaces caused by the wives because of the competition between the wives' families. Marriages were not taken lightly and they were primarily political unions. Jigdal Rinpoche undoubtedly would be expected to marry a noblewoman. I was not from a high-placed family and had no political links to power. Our marriage might mean a loss of face for the Phuntsok Palace.

Uncle Tülku-la immediately requested that the entire family have the Kyedor initiation, the empowerment known in Sanskrit as Hevajra. Jigdal Rinpoche was protected by deities, as his family had been for generations. Thus Uncle Tülku-la reasoned that I too should have the initiation that would protect me against obstacles. Kyedor is the tutelary protector featured in the primary initiation of the Sakya school. The two-day intensive ceremony entered me into the maṇḍala, the magic diagrams that are offered to deities in tantric Buddhism. The vows, which few laywomen received, involved lifetime commitments to Buddhism. The initiation was conducted by Drolma Kyagon Ngawang Rinchen and was a significant step in my spiritual life. It also was important in that the initiation was given me by a member of the Sakya lineage that had been unbroken for centuries. The Drolma Kyagon thus became my principal spiritual teacher.

Soon after, Uncle Tülku-la told the parents of their son's request when they visited the Gorum. Although they had suspicions of a friendship between the two of us, mainly from servants' hints, they certainly were not prepared for a formal request for marriage. Indeed, I thought, they already had someone in mind for Jigdal Rinpoche. Such marriages always were arranged, in many cases years earlier.

With Jigdal Rinpoche's parents thoroughly upset, I stayed away from the palace and my afternoon visits with Tsegen-la and Chimi-la. But I still received messages from Jigdal Rinpoche. Actually, we felt some degree of relief that his parents and Uncle Tülku-la knew. Jigdal Rinpoche felt that we no longer had to hide. He was determined to win in an uphill battle that often seemed hopeless to me.

Uncle Tülku-la, who had been sitting so long in the lotus position, was having trouble with his legs and delayed his trip home. This further complicated any progress toward an answer to the question that was upsetting everyone, or at least so it seemed. My unhappiness increased just knowing that I had placed Uncle in the position of handling an issue that under ordinary circumstances he would have had no connection with whatsoever. Monks and lamas usually do not rule on family problems; that is the duty of the father or head of the household.

Jigdal Rinpoche's mother, after some thought, said she

wished Uncle Tülku-la had given an emphatic no to the request and her son thus would have had no hope. Uncle, in a mild manner, was thereby blamed for indirectly encouraging our love. By custom, the man I now hoped would be my husband did not approach his parents directly, even though they lived in the same palace and saw each other daily. One acted through an intermediary. Thus a new duty befell Uncle. Carrying the traditional ceremonial scarf, he went to Jigdal Rinpoche, stating the extreme parental distress over the romance, and suggesting that it would be best if we forgot each other, adding that our family soon would make arrangements to go home to Kham. Uncle said he wanted no trouble.

It was a blow, but not a fatal one, for Jigdal Rinpoche. As for me, I was helpless. Doubt and unhappiness plagued me. Being the only child, I was expected someday to bring home a nice young man, who, after our marriage, would live in our family home in Thalung. By a marriage to the next Sakya Trichen, I would deprive my family of what they rightfully deserved. It would be, one could surmise, the end of the family.

Jigdal Rinpoche had great respect for his father and the future role he was expected to fill. But the man I loved also had his own weapon. If he were not allowed to marry me, he said, he would live the life of a monk and never marry. This would disgrace the Phuntsok Palace side of the Sakya line—a disaster.

Through all of this, I had a confidante and ally in Grandmother. We always had been close, of course, but she liked Jigdal Rinpoche and didn't want us to be separated. Each day I still went on kora, said my prayers, and studied with Ani Chimi. Womanhood was upon me. I now used makeup, face powder and cream, perfumes, and good-smelling soaps—all gifts of Jigdal Rinpoche. But I used them all in good taste, thanks to my mother, who was a stickler for good grooming and health habits. Some parents objected to cosmetics, but not my mother.

The general climate being tense, our family moved out of

the Trichen's summer palace and into the main town, settling in a three-story residence. Jigdal Rinpoche came to visit often. One day his sister, Thubten Wangmo-la arrived at the house, saying she was sent by their parents to determine my romantic intentions in regard to her brother. This time she conversed with me in the honorific style of speech, the style used for persons of high rank, and remarked that I was growing up. She was accompanied by two servants, a monk and a nun, each of whom held a big tray filled with money wrapped in white cloths. At first she offered to pay my transportation and escort home to Kham and any other costs related to my leaving. She said she was doing me a favor, that Jigdal Rinpoche was not dependable in matters of marriage. The parents would never accept me because they had arranged another bride for him, she said. I should not waste my time further in remaining at Sakya, she said. Astonished, I reacted strongly to any idea of a "business arrangement" in regard to Jigdal's and my relationship. Foremost, I was deeply hurt that she would say her brother was not dependable. "This is not a playful game, but a serious matter," I said with polite sternness. "This is a deeply serious situation for both of our lives. I will not give him up, nor will he give me up." Further, I declined any transportation or other assistance. After tea, the sister, with a somewhat changed attitude, said she would do her best to convey the message to her parents.

Aunt Chacha had heard the two servants remark that that little girl from Kham is no longer a little girl, that she would not easily change her mind or be bought off. This was the first time that I had challenged the family for my rights.

Soon after, the Trichen, his wife, their youngest daughter, and Trinly Rinpoche went on a month-and-a-half-long pilgrimage to India and Sikkim. Jigdal Rinpoche remained at Sakya. He came frequently to our home and the entire town knew of our romance. It was a time of great strain.

Uncle Tülku-la at this time received a monk from Gaba who came bearing a letter from Uncle Kunsang Nyima in Thalung. The letter said the Nationalist Chinese leaders in

Sining had ordered twenty-five district leaders in the western area of Chinghai province to bring a thousand horses and mules and two hundred men with rifles to Sining. No reasons were given for the order. Uncle Kunsang Nyima said that he would be among those going to Sining with the Drawu-pon, our district leader in Jyekundo and hereditary ruler of Gaba. The letter indicated that the Kham area was not peaceful as before and that people no longer could trust the many strangers passing through. We assumed from all of this that the Chinese Communists might be taking over in Sining. The letter had been written two months earlier, so we were worried about what had occurred since then. However, none of us greatly feared an easy takeover and didn't foresee how this new move could affect such small towns as Thalung. Uncle Tülku-la, whose legs were feeling better now, was anxious to go home to his monastery in Thalung. I was too young and far removed from eastern Tibet to be deeply concerned about what was occurring on the world scene at the time.

Shortly after the Trichen's family returned from their Indian trip, I said goodbye to most of my family. Uncle Tülku-la's religious work was finished here and my mother, grandmother, Ani Chimi, and Uncle Kuyak, then in Shigatse, were anxious to return to Kham. Aunt Chacha and I again moved, this time into smaller two-story rented quarters. My family couldn't wait any longer, for who knew when the Trichen would look favorably on my entering his family. If the final reply were negative, then I was to come home with Aunt Chacha in the company of a trader friend of Uncle Kuyak who lived in Shigatse. He would care for us, as he made a yearly trip to Kham.

My family left in the early fall of 1949. We did not know then that the Nationalist Government of China would soon fall at Chungking and that the Communists would take over the mainland.

When his parents returned, Jigdal Rinpoche decided to submit to the Sakya nobles a formal request for our marriage to take place. The Sakya Shapé, the highest government noble, Drungyik Chenmo, a chief secretary, and several other nobles took the message to the parents at the palace. This was all according to established protocol. Every time someone approached our house, I thought, "This will be the bearer of the message." There was no reply. Time seemed to drag.

One afternoon about a week later while Jigdal Rinpoche was leading prayers in a sacred shrine room attached to the palace, he was given the message that the nobles would come by later to confer with him, if he were available. Although Jigdal Rinpoche was busy, he said they should come along. Ordinarily, he would have suggested waiting a day, but he had a feeling they had some news.

He received the nobles in the temple. Shapé and Drungyik Chenmo told him that he was permitted to marry me. The Trichen, the nobles said, had summoned them to his throne room and announced his decision. We could be married anytime, they added. Jigdal Rinpoche was elated with the edict. However, he also saw something deeper in the announcement that dimmed his joy. He wanted the traditional ceremony for me, complete with the prestige and presentation of jewels and costume due the wife of the Sakya Dagchen-to-be. The Dagchen title is an ancient one, meaning "second to the Trichen in the Sakya family." It is bestowed only upon marriage. The nobles were very surprised at his reaction. They returned to the parents with Jigdal Rinpoche's message that he sought the traditional ceremony for our alliance. Several days later the parents agreed to the honors of the rite.

Jigdal Rinpoche then talked face-to-face with his parents, telling them in person what he wanted for me. He won his case. His mother promised to do her best to make it a meaningful ceremony. Actually, I didn't want a large ceremony. However, a woman who marries a member of the Sakya family simply cannot slip quietly into marriage. Especially in recent years, with the rivalry between the two palaces, weddings were important to carry on the Sakya religious lineage and followed long family tradition.

Meanwhile, I knew nothing of this until two days after the

parents gave their permission, when Jigdal Rinpoche came to my house accompanied by a couple of servants. I was practicing writing Tibetan script when he arrived. Aunt Chacha joined us in tea. Then Jigdal Rinpoche brought the message I so long had wanted to hear. I was numb, scarcely able to speak. I thought of home, realizing how attached I was to my family and that I was a Khampa at heart. But I also had a strange feeling of being afraid of what to do. After months of struggle, the sudden impact of victory was upon me. Decisions clearly were out of my hands, yet I felt the full responsibility for them.

Jigdal Rinpoche assured me that the problems with his parents would be resolved. Earlier he said that he had gone secretly to the Trichen to ask his permission to marry me. This surprised me, as all along I thought he had not spoken face-to-face with either of his parents about our possible marriage. The Trichen told him that as the eldest son he had good judgment and should do what he thought was right. The Trichen had said he had no objection to the betrothal, which brought Jigdal Rinpoche great relief. Jigdal Rinpoche then told me that he would have abided by his father's decision, no matter what it was, because the Trichen was not only his father but his principal spiritual teacher.

Jigdal Rinpoche also told me about a significant dream he had had while visiting in Lhasa, when he was married to the prime minister's daughter. The marriage, arranged by his parents, had lasted only a month. The Trichen and his family had gone to Lhasa at the government's invitation. While there, they had taken part in a special three-day religious ceremony at the Ramoche Temple, the second holiest spot in the capital. During the rites, the Trichen had told Jigdal Rinpoche to report to him about any dreams. Jigdal Rinpoche dreamed that he was surrounded by finely dressed and beautiful women. Among them was a girl, who handed him a small gift. He didn't know the identity of the gift, but felt it was very precious. He asked the girl her name; it was Sonam, which means merit. When Jigdal Rinpoche told his father about the dream, the father laughed, but said it was a good dream. "You will have a strong connection with a person who has the names 'Tshe' and 'Sonam' (life and merit)," his father predicted. Jigdal Rinpoche said he had kept that prediction in his heart, but he thought it strange that the woman he had married about two weeks earlier did not have those names. He reminded me about our first meetings when he had repeatedly asked me my name. I had mumbled my name several times until finally he had asked my mother my name, Sonam Tshe Dzom, which means "a gathering of life and merit." This was just one of the signs that told him our marriage would be a good one, he said.

There was no way to tell my family that at last I was to be a bride. One had to wait until someone was bound for Kham to convey such a message.

It was comforting that our proposed marriage had the support of Khanchen Sangye Rinchen, Jigdal Rinpoche's former teacher and now the abbot of the Great Temple of Sakya, and of many government nobles. The abbot was a very learned monk who was the forty-fifth Khanchen of the Great Temple and a good friend of Uncle Tülku-la. Khanchen was the highest abbot in the Sakya school of Buddhism. Earlier the abbot, along with Jigdal Rinpoche, had visited my house one evening. Although often aloof to women, he seemed to like me and was warm. Later he had sent me beautiful red silk material for a blouse, and cookies and fruit, saying that if I had any problems during Uncle Tülku-la's absence, I was free to consult him.

Khanchen was a born teacher, one whose words contained elements of instruction or stories of the past noble deeds of Sakya's feminine leaders. I received a second Kyedor initiation from him. It was a two-day event that took place in Khanchen's quarters in the Great Temple. I renewed promises and vows. Henceforth I was to do more daily prayers. A highlight of the second evening was receiving a special name. The name was written on a small piece of paper and then the paper was eaten. I promptly swallowed the paper, but completely forgot the name!

An auspicious day for the wedding ceremony, only about two weeks away, was selected by an astrologer at the Great Temple. It was a day early in 1950, by the Western calendar, in about the month of March.

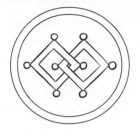

6

The Wedding

Our wedding date was announced by the Trichen first to the Sakya nobles, who, in turn, came to my house to tell me. I was to be wed in the Phuntsok Palace early in the morning in a semiprivate ceremony. One month after the wedding there would be a party in celebration of the event.

Money and white scarfs were sent to eight special temples in anticipation of the upcoming event. Prayer flags were placed in several mountain areas near Sakya to please the mountain deities as a protective measure. Our names were placed on some of the flags, which were taken to their lofty sites by men hired for just such ceremonial chores. Because I was born in the year of the Wood Dog, my prayer flags were green. Jigdal Rinpoche, whose birth year was that of the Earth Snake, had yellow flags. These prayer flags, printed from woodblocks, first were blessed in an early morning ceremony. Monks dressed in official robes then came to my house. They said prayers, beat drums, cymbals, and burned juniper in a ceremony on the rooftop. Ordinarily, in central and western Tibet, monks do not participate in weddings and certain other ceremonies. However, because of the religious hierarchy, tradition calls for the monks to participate.

Since there were no newspapers in Sakya, news of our wedding spread only by word of mouth. And that was fast!

Aunt Chacha made a quick trip to Shigatse to shop for fabrics and jewelry. Uncle Tülku-la had arranged for money, tea, and other items to be left in Shigatse to trade for the necessary wedding effects. Looking ahead to my future life, I knew I would be expected to have a more elaborate wardrobe than I had at this point. I had few clothes in the western Tibetan style that custom now would require me to wear.

One of the items Aunt Chacha purchased was a beautiful jewelry-style charm box, a four-inch-square neckpiece of solid gold inlaid with turquoise and other semiprecious stones. Three of Jigdal Rinpoche's sisters came to help us with the tedious task of stringing the jewels that held the charm box around my neck. There were turquoise, onyx, coral, and many small pearls. My wardrobe also included a brocade silk hat with a wide orange silk brim, a style worn by women of high rank. Tailors from the palace came to the house to sew my trousseau, and I was busy with fittings. They sewed several chubas and blouses in bright colors and appropriate jackets.

There also was the task of going through my clothes and sorting out those I would no longer need. On the whole, this was not a sad undertaking for I liked Sakya-style clothing, as western Tibetan garb fits closer to the body. Two or three garments had been through the pilgrimage; others were too small. Some articles I kept for sentimental reasons. Still other things went to the poor. By custom I also had to save some of my clothes for historical reasons for storage in the palace. Over the years there had been amassed a museum collection of Sakya family attire. Some of these women's outfits—worn on special occasions only—were stored in heavy wooden boxes with metal corners, labeled, and locked. Some of the wearables were elegant, made of silks and gold brocades that glimmered when they were brought out in the sunlight on rare occasions.

There were many Khampas in Shigatse, who sent gifts of rugs, china, aprons, and even tassels for my hair. Since my betrothal had been confirmed, I had worn my hair in the style of a married woman, parted in the middle with two long braids that stretched to my waist. In Kham all tassels were red, but here they were of many colors, all braided into my hair.

In the meantime, Jigdal Rinpoche was learning to play the *tungchen*, a six-foot long trumpet used in religious ceremonies; and I turned my attention to writing. My instructor was a close friend of Khanchen, Jigdal Rinpoche's teacher.

The day before the wedding I was busy with a hair-washing ritual and packing four "trunks," which were actually leather-covered boxes. Aunt Chacha helped me with the packing of these few belongings. People called at the house offering to help me, but I was too busy to spend much time with them. According to custom, I did not see Jigdal Rinpoche the day before our wedding. He sent over a servant who asked if he could help, but I didn't need him. Jigdal Rinpoche was involved with packing and moving into our honeymoon home, the Sakya family's summer palace. It had been redecorated and refurnished for us by his parents. My husband and I were to have some twenty-four rooms at our disposal, including our own shrine room. Whereas earlier with my family I had lived in only six rooms in the palace's north wing, now the entire palace was our home. This included vast storage areas, a garden behind the palace, and a large courtyard. I was delighted to be moving into familiar surroundings. It would be handy to the Phuntsok Palace, but far enough away to guarantee our privacy, I thought. Aunt Chacha was to move with me so that I could have her help in learning household routine.

By custom, washing a bride's hair before her wedding is done by a young woman astrologically compatible with the bride. Tibetans consider hair the most precious ornament of a human being, associated with wealth. One must make sure that the hair is washed according to astrological symbols so that the bride will bring prosperity to the marriage. A thirteen-year-old girl from Sakya with whom I was acquainted was selected for this honored job by a lama-astrologer at the Great Temple. She was born in the Earth Tiger year and thus was thought to be in harmony with me. She also had to have both parents living, be of good family and character, and have a proper and meaningful name. Chödron, which means the lighting of religion, was her name.

The prized token of affection given by a man to his bride is a piece of turquoise or other precious stone for her headdress. This is roughly equivalent in significance to the engagement ring in Western culture. After the hair procedure, I was required to purify my body by bathing in cold blessed saffron water, making me shiver.

That afternoon Aunt Chacha and a distant cousin of mine made the rounds to eight shrines at Sakya giving white scarfs and money to the monks.

On my last evening as a single girl, Aunt Chacha and I ate in the kitchen. She reminded me that when I was in the presence of Jigdal Rinpoche's father I was to be polite and exert my best manners, to bow at the proper times, and so on. And above all, she said, I was not to be too shy and timid. A feeling of being inferior in the presence of this family long had been my trait and I wondered how I was going to banish it now. The Trichen's word was the supreme law of Sakya, and many feared him, including me. Other members of the family and even Jigdal Rinpoche treated the Trichen in a formal fashion. Since his return from India, he had not been in good health. He was fifty-one, which by Tibetan standards is getting along in years. Both of his legs had swelled, bringing dramatic change to this quick-footed man—usually the first one up the mountain.

Jigdal Rinpoche had grown much closer to his father since then. They lunched together frequently, sometimes with Jigdal Rinpoche's two eldest sisters joining them; at other times he was at his father's side, massaging his legs when necessary.

When I retired that night, my mind raced with all the instructions about being polite to my future parents-in-law. How glad I was that it was to be a semiprivate wedding ceremony. I prayed for my future life that evening. Usually I slept soundly, but not this night. In a dream I was again surrounded by hundreds of people and creatures, some curious, some admiring, who questioned me. The dream was similar to the one I had experienced the night I arrived at Sakya.

On my wedding day, Aunt Chacha came to arouse me about five o'clock, but I had been awake for some time. She was very happy for me this day, doubtless feeling like my mother. She was responsible for me in my mother's absence. I was the daughter Aunt Chacha would never have. I put on a dark-green silk chuba, a red silk blouse, fancy embroidered boots, and an apron in the style of a married woman. It was not a bride's costume in the Western sense, but rather the outfit of a high-ranking lady.

Aunt Chacha brought me the traditional *desee*, a sweet rice dish, for good luck. It was mixed with sugar and raisins. There also was droma, the small sweet-potato-like vegetable. "You must eat some of this," she said. But I ate lightly, taking a pinch of each of the dishes and tossing a pinch of them in the air as an offering, sampling the rest. A senior monk astrologer and his monk servant had arrived, she said. I invited them in.

The astrologer began a chanting and asked to see both of my hands. He then drew astrological symbols on my palms, after which I was asked to turn to each of the four directions of the compass while he continued praying and chanting. All of this was done to insure a good marriage that would continue the long line of Sakyapa sons and combat bad luck and evil stars in Jigdal Rinpoche's and my horoscopes.

It was beginning to be light when three officials and their four servants arrived for me. I kept them waiting about ten minutes, then donned my brimmed hat and red embroidered scarf. When I went out the front door, I was careful to step over the threshold with the right foot, for good luck. The officials, acting very differently than in the past, bowed politely to me. I walked to a three-foot-high rock used for mounting our horses. I stepped gingerly, again with my right

foot first, on a *yung-drung* made of grains of wheat that had
been placed on the stone. The yung-drung, or swastika, is
regarded as a design of good augury and represents the
ceaseless becoming of Buddhism.

Under the neck of my white horse, which was furnished by
the palace, hung two yak tails about a foot long and dyed red.
These were designations of rank, and a new mark of prestige
for me. Two more officials joined us for the fifteen-minute
ride to the Phuntsok Palace. Two men, one on each side, held
my horse's bridle. On public occasions the trappings and
heavy headdresses of Sakya women necessitated a slow stately
gait. Having these grooms, even with an extremely gentle
horse, gave me a premonition that from now on I would never
again be able to ride the spirited horses I had so enjoyed in
my youth. Suddenly I had become precious. They would
now fear for my safety on a spirited animal.

En route to the palace we saw three women carrying
wooden containers of water on their backs. It was a good
omen because the big buckets were full. The noble leading
our party gave each of the women a white ceremonial scarf,
carefully draped over their buckets. They were obviously
thrilled and sensed that this was the bride's procession. The
Sakya populace knew this was the wedding day but were
unaware of the exact time the ritual would begin.

I was beginning to feel nervous. As we approached the
palace entrance, two mastiff watchdogs barked and snapped
at the party, startling me. "My first rejection," I thought,
"and even from dogs." Some ten servants, carrying scarfs,
chang, and silver trays with tsampa, wheat, and decorated
butter figures, came out to greet us. I had plenty of assistance
dismounting, and the servants bowed upon seeing us. As we
went up the stairs to the second floor, I was happy to see a
familiar face. It was the Gyayum Kusho's personal servant, a
nun I had known earlier. She removed her pointed cap,
bowed, and then replaced the headgear.

Heavy portieres were lifted back as we entered what was
called the Gold Room, where the Trichen spent his days

receiving people and praying from atop his thronelike seat. The ceilings were covered with richly embroidered Chinese silk. The walls were of wood, with many cabinets with carved doors embellished with gold.

Everyone upon entering the room had performed the chatsa, the ceremonial prostrations, before the Trichen. How different events would have been had I been married in Kham in a ceremony like Lhayag's, I thought. The first noble bowed to the Trichen and the others followed. The Trichen had a slight smile on his face. I was greatly relieved, not having seen him for months. I kept my head down, as was customary in his presence, looking up only occasionally. Seated on a silk-covered double cushion, I waited some ten minutes before Jigdal Rinpoche and a servant entered.

This ceremony was not a social event. Rather, it was a Sakya family custom developed over generations. Only the two ruling houses of the Sakya school observed this type of marriage rite. In contrast, the Sakya nobility had large weddings. With Jigdal Rinpoche's arrival, the nobles left. Besides we three principals, there were only three monks attending us. Thus I was the only woman present. Jigdal Rinpoche and I knelt in front of the throne and received the Trichen's blessing. One of the monks in attendance anointed us with water from an ornamental vase. The water contained tiny bits of a Nepalese flower, the saffron. We moved up a step for a special blessing after which the Trichen tossed sesame seeds over us. The Trichen touched our heads with his prayer beads and with a large charm box containing small images of deities.

During the last blessing, a monk moved about with cymbals, a bell, and a censer which gave out aromatic smoke. I received from the Trichen a special name that was written on white paper, folded, and tied with a small scarf. This name, to be used henceforth for all formal writing and records, was Jamyang Pema Palgyibutri, meaning "the deity of wisdom, the lotus who brings forth many sons."

While the wedding ceremony was in progress, monks were on the roof of the palace praying, using drums and incense

and consecrating prayer flags. As the Trichen was finishing
the blessings, these monks came down to the Gold Room
carrying a large tsampa pyramid decorated with butter. Both
Jigdal Rinpoche and I pinched off a tiny bit of the tsampa and
butter, waved them in the air, made a wish, and then ate the
tiny pieces. The monks also brought in a silver and gold bowl
containing chang. Three times the Trichen, Jigdal Rinpoche
and I each dipped our ring finger of the left hand into the
chang, flicked it into the air with the thumb, and then touched
the finger to our tongues.

Jigdal Rinpoche and I now were husband and wife.

The nobles returned and it was time for tea, cookies, fruits,
and candies. But all this food was barely tasted. Each of the
officials had brought with him a white cloth in which to wrap
food to take home. The nobles told the Trichen about seeing
the three women carrying water and how they had given the
three the scarfs. He seemed to be enjoying himself and I began
to be at ease. He talked about our home and its new look. But
I responded only, "Yes," to his remarks.

The nobles left first and then my husband and I. As we
departed, I felt confident and assured him I was not apprehensive about seeing his mother after all these months. We went
down the hall to the Gyayum Kusho's room, where Jigdal
Rinpoche formally exchanged scarfs and touched foreheads
with his mother. She seemed friendly, I sensed, and I welcomed her suggestion that we make ourselves comfortable and
at home. She and I exchanged scarfs, after which the three of
us had a polite half-hour conversation over tea. Later, while
the Trichen stayed in the Gold Room, we had lunch served on
trays, with Jigdal's mother and three youngest sisters.

Escorted by servants, my husband and I walked to our
honeymoon home, the summer palace. Aunt Chacha had
already moved in and taken my old bedroom. Jigdal Rinpoche
and I were to have the bedroom formerly occupied by Uncle
Tülku-la. Everything was beautiful and clean, I observed. My
husband had brought along many religious items to decorate
our quarters, including statues, books, and tankas. His

mother, who had inspected our quarters and found them in good order, dropped by in the late afternoon with fruit and cookies. His sisters also came with scarfs and gifts.

I felt tremendous relief from a burden that had been long in the making. It had been months since I had communicated with my future parents-in-law. We were like strangers. However, my continuing friendship with my future sisters-in-law had provided me with some insights into my future role of the obedient daughter-in-law. Now no longer were we sending messages, but actually dealing face-to-face with my husband's family.

Though I knew that at heart I would always be a Khampa, I sensed more than most brides a severance with the past. Now I was part of a historical family. Heavy responsibility for religion, tradition, and western Tibetan culture were mine at age sixteen. How fortunate I was to have a kind and generous husband, who had demonstrated his devotion by fighting fiercely against the highest odds to win me.

7

Palace Life

The responsibility of learning the routine of the Phuntsok Palace was thrust upon me only days after our wedding and a brief honeymoon at the hot springs. There was little time to adjust, even to the routine of daily life in the summer palace. I soon was spending several hours of my day in the big palace, learning operations under the tutelage of my mother-in-law. I was being taught these tasks in preparation for the day when I would take over her role.

At first I just visited my mother-in-law and observed how the palace's goods and services were managed. She was a very efficient woman who believed in having a direct hand in the important task of receiving and allocating food and supplies. Since she did not hear well, it was difficult to carry on a normal conversation with her. She also frequently did not understand my Kham dialect, and we needed an interpreter. Everyone spoke louder than usual to her. Even if we happened to be in the same room with her, she always demanded to know what we were saying. This made me nervous and I was always hesitant to talk to her.

A sincerely religious person, my mother-in-law spent from an hour-and-a-half to two hours each morning in religious observance in her room. No meat was eaten by either of us before prayers.

Those were tense and unhappy days for me. "In every move, I'm being tested," I thought. When my husband returned to the summer palace at the end of a busy day, he frequently asked, "How did your day go?" "It went well," I always replied, often relating to him some new routine I had learned.

Because of my earlier rejection, he too probably was worried about how well I would fare in my new role. He had his own concerns of my fitting into what essentially was a royal role. But I never burdened him with problems as I continued with efforts to please my mother-in-law and the four sisters-in-law who lived in the Phuntsok Palace.

Although many in the palace respected me and my efforts, some sensed that I still was a little childish. I too could see my childish ways. Sometimes, for example, when my mother-in-law received fancy wrapped candies from Sikkim, her daughters were waiting for a handout. She passed the treats to them, forgetting me. I was considered an adult now and not eligible for such special treatment. When she gave her daughters jewelry or yardage for new clothing, I thought nothing of it. But with the British-made candies, it was different. I wanted my share. Sometimes she saw my disappointment, especially with the orange juice that also came from Sikkim, and gave me a tablespoon or so too.

The Phuntsok Palace was supported by its nearby estates, on which were great yak herds. A record was kept of every animal in the nomadic herds. If one died, its horns and skin were brought in as evidence that the animal had not been sold. Nomads from estates came and went several times a month, bringing butter, cheese, yogurt, meat, cream, yak dung, and yak hair. Sakya monasteries from throughout Tibet helped support the ruling palace, but their contributions did not arrive as routinely. The nomads would come with twenty-five or thirty yaks loaded with supplies. They would take back items such as grains, tea, tsampa, and yard goods for making clothes. The poor and jobless of Sakya also came to the palace asking for wool, half of which they returned as finished yarn.

From these items I learned to dole out supplies for the two households and some thirty servants. Servants did the actual measuring and counting while I gave directions. At first I was assisted by Jigdal Rinpoche's younger sisters. It was a nerve-wracking job, for if I gave out too much, I was admonished by my mother-in-law. And if I gave out too little, I earned the scorn of the servants. One day I was scolded by the Gyayum Kusho for the way I allotted some partly dried lamb, having given away what she thought were too generous pieces.

To carry out this master storekeeper's job, I carried a huge ring that held dozens of keys to the various storerooms. Each key was attached to the ring by a strip of leather. Some keys were of iron, six to eight inches long. The ring was kept on a post in the center of the Gyayum Kusho's room so that it could not be stolen.

One duty I found difficult to master was tasting the chang that had to be in constant supply for palace affairs. Even though she didn't drink, my mother-in-law could tell imme-diately the brew's general quality, and if the barley was overcooked or undercooked. To me, all chang tasted sour. The barley left over in the brewing process was rather sour and was fed to the dzomos and horses, whose diet also included tea leaves and tsampa.

One woman and her helper had permanent year-round jobs as the palace chang makers. Chang was given freely at Sakya and used for many occasions, as it was very inexpensive here— about a fifth of what it cost in Lhasa. Not much water was drunk at Sakya. Field and harvest workers sipped whey, buttermilk, and chang in addition to the ever-present tea. There was also chang soup, traditionally served before break-fast on New Year's or when it was especially chilly weather. This was made with the chang, dried cheese, and droma.

Most of the populace made chang at home, but one also could buy it at taverns, which stayed open twenty-four hours daily. Women operated these establishments. They had regular customers, some of whom paid in whatever exchange they could offer, as was the case at other shops in Sakya. It was not proper for anyone in the royal families to make a purchase in a tavern, however. Someone else would buy the chang if we happened to run out.

It was a western Tibetan custom to make a chang yaka, or good luck mark, when drinking. This was accomplished by placing pinches of barley flour on the edge of your drinking bowl or cup. When tipping the cup to drink, the flour made a mark on your forehead. The custom was similar to the Western "bottoms up." When drinking chang, imbibers sang and said "Yaka gyap" or roughly, "Put on the yaka."

On my wedding day I was assigned a personal servant, a nun named Tashi Sangmo, from a Sakya nunnery about four miles away. She too was a stranger to the Sakya hierarchy and just as fearful as I of erring. Tashi Sangmo was about twenty-two and likable. As we would be attending monastery affairs often, it was natural I should have a nun as a personal servant; an ordinary woman would not be admitted to such events. Tashi Sangmo was at my side most of the time, performing duties that included serving me meals.

Food was prepared in the main kitchen of the Phuntsok Palace and then brought to the summer palace or to wherever members of the Trichen's family were. I had no direct hand in the immediate supervision of the food preparation. However, our summer palace had a small kitchen that was used occasionally to prepare Khampa dishes and specialties such as cookies, a favorite in eastern Tibet.

The first few days after the wedding many people brought wedding gifts, some of which were delivered by servants. Although I saw these gifts, immediately after they arrived they were taken to the Phuntsok Palace and given to my mother-in-law for use there. The gifts included a silver and copper teapot, chang, and money rolled in scroll-type paper inscribed with wedding greetings. Servants drank most of the chang. We wrote down names of the giftgivers and what they brought. Later they would be invited to a postwedding party.

At the beginning I didn't like life in the Phuntsok Palace and often dreamed of Jigdal Rinpoche's promise that we could visit Kham. My life was confined mainly to the palace and monastery, with social events being family affairs. No longer could I enjoy such simple pastimes as going shopping in the town's bazaars.

There were morning prayers, read from a prayer book, before I went to the Phuntsok Palace. Some of my free hours were spent with beadwork, including making the eight Buddhist symbols. When completed, some of these items were given to friends or sent to my eastern Tibetan girl friends. My tutors for this work included Jigdal Rinpoche's eldest sisters and a woman brought to the palace for a week to teach us how to make the designs.

For high-ranking women weaving was taboo as it was considered ordinary and unskilled labor, but knitting was permitted. I continued to practice writing and reading, and made renewed efforts to improve my grammar. Constantly I strove to rid myself of the Kham dialect.

About three weeks after my marriage I received from the Gyayum Kusho several items of jewelry and special clothing for monastery visits and other important religious and state occasions. There was an elaborate charm box with seven major large stones, a neckpiece more lovely than the one Aunt Chacha had obtained in Shigatse, and a bow-shaped headdress that extended about one foot out from each side of my cheeks. The headdress weighed about twenty-five pounds and severely limited one's movement. In just a short while, balancing this headpiece brought a stiff neck. My mother-in-law wore a headdress daily, and I foresaw I would be expected to do likewise when I became the Gyayum. Now I routinely went bareheaded in the palace.

The jewels and headdress were delivered by a secretary and one of Jigdal's sisters, Thubten Wangmo-la. When I unwrapped them, I was very pleased to see and have my own headdress and special jewelry. Jigdal, however, was not impressed.

"Take this headdress back," he ordered. "She's not going to wear it."

I was shocked. It looked exquisite to me.

"I'm embarrassed in having you wear this," he said. "The jewels are mismatched in size and oversized. They are not fine quality."

I protested, but he persevered. "This is junk. Sakya Dagmos don't wear this kind of jewelry."

"You should be pleased," Thubten Wagmo-la said. But she too knew it was not top quality.

"If this is not changed, she is not going to wear it," Jigdal said.

Two days later, a more lavish headdress arrived. But even then, Jigdal Rinpoche was not fully satisfied.

About a month after the marriage, a wedding party in honor of my husband and me was staged by the Trichen and his wife. Some seventy persons, many of whom I didn't know, were invited to the event on the second floor of the Phuntsok Palace. The guest list included nobles, friends, and noble monks. The affair was typically long, lasting from about two in the afternoon until two in the morning the next day. I wore my best jewels, including my new headdress, with its corals, turquoise, pearls, and rubies, mounted on a frame of bamboo wrapped in red silk.

My husband's parents sat in one room where high-ranking citizens made their way to pay respects. My husband and I and his sisters remained in the main room, seated on high silk-covered cushions. Guests presented us with white scarfs, festive foods, and other gifts.

Pillows for seating were scattered around the room, which also contained the long low tables carved with auspicious symbols. Food was served on individual trays. An entire room in the palace was designated for storing these trays in tall piles, but two or three dozen were always kept handy for quick use. They varied greatly in design, though most were of carved and painted wood. Many were for serving visting monks. Members of the Sakya family had their own special trays. Those of the Trichen, Jigdal Rinpoche, and his brother were of heavy silver embossed with gold.

Noblemen danced side by side in pairs, to the music of the *dranyen*. There was also dancing and singing to Tibetan and Indian records, but when Chinese records were on people usually just listened. Besides the dranyen, there was an instrument resembling a flute. My favorites among the entertainers were the *tungshumas*—women paid to sing, dance, and serve chang. Two of them served the chang from a container in the center of the room. They had lovely voices.

It was Jigdal Rinpoche's job to designate some of the guests who would sing and dance for us that evening. Two noblemen performed on a big wooden platform in the center of the floor, their yakskin-sole boots making a great clopping noise. I didn't consider their style as graceful as that of our dancers in Kham.

It was a tiring party, and we rested periodically by going to one of the other rooms of the palace for a half hour or so. The second dinner was served about eight o'clock, and we left some two hours later. "Less than a year ago," I thought, "when I accompanied the Trichen's family on a visit to Chökor Lhunpo Monastery for a week, I was just a playmate for Jigdal's sisters. Just a little Kham girl. But now I am the center of attention." This convinced me of the impermanence of our existence. Apparently I had been received with approval.

As the weeks wore on, I was becoming more like one of the family. The Gyayum Kusho taught me to pray to the Green Tārā, the deity to whom she was especially obliged to give reverence as wife of the Trichen and mother of Sakya sons. So I now was saying prayers to the White Tārā, my deity, as well as the Green Tārā, for some two hours daily.

My husband was so generous that I was getting somewhat spoiled. Never in my life had I actually wanted for any necessity, but now when my husband came home at night he would frequently bring me a gem, a piece of jewelry, silk yardage, or sweets that had been given to the family by one of his followers.

One evening soon after our marriage, Jigdal Rinpoche brought me a lovely turquoise center jewel for my headdress. The turquoise had been his mother's. He took it out of his chuba as a surprise, but after hints from his sisters, I had guessed that it would be coming. This gem was comparable to a wedding ring denoting that its wearer was married. "This is genuine Tibetan turquoise," my husband noted. I placed it on the forehead of my headdress and planned to wear it the rest of my life.

Khawu was a resort area southeast of Sakya, about a three-hour trip on horseback. The Trichen and his wife were carried on sedan chairs for a three-week vacation there. My father-in-law was going there for treatment of his legs. Ordinarily under these circumstances, Jigdal Rinpoche would have stayed home to oversee palace affairs, but since we had had only a brief honeymoon, his parents insisted we accompany them. We were delighted to get away from our routine duties and welcomed the opportunity for leisure. Trinly Rinpoche was left in charge of the palace.

Some thirty people from the palace went, many bathing in the spring three times daily. These vacationers often dressed up, making the vacation a social event of sorts. The residence for the Sakya family had three pools, plus two pools for servants and one for the family's teachers. Furnishings were kept in the residence the year around.

The hot springs had a semiretreat atmosphere. The water in the springs was a milky-white color and was good for many kinds of ailments.

Many people came to public pools in the area. When the Sakya family was not in residence, other prominent families rented the quarters. Monks went there on vacation, as did honeymooners. People took many prayer flags to put around the waterfalls in the area.

Games were the main entertainment. There was *onju*, a game in which a hole is dug and coins tossed into it. Some persons preferred *sho*, a very old game of chance using dice and shells. My favorite game was mahjongg, which I had recently learned in Sakya. Still others kept amused with *bebag*, a game similar to mahjongg, only that one uses a kind of domino for it. Some sets were in ivory. A simple entertainment for the young people was to go down to the river in the daytime and splash each other. They came home with their chubas soaked, having had a wonderful time.

A servant came each day from the Phuntsok Palace with reports for the Trichen from Trinly Rinpoche on the progress of some major construction at Sakya. Construction work and repair had been in progress at the Great Temple of Sakya for several years. It was a costly project. My husband's mother had been buying wood and timbers for the construction for several years. Each year the woodsmen would bring timbers on yaks from a place about five days from Sakya. Some of the cuttings were more than a foot thick.

When we returned to Sakya, as always hundreds of people turned out around the palace to greet us. Soon after we came home from the hot springs, some one hundred fifty workers and volunteers from all over western Tibet came to repair and remodel the Phuntsok Palace. A new modern front, with larger windows, was installed. That summer the exterior work on the palace was finished. To work on temples, monasteries and lamas' residences is virtuous and helps accumulate merit, according to Buddhist scriptures. The workers were housed in homes owned by the Sakya government and in the Phuntsok Palace, and they were given food by the Trichen. Both men and women worked carrying stones and water. On a nearby mountain, workers would break up the rocks into varied sizes. Then they were brought by oxcart down to Sakya. As the men and women brought the carts down, they would sing together, sometimes as many as twenty or thirty of them. I loved to hear them.

At about this time we received a letter from Thalung saying that my grandmother had died at home at the age of sixty-seven. She had been closer to me at times than my own mother. Jigdal Rinpoche was also very fond of her. This was the first family death I had experienced. The sad and obviously hastily written note made no mention of the Chinese. Following custom, money and scarfs were sent to the monks and lamas at the monastery, asking them to say prayers for grandmother. Aunt Chacha tried to comfort me, attempting to hide her own grief.

Lhamo Chö, a one-day celebration saluting the deity Palden Lhamo, came in the fifth month. The event is an offering to Palden Lhamo, the wrathful manifestation of Tārā, mother of all beings. In all large Tibetan temples, Palden Lhamo presides over wrathful deities as a protector of Buddhism. Palden Lhamo also is the Phuntsok Palace's principal protector. This was the day of the Sakya yearly picnic, an observance that began with prayer and ended with horse races. On this day all food and chang was furnished by the monks but financed by the Sakya government. Sakya residents picnicked en route and generally made it a holiday, returning home in the early evening.

A statue of the Lhamo was housed in the Samling Monastery about four miles away in a mountainous area. Six chief groomsmen, representing the two palaces and the government, carrying prayer flags and rifles headed the parade up the mountain. On this day they also wore big silver and gold ear ornaments inlaid with stones, and gold and silver ornaments on their hips.

About twenty-five to thirty horses were entered in the races. A month or so earlier the horses had been put on a special diet to build them up. There was no betting, but competition was very keen. The jockeys were usually sixteen to twenty-five years old and selected by the Sakya government. Sons often followed their fathers in this sport. They wore brightly colored pants and shirts and sported bells on their shirts, belts, and boots. There also were bells on the horses, so there was plenty of noise. The jockey's fancy hats had colorful feathers, including peacock feathers. There were winners to the fifth place, and all received rewards of white scarfs and money.

It was believed that if the winning jockeys were from the

Phuntsok Palace, it was a good omen for the palace for the year. If one of our friends won, we also would give him a scarf.

Some horses were from eastern Tibet, but I thought the racing quite unspectacular compared to our racing in Kham. There, riders had to perform more complex feats, such as reaching down to pick up a stone while riding, or shooting with a rifle after twirling it, much like a drum-major's baton. I wore my big headdress that day and was uncomfortable.

At the end of the races, three huge silver bowls were filled with chang. One was placed before the statue of Palden Lhamo in Samling Monastery. The other two were passed to the Sakya families in hierarchial order. These family members then flipped some of the chang off their thumb and third finger, left hand, into the air as an offering. Then the chang was consumed by the officials, nobles, monk nobles, the chief groomsmen, and jockeys. Amid songs to the Lhamo, the bowls were filled again and again.

The fourth day of the sixth month was one of our palace's most important religious celebrations, the Chökhor Duchen, which marks the anniversary of the Buddha's teaching of the Four Noble Truths at Sarnath, India.

It was also the nomads' annual accounting day. More than twenty families came, bringing butter, cheese, yogurt, milk, and other items. In return the Sakya family gave them bricks of tea, new summer clothes, and other necessities. The Gya-yum Kusho had the job of deciding what they would be given in return for their dairy offerings. Records were kept of the nomads' gifts and what they had received in return.

The reception for the nomads was held in the servants' living room of the palace, where food and chang were served. On this day the nomads could eat and drink as much as they pleased.

On this sacred occasion the Trichen and my husband prayed all day. Thousands of butter lamps burned in the palace as an offering to the Buddha. I helped the servants fill the butter lamps. The making of butter lamps was an exacting skill which I had learned as a little girl from my great-uncle. The butter was clarified, but must not be overcooked. One kept very clean hands and fingernails, adhered to general standards of purity, and did not breathe directly on the lamps. Sometimes a mask was worn over the mouth, as was the case in making certain other religious items.

That evening, after the nomads had left, we made the kora around Sakya by the light of the moon. It took about two hours; we chanted our mantras as we walked.

Meanwhile I had learned that I was to be a mother sometime early in 1951. My husband was very happy, as were my parents-in-law. I too was happy, but somewhat afraid. The Gyayum Kusho advised me how to care for myself, including what to eat. My father-in-law's doctor was consulted, but the service he rendered at the one examination was by Western standards very limited.

I also had received letters from mother and Uncle Tülku-la in Kham saying how happy they were to hear of the marriage and of their pleasure at the union. A large reception was held at my home in Thalung to celebrate the event. Some relatives were happy, but some were sad that the only child would not be returning to Kham.

Two months later another letter and gifts arrived from my family. Uncle Tülku-la's letter indicated that all of the districts in the Chinghai province, including the Jyekundo area, were now under Communist control. There was no fighting in the Jyekundo area and there were no prohibitions on the practice of religion to date. The Communist takeover so far had made no difference to life in Thalung. He told Aunt Chacha and me not to worry and he said that Uncle Kunsang Nyima and the Drawu-pon's group had arrived home safely from the trip to Sining. The presents accompanying his letter included gold dust, silk yardage, silver money, and a white scarf. The gold dust, he said, was to be used for jewelry for both my husband and me.

The palace life that I had at first so feared was now nearly routine, and I had come to enjoy it. It was a blissful life, far from the world's troubles. This role of the contented bride changed abruptly one late summer day in 1950.

The Trichen had not been feeling well since his return from India. Monks prayed for his long life. The Trichen's condition worsened and visitors were kept to a minimum. He died one midmorning with his family at his side. Jigdal Rinpoche's monk servant came to our quarters and announced simply: "Finished." Puzzled, I queried as to what he meant. "Dorje Chang has gone to heaven," he said. The title Dorje Chang, or Supreme Bodhisattva, is given posthumously to high lamas. My first thoughts were for my husband, who was so close to his father.

The Trichen was particularly unusual in that he was the second of the Sakya lineage to die in the same room where he had been born. The first had been the Sachen Kunga Nyingpo, founder of the Sakya school in the eleventh century.

Forty-nine days of mourning began. Messages were sent to all the Sakya monasteries throughout Tibet that their leader had passed on. During the mourning period more than twenty high lamas and monks came each day for prayers in the Phuntsok Palace. We now moved from the summer palace to the Phuntsok Palace in order to help the Gyayum prepare for these activities.

Cremation, which is the disposition for most lamas at Sakya, took place a week later. For the first time, I saw the extraordinary multicolored fire and ceremonies during the cremation of a high lama, held in the cremation room only for sons of the Sakya lineage in the Lhakhang Chenmo, the Great Temple.

The washed body, wrapped in a special white cloth, was placed in the seated lotus position. The hands, holding the bell and dorje, symbol of wisdom and skillful means in mahāyāna Buddhism, were tied across the chest with a scarf. During the week prior to the cremation, the public came to view the body in an east room on the third floor of the palace, known as the Immortal Room.

After the week of viewing, the body was moved ceremoniously to the Lhakhang Chenmo for cremation. In strict accordance with astrology, my husband carried the body from the Immortal Room to the palace courtyard. This signified the carrying on of the family lineage. The body rode in a sedan chair, carried by four men in colorful outfits with red silk-tasseled hats. The four, taking turns with four other men, were the sedan-chair carriers who had transported him since he became Trichen. Solemn lamas and monks passed in a procession, chanting prayers.

The step-by-step ceremony was led by my husband. The body, placed in a simple white-painted dome, was burned with many kinds of fragrant wood such as juniper and sandalwood, and melted butter. This cremation dome had been used for generations of Sakya sons. As the fire ceremony progressed, lamas and abbots, sitting in the four directions of the compass, performed tantric rites. As monks and lamas solemnly carried out their duties, our family viewed the beautiful fire of cremation.

Five days later, in another smaller ceremony, the sealed door of the cremation dome was opened and the ashes removed. Most of the ashes were made into a small chöten that would be placed inside the larger, memorial chöten.

According to tradition, high lamas left at least one of three body parts—the heart, eyes, or tongue—as a symbol that they would soon be reincarnated to carry on their Buddhist teachings on behalf of all sentient beings. In this Trichen's case, we found his tongue still lifelike amid the ashes. I was astounded at this phenomenon. It meant his teaching work was not yet finished and would be carried forward again on earth.

There was a room in the Great Temple especially for chötens of sons of the Sakya families. Later, smiths arrived from many parts of Tibet to build a magnificent three-story chöten in memory of the Trichen. Faced with copper and gold and encrusted with precious jewels, the chöten would take several months to build. At this time, the Phuntsok Palace was busy collecting gold from many parts of the country and India for the memorial chöten. We gave our fine gems, as did other patrons for this project. It was very costly for the Phuntsok Palace and for the Sakya school generally. During the Trichen's illness we also had given generously to many other monasteries to say prayers for his health.

In the past, the post of Trichen had automatically passed to the eldest Sakya son of the two palaces. Only once in recent times had this not occurred. During the illness of the Trichen, Jigdal Rinpoche had performed most of the religious duties and affairs of state associated with the office. For most of the Sakya people, I felt, there was no question as to who would be the successor. Some already were looking forward to the installation ceremonies for my husband.

At this time, the Phuntsok Palace had not sent any request to the Lhasa government to obtain the formal trichen title. During the coming winter Jigdal Rinpoche planned to complete all requirements for the post of Trichen, including an examination before Sakya abbots and monks.

Our first offspring, a tiny baby girl, was born one February day in 1951. The Gyayum Kusho, who had given birth to many children in her lifetime and delivered them all herself, acted as midwife, assisted by Aunt Chacha and a nun servant. Jigdal Rinpoche came and caressed his new daughter, who was wrapped in a soft blanket made in India and held by proud and childless Aunt Chacha. In keeping with Sakya custom, immediately after birth my mother-in-law drew a line of soot down the length of the baby's nose using the third finger of her left hand. This was done to scare away evil spirits and demons that might harm her. For long life a bit of fresh butter was placed on the baby's tongue.

Traditionally, a son is eagerly desired by all Tibetan families to carry on the family name. And each day of the year throughout all the Sakya monasteries, monks prayed that the Sakya family would continue to have sons. Thus I felt strongly that many would be disappointed that their wishes were not realized. Everyone in the palace pretended to be pleased, but I could see disappointment in some faces, even those of my husband and his family. Although I still was young and there was plenty of time for male offspring, I felt something of a failure. Aunt Chacha emphasized our good fortune that the infant was healthy.

But it was my husband's elderly great-aunt who was especially diplomatic about our new girl and made me and my family feel better. "This is best," said the aunt, a nun about ninety. "Now we can get lots of baby boys." She and other family members had come to view the baby about three days after her birth, leaving white scarfs and gifts. Highly respected and influential, this aunt gave advice to many and was widely consulted on many topics. She was especially schooled in the traditions and customs of Sakya. Among her many nieces and nephews, Jigdal Rinpoche was one of her favorites.

Jigdal Rinpoche bestowed upon her the honor of naming our daughter and she chose Tenzin Chödron, which means "the one who maintains the teachings, the lamp of religion."

The baby's birth was not announced publicly until she was a month old. On that day the baby, servants, and I went on horseback to visit each of the eight main temples of Sakya to make known the birth and to ask blessings for our daughter. Monks greeted us at each of the temples. A smiling public met us passing from temple to temple. Since Tenzin was wrapped in a maroon blanket, people knew immediately she was a girl. Had she been a son, the blanket would have been orange or yellow. Afterwards many friends came to the palace bearing gifts. Tea was served while a servant held the baby.

Weeks passed and my husband continued both the daily work of the Trichen and his other religious duties. There were many conferences between the Phuntsok Palace family and Sakya government nobles. My husband's trusted adviser through all of this was his teacher, Khanchen.

Jigdal Rinpoche's other primary religious duties involved Lay-Rim and Lam-Dray. Lay-Rim is the higher and more specialized ascetical-mystical training in the Sakya school, taught only at the monastery of Sakya itself. Drawing on the rich tantric-mystical experience of Tibet, this path was reserved only for the lamas and most promising scholars of the

Sakya order. The training prepared them for their roles as teachers and leaders in the Sakya world. My husband did this memorization, reciting, and performing of ritual before groups of monks over a period of more than a year.

During this time he also taught Lam-Dray, in memory of his late father, his principal lama. Lam-Dray is the regular course of religious studies and training of the Sakya monastic order that was followed in all Sakya monasteries throughout Tibet. The content of the course is based on teachings dating back to the Indian master Virūpa in the tenth century c.e. and is distinguished by its discipline. The Tibetan text and collation of this teaching was the work of the great bodhisattva Sachen Kunga Nyingpo, who lived from 1092 to 1158.

Tsegen-la and Chimi-la, more than two hundred monks, and I received this instruction for about three months. Sessions were held in the afternoon and evening in the main palace. Ordinary lay men and women were not allowed this instruction because it involved taking sacred vows, forbidding, for example, any fieldwork that might involve killing of animal life in the ground. This for me was an important step in my role as a Sakya family wife.

With the Lam-Dray successfully completed, the Sakya government sponsored a ceremony in appreciation of this treasured teaching known as "the fruit of the path." With this my husband's title was changed to Dagchen Rinpoche, signifying that he was second in rank in the Sakya religious hierarchy. But actually he was performing the duties of the Trichen.

Meanwhile, there were continuing invitations for my husband to visit eastern Tibet. Dagchen Rinpoche's marriage to a Kham girl had heightened the easterners' interest in such a trip. I wanted to go, but with new responsibilities facing my husband, I dared not even hope.

As the months passed, it was evident that little Tenzin—who now was getting long hair and was cute and cuddly—was not well. She cried frequently. During her illness, I also was very concerned for Dagchen Rinpoche's health. He was still in mourning for his father; he was assuming more Sakya governmental duties; he was teaching at Lam-Dray; and evenings and mornings he was giving blessings for the health of Tenzin. Seldom eating, he lost a great deal of weight. My mother-in-law examined the baby one day and declared that nothing much appeared wrong. My hopes rose. But Tenzin continued to worsen—from what we did not know. I held Tenzin in my arms both night and day. A few days later, the Gyayum came and examined Tenzin.

"Give Tenzin to me," she said.

"Is she going to be all right?" I asked anxiously.

The Gyayum Kusho nodded her head negatively. Aunt Chacha left the room in tears. The Gyayum Kusho then sat down and held Tenzin. She then ordered the secretary to summon an astrologer and monks to conduct prayers. At just over three months old, Tenzin died in my mother-in-law's arms one evening in the main palace, plunging the family again into the customary forty-nine-day period of mourning. Because of this I missed the final ceremony for Lam-Dray. But my husband could not stop his important work. Nearly three hundred people were depending on him.

The astrologer decided that Tenzin's body was to be embalmed in brine and placed in an urnlike vessel in a lower room of the palace. This seldom-visited room, which was locked and sealed with wax, was reserved for religious artifacts. The vessel was placed inside a wall of the room and the proper inscriptions made.

Events of recent months had left me depleted physically and emotionally. My mother-in-law insisted I get a rest in new surroundings. I spent a month at the hot springs in the company of Aunt Chacha and three of my sisters-in-law, who were very comforting. There were occasional visits from Dagchen Rinpoche, too. Then I quickly returned to the busy palace pace.

Shortly after the Trichen's death, Ponsho Thejei, an associate cabinet minister in the Kashag, had come to Sakya from Lhasa concerning the remodeling of the Great Temple, the famous thirteenth-century structure. The Kashag is the council of ministers of the Tibetan government who were to help finance and supervise the work. Ponsho, a cousin of the Drolma Palace's Dagmo Kusho, stayed in their summer palace for several months. He was a powerful political figure whose maneuvering was to change all of our lives dramatically.

Some three months after the Trichen had passed away, the Gyayum and my husband's brother, Trinly Rinpoche, moved out of the Phuntsok Palace and into the summer place. The Gyayum's power in political affairs was diminished, or so we thought, and I automatically took over her duties. She retained the title of Gyayum, however. In the past I had not known much about the duties of the Trichen, but I was learning them quickly now. There were many officials and other visitors who came to the palace daily to confer on government business, to ask blessings, and to make requests for religious functions. Family mourning continued for the Trichen.

The Gyayum asked that the remaining Phuntsok Palace estate lands and wealth be divided evenly between the two sons. My husband's sisters earlier had received their rightful shares of property. My husband and I immediately were skeptical of this proposal, fearing that it would increase family disputes and lower prestige of both sides. The Sakya nobles and many people of Sakya also opposed the split of property. This proposed division was opposed by my husband and me, the Sakya nobles, and many of the people of Sakya. The Gyayum's will prevailed, however, but the division of assets was not on a fifty-fifty basis. Generally, the wealth of the main palace was greatly depleted by this move.

Ponsho had a young daughter who was of marriageable age. There were exchanges of gifts between my mother-in-law's household and the Ponsho's family. There were also numerous dinner parties between the two families.

My mother-in-law, from her new outpost in the summer palace, thus again tried to get a high-ranking noble's daughter into the family. She planned a marriage between Trinly

Rinpoche and Ponsho's daughter, which, from all appearances, would be mutually beneficial to both families. Trinly Rinpoche, as a high-ranking member of the Sakya family, was considered a good candidate for the daughter's hand. It would be to the advantage of the Sakya family to have a close link to a Lhasa noble, and Ponsho would greatly enhance his own power among the noble families there. Both my husband and I were pleased to hear belatedly about the proposed union, which had been arranged secretly.

Trinly Rinpoche, however, when told of the arrangement, would have no part of such plans. He informed his mother that he wanted to be a monk and live a celibate life, as he had frequently mentioned to many friends and family members in the past. He went quietly off to Ngor Monastery, shaved his head, and took the vows of celibacy from a distinguished abbot there. This was a great honor for the Ngor Monastery, since it was believed to be the first time that a Sakya son had come there for that rite.

Insulted by the rejection of his daughter, Ponsho began a grand scheme with the Drolma Palace. At a meeting of my husband and the head monks at the Great Temple we learned what was going on. The marriage, we discovered, was to have been much more than that. It was part of a plan by my mother-in-law to make Trinly Rinpoche the Trichen.

From the day of his birth my husband had been trained to be the next Trichen. To us it was unthinkable that the second in line would be her choice. There was some resentment obviously caused by me. I was never to be accepted fully by my mother-in-law, it seemed, for being a Khampa and not from one of Lhasa's noble families. This intrigue left my husband and me heartsick and unbelieving. It was even more of a shock because the two brothers were close and had never been rivals. Although deeply hurt, Dagchen Rinpoche continued to see his mother and pay her the proper respect. It was a very unhappy time of our lives. I seldom left the palace those days.

The failure of the marriage plans was especially embarrassing to Ponsho, for he had backed the Gyayum when she made the formal request to the Lhasa government to have Trinly Rinpoche made the next Trichen. It was clear that Ponsho had been well paid for his efforts. However, now he had not only lost a future son-in-law, but he and his family also had lost face with many people of Sakya. During Ponsho's mission to Sakya for the remodeling of the Great Temple, many valuable porcelain bowls, pieces of jewelry, and antiques were removed to accommodate workmen. Somehow many of these valuables never got back to their rightful places. It was believed that many of these items were taken to his estate in Gyantse for Ponsho's personal use. Two years later, after his sudden death in Gyantse, his widow returned some items to the Sakya government. The widow said the items had brought tragedy in her home, including the Ponsho's death, and bad luck. She returned the valuable antiques, asking monks to pray for the surviving family. She also apologized for the mistake in the taking of Sakya property.

Soon we begun to notice strange differences in the routine at Sakya. For some time we had wondered why the Drolma Palace was not making the usual requests to the Trichen for various Phuntsok Palace services. For example, when monks were needed for Drolma ceremonies, it was customary to come to the Trichen's palace to obtain permission for their services. Sadly, we came to realize the reason for these discourtesies and other suspicious occurrences. The Drolma Palace had become aware of Ponsho's scheme with my mother-in-law to promote the marriage. The Drolma Palace family felt that if the eldest son, my husband, were not selected as Trichen, the title then should go to their family. It would be their turn, they said.

Indeed, the Drolma Palace had made its own bid for power. The next in line there was a young lama, eight years old, Ayu Rinpoche. His father, Kyagon Ngawang Rinchen, my principal lama, had died just before the Trichen had passed away. The young lama's stepmother, Drolma Dagmo Kusho, who also was his aunt, had sent a delegation to the Kashag in Lhasa asking for the Trichen post for Ayu Rinpoche. Ponsho joined the Drolma Palace in its fight for political and religious control of the Sakya school. He was upset by the failure of the proposed marriage, and by siding with the Drolma Palace, he was helping one of his own relatives, as Ayu Rinpoche's stepmother was his first cousin.

Meanwhile, since we were absorbed with internal matters at Sakya, we were virtually isolated from the greater problem that faced our country. By late 1950 the Chinese Communist forces had strongly established themselves in eastern Tibet and were getting a foothold in parts of the West. After a failed appeal to the United Nations, the Dalai Lama moved to the Chumbi Valley, from which he could flee to India in the event of a future emergency. Then, after months of exchanging messages with the Chinese government, a Tibetan delegation went to Peking to begin negotiations. This resulted in the Sino-Tibetan Agreement of May 23, 1951, which called for the "peaceful liberation of Tibet." Thus began the complete physical domination of my country and the Dalai Lama's government by the Chinese.

At this time the Dalai Lama had left in charge in Lhasa one Lhukhang Sawang, who held the title of prime minister in the Kashag. The Drolma delegation told Lhukhang that the Trichen post alternated between the two palaces. However, this was not the case. Rather, by tradition, the eldest son of either family automatically became the Trichen, no matter from which palace he came. This had been true except once in the early 1700s, when a second son reigned for a few years in the absence of his elder brother. Later in the 1700s, the eighth Dalai Lama clearly established the rule that succession went to the Sakya family's eldest son. The Drolma Palace emphasized too that my mother-in-law had not favored Dagchen Rinpoche's marriage to me.

Thus, Lhukhang Sawang, whose palms were greased we felt, and who was related to the Drolma Palace's Dagmo Kusho, made a decision in favor of the Drolma Palace. This persuasion was passed to the Kashag, whose other ministers agreed. We were never consulted by anyone in Lhasa about the Trichen post.

The arguments in favor of the Drolma Palace's young lama were refined and then sent to the Dalai Lama. By this time it was July of 1951 and he was returning from near Yatung in the Chumbi Valley, stopping at Gyantse. His Holiness was traveling with General Chang Ching-wu, whom the Chinese had named the new commissioner and administrator of civil and military affairs in Tibet. His Holiness quite naturally was concerned with the grave problems confronting his people— problems that overshadowed the case of the Trichen post, we felt. Then he too put his seal on the succession paper.

About a month later several Sakya government officials and monks from the Great Temple sent a letter to Lhasa to Pandatsang, a Sakya patron and the wealthiest man in Tibet. The letter again explained the long-established rule of succession and Dagchen Rinpoche's right to the post and requested that Pandatsang again raise the matter with the government.

Pandatsang responded that the request would be of no use at this time, that the Dalai Lama would not change his mind, and that political affairs involving the Chinese had precedence. We also learned that Pandatsang, a powerful figure, had won the support of the Drolma Palace group. Thus the Sakya nobles had no choice but to drop the issue temporarily, but it was by no means forgotten.

Thus my husband, having served as Trichen some eight months, entered a new, entirely unexpected phase of his life and an uncertain future. Although he had lost the Trichen post, he still remained a high lama with followers throughout the country. He would retain his title of Dagchen, a title in the Sakya family dating from the time of the Mongol Khans.

"Now I know why the Gyayum Kusho wanted a ranking noble's daughter for Dagchen Rinpoche," I thought, feeling helpless. "I have no relatives to argue this historic issue behind the scenes." All I wanted was to prevail for the sake of Sakya history. Many times I had been advised that the Sakya lamas never intentionally engaged in the two palaces' competition. It was the mothers and wives with connections to the high government who, in power plays, caused the dissention.

At this time, the fourth family death in about a year was made known to me. Dagchen Rinpoche and Aunt Chacha sadly told me about the passing of Great-Uncle Nawang in Thalung Monastery at the age of seventy-nine. He had known he was going to die for about a week and left messages for all of us, Uncle Tülku-la said in his letter. I was deeply grieved, and being so far away, I felt helpless and homesick.

8

On to Kham

Several months elapsed, during which my husband again decided not to bring up officially the decision on the Trichen post. We doubted the question would get a fair hearing. We believed that government nobles who were interested in amassing wealth were not concerned about truth and justice. Instead, after long deliberations and much urging from eastern Tibetan monks, we decided to visit Kham and make our case for the Trichen post upon our return. My mother-in-law opposed the Kham visit, feeling that this was the proper time to approach the Tibetan government.

Sakya officials approved our planned two-year trip, but some people opposed this on grounds that Dagchen Rinpoche was the eldest of the Sakya sons, was considered precious, and was needed in Sakya for the many religious duties he performed. He insisted on making the journey, and thus dozens of followers requested to accompany him. They felt that Sakya had been spiritually active in the immediate past years and they sought to be with Dagchen Rinpoche because of the religious atmosphere he created. Without him, they feared, this spiritual atmosphere would be diminished, at least temporarily. Also they knew that if they too went, they would share in receiving the teaching of learned lamas in eastern Tibet.

Actually, there were strong forces drawing us to Kham. On at least eight occasions over the years, monks of the Lhagyal Monastery had asked Dagchen Rinpoche to visit. It is the custom that if one is the incarnate lama recognized by a specific monastery, one must visit that monastery sometime in his life. Dagchen Rinpoche planned to spend about a year at Lhagyal working and teaching monks. Another highlight of the trip would be getting to spend about a year with Dzongsar Khyentse Rinpoche, a famous lama in the Derge area with whom my husband planned to study. My husband also genuinely liked Khampas and would feel very comfortable with them. I envisioned showing him the home where I grew up and introducing him to my friends.

We had two months to prepare for the journey. I sent a letter to my mother in Thalung via two overjoyed monks from Lhagyal who went ahead of us with the good news. There were many arrangements to be made for the Phuntsok Palace during our absence. Tsechag, a noble monk, was to take over my duties of managing the palace. Warm hats, sturdy boots, and even fur-lined pants were made for my travel wardrobe.

I selected Tsechag's niece, Wangmo, to be my new personal servant for the trip. Wangmo was a Sakya girl a year younger than I. Both her parents were dead and, thus, since she had no immediate family, she was asked to come along. Although she had not been a servant before, she was very competent and trustworthy.

Family life took an upward turn just before our departure when I learned that I was going to have another baby. Once again, I wished for a son. Since little Tenzin had died here at Sakya, it was well, I felt, that the new child would be born elsewhere.

A week was devoted to visiting chapels and monasteries at Sakya, during which we made offerings of money and scarfs to ensure safety on the road.

An auspicious day for the departure was chosen by the

same learned monk who had selected our wedding date. It was the first day of the seventh lunar month, 1952, or September in the Western calendar.

Thirty-three persons and more than sixty horses and mules made the first leg of our trip to Shigatse. Three days earlier some servants had left with the heavier belongings on yaks and pack donkeys; they would meet us in Shigatse.

My mother-in-law was grief-stricken as we said goodbyes, declaring that she didn't think we would meet again. Despite my joy at the prospect of going home, I too felt a trace of sadness about leaving. Regardless of all the tragedy and sudden change that had characterized life there, the Phuntsok Palace had become like home.

The man who would have a large role in directing our destiny in the next years, Phuba Tsering, was the party leader and head horsekeeper. He would direct our daily movements on the road, deciding when and where we would stay overnight or camp. Phuba Tsering was a colorful figure, immediately recognizable as the party leader. He wore large earrings set with heavy stones, a fur-lined and silk-covered hat, and a colorful wool chuba with a leopardskin collar and designs woven into the fabric. I too traveled in finery that included my big headdress.

After the departure ceremonies, we rode out a half mile to a spot where the palaces still were visible. Then, abruptly at the signal of the monk on the lead horse, we turned back about a half block, then resumed our outbound journey. We did this maneuver three times with everybody chanting prayers symbolizing our safe return home. When I looked at many people who had come for the farewell, I saw smiles, but tears were in their eyes. We waved and tried to smile too, but I was emotional and understood their feeling of being left behind for a long period. Usually Sakya lamas of this rank left only for a few months at most; it was considered exceptional to be gone two years.

Beyond the town of Shap, where we were warmly greeted, we had to cross the Shap River. There had been heavy rains and we were required to lash our yakskin boats together for the crossing. Muddy water swirled around the rocks. Although it was only about a two-hundred-foot crossing, I was nervous since I was always afraid of water. As a girl in Kham, I had heard of many deaths in the Dri River that passed four miles from my home. "Be careful crossing rivers," Great Uncle Nawang Nyima had said. While I prayed, I covered my eyes and concentrated on the sound of the paddles. It was the first of many jolting adventures—traveling experiences that any mobile Tibetan knows he will encounter.

We arrived in Shigatse and spent an enjoyable three weeks, making our headquarters in a home obtained through a friend of Uncle Tülku-la. Dagchen Rinpoche's uncle, the powerful governor of Shigatse, helped us arrange for the trip from Shigatse to Lhasa.

Although my husband did not travel extensively in the city, the people everywhere paid their respects. His wife, too, I soon learned, was the object of much curiosity; this was my first trip out of Sakya since our marriage.

Shigatse was the site of Tashilhunpo, home of the Panchen Lama and one of the great monasteries of the Yellow Hat school. One of his government aides was married to my cousin, Drokar, who was from Jyekundo. It was in her home that I was introduced to many of the ladies of Shigatse. Many of them invited me to their homes, but I generally preferred the gatherings at Drokar's. I was the guest of honor at several of these combined tea-and-dinner parties held for women only. Usually eight or nine women attended, each accompanied by servants, whose duties included serving tea and caring for the children.

Each woman dressed according to the rank of her husband and was similarly addressed. They complimented each other on the beauty of their chubas, blouses, aprons, and jewels. But one never said, "Thank you," as it was not proper to accept compliments or flattery as in the West. Instead we shrugged and replied, "It's nothing," or "Don't mention it."

Conversations at these events were different from what one

would expect at such a gathering in the West. We observed formal rules, asking each other in turn, "How old are you? How many children do you have? Where were you born? Where are your parents?" Being asked one's age was quite appropriate, as age is respected in my country.

Mahjongg was played for money, with part of the winnings going to the servants. Politeness was the rule, and the highest standards of etiquette prevailed. There was never any expression of disappointment if one lost.

On the day after our arrival in Shigatse, the Panchen Lama sent us a magnificent array of gifts. The gifts were hugely proportioned—a whole animal for meat, a large bundle of butter, sacks of rice, and large boxes of tea and tsampa. Our request to visit the Panchen Lama was granted by his regent, who held power until the Lama was considered old enough to rule. About a week after our arrival we called on the Panchen Lama, then about seventeen years old, in Tashilhunpo Monastery. Our group gathered in a large room where he received us.

The Panchen Lama, a few years younger than the Dalai Lama, had arrived in Shigatse that year from Amdo. I wondered which dialect or language he would speak—Amdo, Kham, Chinese, or Mongolian—as I had been told he knew them all. He looked much older than seventeen, I thought. He appeared to be a bit shy, but perhaps he just was attempting to add solemnity to the occasion. When he spoke, it was rapidly and in a low voice to a monk attendant, who repeated his words. Much of his speech suggested the Amdo dialect. He was seated on a rather low type of cushioned bench. He first gave a short blessing to all in the party, after which all but five of us left. We were served tea, rice, dried fruit, and fancy cookies. This man was very gracious. He offered to help in any way that would make our trip easier.

Although the Panchen Lama traditionally is of the Gelugpa school, he called our attention to ties to the Sakya lamas. He mentioned that the first Panchen Lama was a reincarnation of Sakya Pandita, and that the fifth Panchen Lama had studied at Sakya. His knowledge impressed us, especially Khanchen, who was very scholarly. While at Shigatse near the Nyang River, we picnicked at a big park with a zoo, owned by the Panchen Lama.

Twenty-one of us set out for Lhasa on one of the most rugged of the three routes to the capital; but it was the route that had the best forage for our animals. Among newcomers in our party was Yeshe Gyatso, a Mongolian who had recently come west with the Panchen Lama's party. Yeshe, who had been trained at the Amdo monastery of Kumbum, spoke Chinese fluently and would be our interpreter when needed.

We first stopped at Serdogchen Monastery, in an area famous for its peaches. It was the season and we indulged. Uncle Tülku-la had told me so much about this famous old Sakya monastery, a very holy place, but I was disappointed that it had no gold roof. However, the place became significant to me for a special reason. For here, among a community of some three hundred monks, I slept inside the monastery— something I had not done since I was a girl of seven and recovering from being gored by the yak. Even though there were special quarters for visiting Sakya lamas and their immediate families, a feeling of superstition—a sense of wrongdoing came over me. I rested uneasily.

Across the Tsangpo River, we stopped at Tsedong, the site of one of the most productive Sakya estates. The best statuary smiths in western Tibet lived here. It also was famous for lumber, some of which had been used in renovating the Phuntsok Palace and other buildings in Sakya. There also were sizeable barley, bean, wheat, peach, and apricot crops.

It was fun traveling as the wife of a high lama and observing the dances and other ceremonies. At each town these ceremonies were a little different. Sometimes this could be exhausting; now and then I had time to relax and remove my headdress.

The day before we arrived in Lhasa we stayed near Drepung Monastery at the estate of a friend. We were greeted by some of Dagchen Rinpoche's relatives and two Khampa businessmen. The Khampas brought news that my mother and Uncle Nyima had arrived in Lhasa and were awaiting us there. Aunt Chacha and I had not seen them in about two years, and we were very happy and excited. Soon we would have our family reunion. I was awake most of that night anticipating all the news from Thalung. Aunt Chacha was particularly anxious to hear news of her husband, Uncle Kuyak.

When we arrived in the capital for a month's stay, we were welcomed outside the three-story noble's residence that was to be our headquarters. It was like coming home; everything had been arranged, and all I had to do was relax.

My mother had planned to make her home with her only daughter in Sakya. But she was delighted to hear that at last we were going to visit Kham, so much so that she enthusiastically agreed to join us and return there.

This was Uncle Nyima's first trip to western Tibet. He planned to engage in further studies at the Chagpori Medical Center and to buy many medical supplies, and then to visit the Ngor Monastery and Sakya, a major lifetime goal. But he too changed his plans and made the turnaround for the pilgrimage to eastern Tibet. He had brought along a number of horses for us, bound for Sakya. Now they too were to make the trip back to Thalung.

Here also I was reunited with my childhood friend, Khando, who had married a Lhasa man. Khando was homesick for Kham. She was like a sister to me, and we saw each other every day. But I now found a new reserve and shyness in Khando, owing to my position as a Sakya lama's wife.

Late one morning, a few days after we had arrived in Lhasa, I had my first formal visit with the Dalai Lama. This was the customary arrival visit made to pay respects to our leader. It was also traditional for high lamas and officials to make a departure visit. We had rehearsed the proper protocol two days earlier, including behavior, manners, and the proper dress according to rank.

This time our family group of about twenty-one rode on horseback to His Holiness' summer palace at Norbu Lingka.

We were greeted by the chamberlain, who was His Holiness' elder brother, Lobsang Samten, and ushered into the chamberlain's quarters on the first floor, where we were served tea and sweets. We drank from elaborate china cups in gold and silver stands. Summoned to His Holiness' reception room, we passed through a courtyard laden with potted flowers and plants. We walked silently in line as we passed through this Jewel Park.

As we entered the big room we saw the Dalai Lama, who was about nineteen, seated on a high golden throne. He acknowledged Dagchen Rinpoche and smiled. I was in awe of this Living Buddha whom Tibetans call "Precious Jewel."

He blessed each of us. When it was my turn to be blessed, I was very nervous. His Holiness spoke rapidly to me in Lhasa dialect. I did not hear him clearly. But I had to respond and blurted out, "I'm eighteen." It is a Tibetan custom to open a conversation with questions about name and age, and I presumed he knew my name. He smiled and nodded. That made me even more nervous, as I was convinced that he had asked some other question. I was silent for the remainder of the audience, keeping my head bowed and eyes lowered.

The Dalai Lama then beckoned my husband to be seated. Others directed me and Trinley, our treasurer, to sit down. The rest of the party withdrew to the next room. After we were served tea, the Dalai Lama asked Dagchen Rinpoche about our forthcoming trip to Kham. My husband answered with brevity and politeness. That concluded our half-hour visit.

Later I asked Dagchen Rinpoche why he had not answered in more detail. He said we had already provided that information when he had requested permission for the trip and it was not necessary to repeat it.

I visited the temples—the Jokhang—nearly every day. But I found Lhasa greatly changed by the influence of the Chinese Communists. One found many more kinds of Chinese goods such as fruit for sale in the shops. There were also Chinese signs and photographs around the city. The Chinese were not yet in evidence at the three major monasteries around Lhasa, but I detected an underlying current of mistrust among the people. One never knew where loyalties were.

General Chang Ching-wu had been here for some time as Mao Tse-tung's government representative in Lhasa. We Tibetans called him "Tanjiwu." His residence was one of several fine Tibetan homes that had been bought, requisitioned, or rented by the Chinese. Our party was given tickets to a program of Chinese history, drama, and music one evening at Tanjiwu's house. The residence was near the center of Lhasa. The program was staged in a large area in the middle of the property, where a tent had been erected.

My opinion of Tanjiwu was neutral. We returned home early, feeling it was dangerous to travel at night. Sometimes we had heard gunfire from the darkened streets. Rock-throwing at passersby was frequent. Some mornings bodies were found in the central square.

On the way to the event that evening I saw, for the first time, an automobile, a Chinese model resembling a jeep. It was a Chinese official's car. It appeared, with its blinding headlights, like an angry beast coming at us. Our horses were frightened, and some of the people in the crowded street were screaming. I too was fearful, wondering if this beast could be controlled or would swerve into the crowd. But my husband, who had seen many cars in India, calmed me.

Another invitation came, this time for dinner at the Indian government mission, Dekyi Lingka, where I first tasted Western food. There was a lovely garden with magnificent flowers, much of the credit for which belongs to Hugh E. Richardson, who headed the mission when it was under the British rule. I saw growing, among other things, sumptuous red tomatoes.

We arrived late one afternoon. We were surprised to see the peculiar blend of East and West in the servants' uniforms. These Tibetan men wore high-collared red jackets and red pants trimmed in braid, in the British tradition. Their hair was worn back in a single braid with red Tibetan-style tassels.

Each wore a big gold earring in the left ear and a piece of turquoise in the right ear.

It was a splendid setting, with lovely white tablecloths and a wide variety of silverware. I had a brief moment of fright when I was beckoned to begin the dinner at my table. Faced with an unfamiliar array, I was stumped. Was I to start with a knife? Spoon? Fork? And what size knife, spoon, or fork? Tibetans use chopsticks, as well as spoons, forks, and small knives when eating, but they do not use the fork and knife together. And the fork is never held in the left hand. My face reddened. Kindly Norzing-la, the wife of a Sikkimese official, quietly directed me to a starting point—a fork. I don't recall the exact menu, but there was a choice of several meats. Whatever the colorful vegetables were, I liked them.

After dinner we went downstairs to see a British film, which included footage of my husband's family. This film had been taken several years earlier when all of the Trichen's family had visited Lhasa.

In Lhasa we also visited the Chagpori, high on a hill, accessible only by climbing many flights of stairs. It once was the home of Thangtong Gyalbo, the eleventh-century ascetic-saint who was believed to have lived to the age of 125 years. The Chagpori attracted many visitors who came to enjoy not only its magnificent view of the Potala but also its old and valuable statues. Three images, covered respectively with coral, turquoise, and conch shells, were particularly treasured.

Here, as was also the case at some monasteries, monks received training in medical practice. Uncle Nyima, who had studied nine years to become a doctor, bought great supplies of drugs, many of which were herbs and pills. Some of the ingredients had been brought from India and compounded here.

Nearby was another tourist attraction, the Dalai Lama's elephant, quartered behind the Potala. The elephant is a precious animal in the eyes of Tibetan Buddhists, in part because the animal is the largest creature living on the dry earth. Many parts of its body can be used for a number of purposes—the flesh, skin, and especially bile for curing diseases. When the Lord Buddha was conceived, his mother dreamed that a six-tusked white elephant came out of the heavens and entered her right side, an omen that the baby was a holy infant who would achieve perfect wisdom. The elephant is also one of the seven precious articles of royalty in Buddhism. At least twice daily, the elephant was watered at the Dalai Lama's well. We watched as the animal bowed his head and then offered water from his trunk toward the palace. He did this three times before he drank. We made the customary offerings of a scarf and money.

After much deliberation, we selected the middle route to eastern Tibet for what was to be a three-month journey. We started in the ninth month, first on the road from Lhasa to Nakchuka.

His Holiness' office provided our party with a letter bearing his official seal in order to facilitate our making housing and other arrangements en route. The letter had not been delivered to us, however, at the time of our departure. A brave and trusted monk from Kham thus volunteered to wait for it in Lhasa and then overtake us.

The monk was supplied with a horse and provisions. For protection on the road he was given a sword and a treasured ceremonial flail, or scourge, of knotted leather set into a wooden handle decorated with silver. After about a week on the road, the monk arrived in the middle of the night, on foot, completely unnerved, and in a pathetic state. Robbers had taken his horse, clothing, sword, and flail, and then beaten him cruelly. His baggage had been rifled, and money, food, and supplies of all sorts taken. But the Dalai Lama's letter, which the robbers apparently considered worthless, was cast aside by them, and thus delivered to us intact. The monk's mission had been fulfilled, for which we were deeply grateful.

The first few nights on the way to Nakchuka, we stayed in homes; later, we began to camp in our tents, mostly in towns and villages, as monasteries were ordinarily off the main route. Our family tent was made in Bhutan of heavy striped canvas, with a window. My husband's tent was particularly beautiful and visible for some distance. This tent was set up when there were enough visitors to warrant it. Made of gold canvas decorated with red and blue dragons and Buddhist symbols, it was used for religious ceremonies. People would come for miles around to see and be blessed by the Sakya Dagchen.

In many of these areas, the nomads would circle our tent on kora almost all night long. The women's jewelry and coins tinkled endlessly as they moved, accompanied by mumbled prayers and whirring prayer wheels. It was nearly impossible to sleep, but we dared not complain. These nomads requested the blessings of the Buddha, the bodhisattvas, and the Sakya lamas. Having limited vocabularies, these people spoke openly and simply whatever was in their hearts. Their faith was deep and they expressed profound respect for all lamas and monks, not just those of our school of Buddhism.

We were several days at Nakchuka, where my husband was busy with religious ceremonies. Here I readied my winter clothes for the serious travel hazards ahead. All of us had fur-lined garments for the venture into wintry Kham, yet I always wore a necklace and jewels. I got out my turquoise silk hat with the fox fur trim. Frequently we thoroughly shook our fine furs, and hung them out in the air. They became freshened and free of odor. To clean fur-lined clothes, the fur was covered with a thick paste made of native Tibetan soda and water. When it dried, the fur was pounded with a stick against the hardened ground or, more often, against icy snow, to remove the soda mixture. Fur dried easily in the dry cold air.

People escorted us out of town, and we began the strenuous part of the journey. Sometimes there was snow. We crossed passes and forded icy streams. Cold winds swept about us. Our routine called for a meal at about seven-thirty A.M. and another at five P.M. Our midday meal was not large. If we were in a nomadic area, nomads would give us hot tea, milk, and yogurt. Each of us had a small bag of dried meat, cheese, dried fruits, and cookies, doled out at the start of our trip.

The formality of our party was greater than when my family and I had made the journey from Kham to the West. Then we had sat around singing, joking, and playing games in the evening. But on this trip, we always prayed before starting out and again at the close of each day.

The eldest member of our party was Khanchen. The youngest was Tsenam, about nine, grandson of the Shapé. Tsenam was a likeable lad and we enjoyed having him along. He called my mother, "Mother."

Frequently along the way, the servants became lonesome for Sakya. But I was going home and my interest piqued the closer we came to Kham proper.

In the nomadic area of Khoma, we stayed a few days with the headman and his family. Their home was built on a foundation of stone surmounted by a tent. These were semi-permanent dwellings, as most nomad families moved about four times a year. The rest of the tribesmen lived in tents. We had a prayer service that night during which my husband blessed everyone.

The Khoma nomads dressed and otherwise appeared quite unlike either Khampas or western Tibetans. The Khoma men wore a single braid wound around their heads. The braids were held with heavy finger rings of silver, brass, and copper, set with coral and turquoise. When these men met lamas or nobles, they quickly unwound their braids as a gesture of respect. The women had many braids and jewels and observed the fashion we call *durkah*, meaning "makeup," made with, among other things, brown sugar, raisin juice, honey, and charred wheat. We believed this was good for our health and helped to keep our skin smooth and protected from chapping and aging. This tradition of beautification was carried out in many parts of Tibet. Men never used these face markings.

We headed into snowy country, where many times the weather was miserable. But often when we stayed with nomad families I found myself relaxed and having fun. We were starting toward Sok Sandalwood Monastery, a community of about five hundred Gelugpa monks. But first we had to cross the Sok Pass, a treacherous one. We began at five A.M., sending the horses ahead, single file. We were on yaks that had been sent to Nakchuka by Lhagyal Monastery. It was snowing heavily.

Since I had ridden on yaks many times as a girl, this aspect of the trip seemed rather enjoyable despite the hardships. But for the western Tibetans it was a new and scary experience. Although the yaks had reins attached to their nose rings, they paid no attention to their riders, but simply went their way up the steep and icy slopes. It was extremely cold and much of the snow was frozen hard. Ice gathered like jewels on my chuba hem. When I walked it made a tinkling noise. Several inches of snow were on my boots. Every few minutes it was necessary to knock snow off the horses' shod hooves.

We paused briefly for lunch, but it was so windy atop the pass that we couldn't sit still and keep warm. The animals got so tired on passes like these that they shook. On the way down, we couldn't ride our yaks as it was too steep. At times I just had to sit down and slide. It was the most miserable mountain crossing I had ever made. Late in the afternoon we somehow reached the bottom of the pass. We paused for tea and to feed the horses and free them of snow.

In this mood of exhaustion, we suddenly heard gunfire. Everyone was terrified. The horses shook with fear, even though we had just fed them barley, peas, and dried turnips mixed with tea leaves to calm them after the exhausting trip over the pass. Surely it was robbers, we all surmised, and we would be raided, but the noise didn't sound like rifle fire. My husband performed a ritual divination and determined that it was not robbers; Khanchen agreed. Phuba Tsering, as head horsekeeper and our group leader, warned that we must stay close together. The horsekeepers' guns were loaded. When the noise grew louder, we decided to send two scouts ahead, so that we could prepare for whatever fate was to befall us. The two went to investigate, returning in about an hour—

laughing. "It was a greeting party," they declared, "in our honor."

Both Tibetan government officials and Chinese officials, who now had a headquarters in the Sok area, were paying their respects. The scouts had seen about fifteen Chinese and two Tibetan government officials with their servants. The guns we had heard were machine guns operated by the Chinese.

What a time to be officially received! All of us looked bedraggled. Our clothes were soggy and dirt covered our faces and heads. About two miles from Sok Sandalwood Monastery a large group of people awaited us. Tibetan officials greeted us with scarfs. The Chinese introduced themselves and led the parade to the monastery. The crowd watched as we entered the monastery, looking far from elegant. I was embarrassed.

The Tibetan nobles were anxious for news from Lhasa, which we conveyed. We also brought mail to these government officials. It was pleasant at Sok Sandalwood Monastery and the first time I had been in an honest-to-goodness house since we had left Nakchuka. We were asked to stay a week, but my husband said we could spare only three days. He was busy most of the time performing religious ceremonies for both monks and the citizenry. When we left, the Chinese again fired their guns in salute!

We crossed the frozen Sok River and moved into an agricultural area. Some four days later, we encountered the first of three parties who had come to meet us. About thirty men were from Jyekundo and Thalung, and my mother knew many of them. They were a great help, bringing us fresh horses and food, and bartering and selling the tired horses.

We entered Bönpo country. Bön is the pre-Buddhist animistic religion of my country. When in the eighth century King Trisong Detsan gave the edict that Buddhism was the official religion of Tibet, many of the Bönpos moved into eastern Tibet, where native religion became mixed with Buddhism. There were several Bönpo monasteries in this area of Kham.

We stayed in one of them, during which I had my first real contact with these people. I thought the Bönpos very pious. They seemed to be praying constantly.

Bön monks wore the traditional red robes as well as white shirts and hats. Among Buddhists, white shirts often were worn by those being punished. I was shown many statues, some of which looked almost identical to Buddhist deities. One monk explained why many of the ceremonies, such as kora and turning the prayer wheel, were performed counterclockwise. "We are going to meet the Buddha, not to follow him," he said.

Proceeding toward Jyekundo, we moved across a high plateau on the way to the Nangchen area. For four days, we endured very heavy snow. When we stopped for tea one day, we met a welcome sight—a group of some four hundred yaks and their caretakers, carrying food from Jyekundo to Chumpotingchen. These men were not traders; they were simply transporting food from China. We were able to move into the trail in the snow broken by these yaks.

On the third day of this rigorous route, we took a wrong turn and went two or three miles off course. My husband had a compass, but it was packed away in a box aboard a mule, along with clothes and other valuables. When we stopped for tea, we searched for an hour for the compass. Under orders from my husband, we consulted our index of boxes. Finally it was located and we had to turn back, again traversing the snowy trail until we found the proper route.

There was nothing to use for fuel in this desolate high country. On the second day we burned a tent pole and a wooden yak saddle. The third day we lost our way again, and again burned a pole and a saddle. We searched three to five feet under the snow for several kinds of large dried plants to burn.

It was a disheartening time, and some wished they had not come to Kham. The only water was melted snow. Animals went thirsty and hungry. Roads were narrow and a couple of our horses died. During the ordeal of the harsh weather, many of us donned warm headgear as well as dark glasses for protection from the glare of the snow. Gradually we left this snowy country and came to a group of settlements where people brought us plenty of food.

We had a week's rest at Tsangda Monastery in Nangchen, home of some five hundred Sakya monks. There was great rejoicing as a highly trained lama and his servants from Sakya were assigned here and they knew most of our people. They asked for news of their friends and relatives back home. What hospitality we got here! Before each meal, they asked Dagchen Rinpoche and me what food we wanted to eat. Trinley was busy fixing poles and other equipment with the help of monks who sprang to his aid.

Leaving Nangchen, a small group of us started out ahead, including myself and Wangmo. Dagchen Rinpoche was delayed slightly by ceremonies. Part of the road followed a stream that was frozen over and just right for sledding. Using large flat stones, Wangmo and I went sliding out on the ice, with Wangmo bending down and pushing my back. It was about half past eight in the morning and we were full of energy, taking turns pushing each other and giggling. From the roadway others warned us that we would hurt ourselves on the ice. As I coasted down, I came to a sloping spot and slid off the rock on a rough piece of ice, badly bruising my seat and hip. Wangmo cut her elbow. There was great anxiety over my fall, since I was expecting my second baby in a few months.

All day following my fall I was unbearably stiff. Could I ride my horse? I had to, but mounting and dismounting was slow and painful. That was the end of my ice sledding. Subsequently, while still in the Nangchen area we stayed in homes with very steep stairs that were difficult for me to climb. These stairs, usually on the outside leading to the second floor, were made of tree trunks with steps hewn out. When one went up the stairs there was nothing to hang on to. These trips were agonizing, but I dared not complain as my accident had been my own fault. Wangmo brought me warm towels to use as packs for my bruise. She sneaked the packs to me, hiding them under her apron. We didn't want to attract attention to my lingering pain. Others in the party looked strangely at my slow gait. I walked like an old woman. But many thought my pregnancy was the reason.

As we crested a hill on our approach to the city of Nangchen-Gar, we saw a crowd of hundreds awaiting us. It was too late to change clothes, and again we were on view in our bedraggled state. I hadn't thought this center would be such a big and important place. There were many Chinese shops with a wide variety of goods on sale.

Soon after we arrived in Nangchen-Gar a Chinese official gave a large dinner party in our honor. Stiff and sore from my accident, I did not attend, but my mother did. There was some bad feeling, and my absence was noted by one Chinese who remarked to Dagchen Rinpoche that he was "sorry your wife couldn't come."

It was here in Nangchen-Gar that we first met opposition from Chinese officialdom. In eastern Tibet, one of the measures of a man's wealth and prestige is the number of guns he owns and wears. Guns are kept in good working order and worn with pride, some having been handed down from generation to generation. It was not uncommon for as many as a dozen yaks to be traded for one gun. An eastern Tibetan who could afford one wore his gun on his back, held by a decorated strap clasped with a silver buckle across his chest. Often the guns themselves were richly decorated with silver. The end of the barrel was protected from moisture with a stopper made of a white yak tail, dyed red and set into a base of brass or silver and attached to the barrel by a short silver chain. Most guns had a case of leather, cloth, or leopard skin. Occasionally a pistol was worn, carried in a hip holster of fine red or black leather, or wood decorated with silver or antimony, coral, and turquoise.

By this time, the Chinese had forbidden Tibetans to own or carry arms. Nevertheless, many Tibetans still secretly hung on to their firearms, at least their best ones, some of which had been inherited from their ancestors. About twenty firearms, some very old, were turned over to my husband by faithful Tibetans here. In the main temple of Sakya in the building known as the Gorum, there was a large collection of guns made as religious offerings. The weapons were offered by those who declared that henceforth they would not take life and wanted to be good men.

The new offerings were to go into the collection. They were tied together in a bundle with leather bindings and readied to be sent back to Sakya. The Chinese administrators were aware of this arms cache.

The morning we were to leave Nangchen-Gar, horses were being saddled and other preparations for departure were underway. Suddenly two Chinese Army officials and a translator approached Trinley, our treasurer, and began their polite—always polite—interrogation. Trinley disliked them, but played their game of politeness. The conversation went something like this:

"Are you leaving today?"

"Yes," Trinley replied.

"Do you have any quicksilver, opium, guns, or wristwatches?"

"Yes, we have guns," Trinley admitted. "We need them on the way. These guns are registered with the Dalai Lama's government."

Tanjiwu had given us a permit to carry guns into Kham. Trinley showed them papers from the Dalai Lama and from the Chinese representative in Lhasa.

"Do you have any guns not registered?" they asked.

"No," Trinley said.

"Did you buy any firearms or have any given to you on the way from Lhasa?"

"Yes," Trinley explained. "Some people gave guns to us for the Sakya temple. They are ready to send to Sakya."

"Do you have any bullets?"

"Some, not many," Trinley added.

How many, they wanted to know. Trinley replied that he didn't remember.

The Chinese asked when we were sending the arms to Sakya.

Trinley replied, "When we arrive in Jyekundo."

The Chinese asked why Trinley didn't show them the guns. Were they Tibetan, British, or Indian-made, they queried.

"They all are going to the Sakya Temple," Trinley retorted. "Why show them to you when we don't use them?"

The Chinese, becoming increasingly brusque, insisted that the guns must be shown, that Kham was under Chinese jurisdiction. Their politeness was vanishing and it became increasingly clear we would be detained.

Trinley conferred with my husband.

"You must display the guns," Trinley advised. "If they insist on having them, give them up."

The firearms were unwrapped and shown to the Chinese, who promptly stated they could not be taken further into Kham. Such action would require permission from Mao Tsetung. He would give the required papers, they insisted.

In desperation Trinley suggested that the Chinese keep the guns and that we would pick them up later. But the Chinese declared that we must wait while a telegram was sent to Peking.

Several days elapsed, but there was no reply. We said we could wait no longer. Trinley suggested the Chinese take the guns to the Nangchen Palace, our next destination. But they insisted that the Nangchen Palace was out of the way, being off the main road, and inconvenient.

At the end of the week, permission finally came. Not for a moment did we believe it was from Peking. We guessed it came from officials in Jyekundo. The Chinese stipulated that we must not fire the guns in Kham or sell them to Khampas. We promised we would not do this. We had to give a detailed report, stating the number of guns and their value. The firearms then were sent temporarily to Jyekundo.

While in Nangchen-Gar, our party had asked nothing of

the Chinese; nevertheless, our presence was a dilemma for them. In order to maintain credibility and stability in their relations with the people of Nangchen-Gar, the Chinese felt obligated to show the proper respect for a high Sakya lama. When we left, about five of them rode out with our party. After going about two miles, they fired a departing salute.

We moved on to a happy stay with the royalty at Nangchen Palace, the capital of a small kingdom that had existed for hundreds of years in eastern Tibet. Only about three such kingdoms, ruled by *gyalbos*, or kings, remained in my country. Another was at Derge, where we would be visiting. The Nangchen gyalbos had existed since the time of Chögyal Phagspa in the thirteenth century. The current gyalbo was not in residence at the palace. Chinese administrators at Jyekundo were trying to diminish his powers, which were few, and required that he stay in Jyekundo much of the time. The gyalbo, on his trips through Jyekundo, dressed in yellow silks and moved in royal fashion, accompanied by guards.

The palace was built high on a hillside, overlooking the farm country of Nangchen province, which was known for its sweet turnips and generally good food, including plentiful butter and other dairy products made by nomads. The palace was an old, three-story structure, lacking the large windows often found in new or remodeled Tibetan residences. The gyalbo and his queen were very religious. The queen had just completed supervising the construction of a new temple housing an unusual collection of twenty-one Tārās, many encrusted with jewels.

The queen, mother of three princesses and two princes, was particularly happy about our visit, as she did not get to see her husband for months on end. Her children had few opportunities to play with other youngsters. Because they were royalty, they were kept from ordinary citizens. I gave the children a phonograph record from Lhasa, which delighted them.

The queen was an excellent hostess, and I enjoyed my rest here. While my husband was busy with religious duties, the queen and I often talked together, sharing religious experiences. We became very close, and when I left, we exchanged rings in a gesture of deep friendship.

One of my duties while traveling was looking after the health of our horses and mules. As a child I had learned this skill from Uncle Kuyak. Careful treatment of these animals was of paramount importance, and they were closely watched.

Besides my trusted horse, Sengerapa (Blond Lion), I had a mule which I primarily used in rugged mountain country and in crossing streams. Blond Lion was a *singta* or show horse from Sining. In my country there also is the *yulta*, the work horse, and the *dokta*, the nomad's horse. My husband also rode a singta, customary for lamas. Blond Lion had an uncanny ability to understand what I said to him. Each morning he would wait outside for his treat—a ration of our tsampa, cheese, and butter. When we stayed in a monastery and I was busy, Blond Lion missed his ration. The next time he saw me he would whinny, clearly asking for his handout. A gentle horse, he also ate puffed wheat, cookies, and buttermilk. We were close companions indeed.

Our medical treatment of horses was primitive, but we were devoted to the task. The principal treatment was an elixir in the form of pills containing blessed medicines. If an animal had eaten poisonous plants, bloodletting the tongue was a common remedy for bloating. The dark, infected blood was removed from a specific vein on the tongue. When they had been poisoned, I always could tell by their ears, which drooped over, and their eyes, which looked down. If they drank impure water, they would shake and became feverish with bloodshot eyes. For this ailment, horses were given a salammoniac from India, ground up and placed in their mouths. When the animals had high fevers, they were raced to sweat out the impurities. Some of these ailing beasts got a kind of cold and flu known as *chamba*, which brought them sore throats and coughing.

On the road I was also in charge of butter for the butter lamps when we arrived at a town, and in charge of *sungdu*.

This is a strip of cloth about two inches wide, long enough to go over the head and hang down over the chest. It has a blessed knot in the center. They were either white, green, yellow, or red, depending on the wearer's social and religious rank. Sometimes a little *mendup*, or elixir-pill, which the monks and lamas at Sakya had blessed, was attached to this in front. I wrapped each of these pills in an appropriately colored paper triangle which, when finished, looked almost like a little flower. Mendup also were worn in a charm box or in a little leather bag around the neck. The latter was folded into a flat oblong shape.

Outside Rashi Monastery, forty monks and the Drawu-pon's uncle Pemadondup came to greet us and escort us to Jyekundo. With him were some one hundred monks and laymen from the Jyeku area, together with many of our friends and relatives from Thalung. It was like a homecoming. The Drawu-pon himself met us outside Jyekundo. When we arrived there, hundreds of people were waiting to greet us. Many prayer flags flew on the nearby mountain and from the houses.

The Chinese were aware of our visit. They sensed it was important and went along with the ceremonies. From my tent outside town I could see the Chinese compound. As a young girl I had picnicked in these open fields. Now they had been given over to growing crops. The compound had a jail and a factory where Chinese foods were processed.

We crossed the Dza River and went on to Jyeku Monastery. As we left, a large group of Chinese circled us, staring and doubtless curious about the visitors they had heard so much about. Five hundred Sakya monks lived here, and our arrival was a big moment for them. There was dancing and singing and a general air of festivity. All of the temples in the monastery were open and the butter lamps blazed with a message of welcome.

However, news supplied by the Chinese the next evening briefly tempered the gaiety of our arrival. According to news received from Peking, Premier Joseph Stalin of Russian had died. It was March 5, 1953. Chinese officials lowered the Chinese flag. Photos of Stalin and Mao Tse-tung were taken down as Communist party loyalists went into mourning. Despite Stalin's demise, Drawu-pon was permitted to fly flags in honor of our arrival. Some Tibetan officials, however, were given black armbands to wear. Obviously, most of the Tibetans found it difficult to grieve.

Nevertheless long-time residents said the ceremonies and celebration marking our arrival were the greatest in their memory. The monks carried banners, drums, and cymbals of gold and silver in procession. There was a cermony in the temple, which the public attended. When my husband was presented with gifts, all of the monks rose, followed by the entire assembly.

Jyeku Monastery was old and very strict. It was considered the "mother" monastery of all of Gaba province. High standards were practiced in all phases of religious life. Monastic police enforced strict rules. Outside the monastery monks could not speak to each other, for example, unless their conversation concerned monastery business. This rule was designed to cut down on socializing.

The palace in which we were to reside was one of three owned by Drawu-pon. It was a big, old-fashioned red structure that formerly had been a lama's residence. So strict was the monastery that Wangmo, my mother, and the other women had to sleep outside the monastery—in the town.

There wasn't much for me to do here except say my daily prayers and await the birth of my child. The food was excellent, however, and I sampled some Chinese vegetables I never had seen.

About a week after our arrival, Chinese officials invited the Sakya party, including the horsekeepers and servants, to dinner. It was an afternoon affair as Khampas eat their heavy meal then, as opposed to the custom in Lhasa, where the main meal is eaten in the evening. We brought woven material, a leopard skin, and white scarfs to our hosts.

There were about fifty guests, mostly men. There was

much fresh and dried fruit—oranges, golden raisins, apricots, figs, and pears, which were a novelty to us. An airplane frequently brought fresh produce from China, we were told. There was an airfield now at Pathang, near Jyekundo. We also had to toast Mao in a manner so reverent it was just like prayer.

After dinner we were invited to watch a basketball game outdoors, which the Chinese obviously regarded as a special treat. But it was a windy, dusty day, and I was very tired in my big headdress. Finally my husband begged off, saying that we must go home and that we would see more next time. Although the Chinese were polite, it was clear they didn't want to get too friendly. Our hosts said they were glad we had come, and that if we needed any help during the visit to inform them.

9

Home to Thalung

The next day several Chinese arrived with gifts of flour, rice, fruit, noodles, and other foods. These gifts invariably were accompanied by propaganda in the form of magazines, small booklets, and pins. The pins had many different designs, but always bore a likeness of Mao. The Chinese also sent a message saying that they had a film to show our party and, if we agreed, they would bring it to the monastery for all to see.

Three days later they arrived with the movie. It was shown on a screen erected in the monastery courtyard. The film had a Communist line that the monks found distasteful and distracting from their religious mission. Sensing the possibility of trouble, we stayed inside the palace and watched from a window. The Chinese had strung up several battery-powered light bulbs. Near the end of the film, some young monks hurled rocks and broke the bulbs. Since some monks were outside, some inside, and still others on the roof, it was impossible to tell who had thrown the stones.

Never again did the Chinese offer to share their films. All of us felt extremely uneasy about the incident, fearing a real clash sometime in the future. The Chinese were becoming more powerful and ruthless, taking prisoners on trumped-up charges. My countrymen knew their goals, but were helpless. Certainly they were not fooled.

Before the Chinese Communists had come to power, the Nationalist government had been busy building roads from Sining to Jyekundo, but many of them were badly in need of repair. Now the Communists began in earnest to repair these roads and to build bridges. There was much secrecy and pretense. The party line said that "now all of the people will enjoy the material goods and food that can easily be brought from China."

Having settled properly at Jyeku Monastery, we began visiting other monasteries in the area. At one of these I saw a young lama named Yudrog Tülku. He belonged to the class of married lamas who continued their lineage through their sons. When I was about eleven or twelve, Great-Uncle Nawang wanted to arrange a marriage between this youth, who was two or three years my elder, and me. The boy's family was wealthy and prominent. The father was head of a monastery and had several estates between Jyekundo and Thalung. A match with him would afford me time and opportunity to keep up my religious practices, my great-uncle thought. But my mother and others in the family, including Uncle Tülku-la, would not consent, for it would have meant my moving away from my family. I felt shy when this lama came bringing gifts to my husband and me—so shy in fact that I continued to avoid another direct meeting with him.

Next we paid a call at Palchung Monastery, belonging to the Nyingma school. This monastery was well off the beaten path, in a cavelike setting high on a steep mountain. I found the lamas here interesting, for they were schooled in necromancy—the cooperation of the spirits of the dead for the purposes of magically revealing the future or influencing the course of events—and emphasized meditation and yoga. My husband greatly enjoyed these "magic" men.

These fierce-looking lamas wore long hair (which they seldom combed) tied around their heads with a cloth that resembled a turban, earrings from conch shell, and huge prayer beads. They also wore black and red hats with black tassels covering their foreheads. They used small trumpets made of human bones. Seeing these men and their ceremonies was a new experience for me. About fifty of them were married; their wives lived in a town near the monastery. I stayed there, too, although Dagchen Rinpoche remained at the monastery.

We crossed a very swift and deep section of the Dri River in yakskin boats. I kept thinking, "this water is from Thalung." It made me feel closer to home. During a stop at Sepa Monastery, the head lama, one of Uncle Tülku-la's classmates and good friends, presented several plates of red dates to me. My father used to send me red dates when I was a little girl. It was such a treat that I overindulged. I became ill, and a lama doctor was summoned and medicine administered. That night the monks prayed especially for my recovery. I was fearful I would lose my baby. This time I couldn't cry, I thought, because I had brought on my own misfortune. But I soon snapped back to good health.

Meanwhile my husband was keeping a diary of his daily activities. Each day he was busy with ceremonies, many of which I did not attend.

During some two weeks at Shewoo-Dogon Monastery, the site of a famous statue of Wangdu Nyingpo, a spiritually powerful Sakya lama who lived some two hundred years ago, I turned to some constructive work. I wanted to have a sense of accomplishment here. We had a tailor from Sakya in the party, so I thought it appropriate to make a new set of garments for Wangdu's statue. I had bought some Indian silk brocade in Lhasa that was ideal for the job. So we went to work making a jackletlike garment, hat, and apron with multicolored silk tassels. The apron is part of the traditional garb of religious statues.

One day when I was busy working on the garments, a monk interrupted to announce that a lama had arrived and wished to see me. Mildly annoyed, I told the monk to ask him to come back later. But the visitor pressed his case, and the monk returned with the same request. I left reluctantly, grumbling about how busy I was. As I passed through the center of the main temple, I stepped in view of hundreds of monks in prayer. Walking to my quarters, I came to a dark hallway outside our room, where I saw the dim outline of a man seated on a chair. He was heavily attired and carried a traveler's charm box on his back. His face was dark and his skin chapped and weatherbeaten. When the man stood up, I thought I'd seen him somewhere before. As I approached, he took a white scarf from his servant. The moment he unrolled it, I knew it was my Uncle Tülku-la!

We embraced and touched heads affectionately.

"Why didn't you send a message?" I asked.

"If I had sent a message, you wouldn't have slept," he replied. And he was right.

Uncle Tülku-la's skin was rough from trekking in the sun, snow, wind, and cold of the northern wasteland, the Changthang. After he had paid his respects to my husband, we began to catch up on the events of our four-year separation. I simply forgot about sewing that day.

The abbot and other officials, hearing of their distinguished visitor, quickly offered to make him comfortable. He, my mother, and I chuckled, for only hours earlier he had been told that the monastery was full. "The Sakya family is here," they told him. They also hadn't recognized Uncle Tülku-la. He stayed only two days, then headed for Thalung Monastery, home at last after a year's absence.

When the statue's costume was completed, there was a consecration ceremony conducted by the head lama of the monastery and attended by some sixty monks. We read from a text offering prayers to Wangdu Nyingpo. The Tibetan word for consecration is *rab-nay* (rab-gnas), which means "to give form to or make permanent." During consecration, objects are ritually blessed. Those blessings remain until the end of the eon, immune from the elements of fire, water, earth, and wind. I was happy to have accomplished this important deed perfectly and in accordance with tradition. I was devoutly determined to undertake many more similar projects in the service of the Sakya lineage.

Later that evening, a celebration was held with the townspeople. Wearing their finest garments and jewelry, they gathered outdoors in a garden around a fire. A troupe of boys and girls danced and sang for us—a poignant reminder of my own dancing days in Thalung a few short years ago. The young people sang a specially written song about the rerobing and my role in it. We gave them scarfs and gifts.

After the consecration, we returned to the palace at Jyeku Monastery and found everyone there concerned about the weather. Last year had been very dry, and it looked at though this year would again lack sufficient rain for crops. The townspeople felt Chinese Communist violations of long-held Buddhist practices were angering the mountain deities. Many who blamed the lack of rain on the Communists also found it disgusting, for example, to see the Chinese, who were short of firewood, burning animal bones for fuel, the foul smell displeasing the deities. Two years earlier the Chinese had been blamed when, just before the harvest, a tremendous storm destroyed the crops.

So my husband and a party of Jyeku monks and lamas made three or four trips to nearby mountain areas in order to pray for rain. The lamas made small fires for these ceremonies, using juniper boughs and incense. One day while they were atop a nearby mountain, I went up on the palace roof. I could see showers in the distance. Ironically, it was raining in the mountains, but not on the fields. Dagchen Rinpoche and the monks celebrated: they thought that the showers had come at last—they were drenched and their tents were soaked. On the way down the mountain, they stopped at a spring that bubbled out of the ground to pray to the *lu* or *nāgas*, demigods of the water. The rest of the way they raced their horses just for the joy of it, they were so happy.

While they were celebrating, my son was born, with my mother acting as midwife. When he arrived at about three o'clock in the afternoon of May 19, 1953, he opened his eyes and gave three lusty sneezes. Immediately a message was sent up the mountain to Dagchen Rinpoche. My husband was not only overjoyed that there was a new son in the family, but also thankful that his son—who was small for a boy—was healthy. Our son was garbed in yellow—the traditional color for lamas—and soot from a butter lamp was placed on his nose. To protect him from harm, many charm boxes were placed around his bed. The monks were called to prayers, although the monastery usually was not told of a new infant son until a week after the baby's birth. It is customary to make such an announcement only after the baby is strong enough to be considered out of danger. No one would want to attract harm to someone so young and helpless.

That evening, rain began to fall in Jyekundo, and it continued in abundance throughout the night. It was a wonderful omen. Many said it was because of my husband's presence; a few who knew of the new baby credited the long-awaited rain to him.

The news of his birth was released publically when he was a week old, bringing joy to thousands of Tibetans, especially Sakya followers. Uncle Tülku-la arrived a week after the birth to attend his grand-nephew. Uncle sprinkled holy water on the baby's head, said prayers and generally stayed close by him for about a month.

My husband and Uncle Tülku-la named our boy after the Buddhist deity of wisdom. The name in Sanskrit thus was Manju Vajra. He would use his Sanskrit name, which we modified to Minzu-la, until he had finished his schooling.

At three months of age, Minzu-la was officially launched into the world in two religious ceremonies. At the first, a flagstaff more than three-stories high was raised in the palace courtyard. It was made of logs brought by monks and laymen from the forest areas near Domthog, a five-day walk from Jyekundo. Its top bore a gold and brass ornament. From the pole hung many colored flags inscribed with prayers. One of them declared that the new lama had been born here, on the appropriate date, in the year of the Water Snake.

In the second ceremony, Minzu-la was placed on a high throne, where he remained for nearly two hours. I was close by, very proud and relieved, for he did not cry once, even when the public and monks passed by him to receive his blessing. He received three offerings, symbolizing the body, speech, and mind of the Buddha—a golden image of the Buddha Amitābha, a sacred Buddhist text, and a small chö-ten, which represents the mind of the Buddha. We supplicated Minzu-la to have a long life, to expound our religion, and to have thoughts like those of the Buddhas. Then figures of the eight Buddhist symbols were presented to him.

Our group was getting used to Jyekundo and felt the people there were hospitable to them. I occupied myself by reading and learning the history of the area. We attended an annual summer festival that took place some five miles from Jyeku Monastery in an area of plains. About seven hundred tents were erected and hundreds of people came for a week of camping, religious ceremonies, dancing, and horseracing. I went later in the week on the day of the biggest races. We saw boys as young as nine performing great feats of horsemanship, some on mounts that were difficult to control. The boys had the agility of circus performers, doing headstands and hand-stands on their saddles. The visiting Sakyapas were im-pressed, not having seen such skills previously. It seemed so tricky and risky that sometimes even I was afraid to look.

Soon after, a disturbing element of Chinese commercialism entered our lives. A photographer in Jyekundo began selling photographs of my husband at an exorbitant price. It all started when a monk, a gifted artist, painted a large picture of my husband. It resembled a tanka, and was hung in the monastery's main temple. Some of the artist's friends asked to have small copies, which he made for them. The requests mushroomed, and monks offered to pay for the copies.

This came to the attention of the Chinese. Twice they sent photographers asking to take Dagchen Rinpoche's picture, but he refused. The Chinese also asked for a photo of the family, but we firmly declined. Then, without permission, they came and photographed my husband seated on his high throne in the temple, conducting various ceremonies. The photos were excellent. The Chinese justified their high price saying that my husband was a "very good lama." Actually they were attempting to get him in their camp and use him for propaganda purposes.

People stood in line to buy copies at government shops in Jyekundo. An estimated several thousand copies were sold, no doubt swelling the Chinese government coffers. At first people came to Dagchen Rinpoche to have him put his official seal or fingerprint on the photos. This soon became too much and my husband advised the public not to buy any more of the pictures and that he would put his seal on a piece of paper for them instead. The Chinese continued to sell the photos in towns throughout the Jyekundo area.

Our next stop was Singdze Palace, one of the homes of the Drawu-pon, where, in contrast to the formal life of the monastery, I relaxed with picnicking and other outdoor activities, even venturing out into the fields to pick peas and wildflowers. Near Singdze was the largest pile of *mani* stones in eastern Tibet, the great "mountain of white rock" that was a very holy place for pilgrims. In particular, pilgrims whose families were struck by sickness or death came here. The mani wall was about a city-block wide, three stories high, and at least a mile long, and ran parallel to the Dza River.

Mani stones are carved with religious inscriptions and symbols, painted, and sold. Mani stone carving was the main occupation of Singdze families. They used oxen to haul rocks from a nearby mountain.

Stones were added to the top of the wall by people standing on ladders, all volunteers, who chanted religious songs as they worked. Near the wall was a shrine that had two enormous prayer wheels, each weighing about two tons. It required two or three persons, pulling on huge metal rings, to make them turn. The interior of each wheel had more than a hundred-million prayers written on paper.

Singdze brought back memories. When I was a girl, I had

spent a month making a thousand koras around the mani wall. In Singdze an old beggar woman had sat outside our guest house telling stories to my playmates and me. She was the town fortuneteller, who practiced her art by twirling a colorful boot belt in her hands, knotting it in a particular way, and then interpreting the patterns thus formed. We had given food to her. She was gone now.

Here we had played for hours with a ball-like toy we called a *teplay*, trying to keep it off the ground as we passed it to each other. It was made of sheepskin, sometimes with a stone or coin sewn inside it for weight, with rooster feathers added in the manner of a shuttlecock. We batted the teplay through the air using our hands and feet.

My husband was getting anxious to see my family home in Thalung. Aunt Chacha and Uncle Kuyak had gone to prepare Uncle Tülku-la's labrang for our arrival, as our house was far too small for the entire party. It was only a day's ride from Jyeku Monastery to Thalung, but we took three days, stopping at monasteries and towns, including the Ranyak and Bamchu monasteries, where we had many monks and lay people come out to accompany our party to Thalung. On the way between Zindah and Thalung we passed many familiar little villages. As their houses came into view, I recalled many of their owners. My mother, Aunt Chacha, and Uncle Kuyak owned some of the fields we passed. People lining the road to greet us chanted a songlike prayer about my husband's arrival and the wonders of the Thalung countryside. Occasionally he would stop to bless and accept some warm tea from townspeople who had waited hours to see him.

Minzu-la made his entrance to Thalung in a silk-covered sedan chair carried by a monk on horseback. Minzu-la enjoyed peering out, and the monks liked to take turns carrying him. I was dressed up for my homecoming in my big headdress. I recognized many of the faces greeting me and smiled.

About a mile from Thalung, my good friend Lhayag, with Khando's sister and several other girl friends, rode to meet our party. All of them were dressed up—and grown up too—

I thought. By glancing at their hairdos I could tell who was married.

We stopped and I touched heads with my friends, and my husband blessed them. I was deeply touched by the songs they sang in my honor. In the songs they used my childhood name of Sonam Tshe Dzom, preceded by the title of Gya-yum, conveying that I was now the mother of a prince. Then they rode alongside. I would have preferred to be more informal, but I had to maintain my dignity as the wife of a high lama from Sakya. With envy I looked at their familiar garb, wishing I could wear Khampa-style clothing again. It was a sunny day, without a whisper of wind—an ideal setting to end a nearly five-year absence from home.

We were led to Thalung Monastery by monks who danced and paraded in ceremonial costumes and masks of animals such as lion and deer. How beautiful the freshly painted monastery looked. Many structures had been built inside the monastery since I left. Familiar faces were everywhere. There were some monks with whom I had played as a girl and two who had been my schoolmates. One of these carried a censer and another blew the trumpet. Others carried a brightly colored silk banner inscribed with a greeting to us. There was a two-hour ceremony in the main temple where a huge drum thundered continuously, frightening Minzu-la.

Across the courtyard and up the stairs of the labrang I hurried. Wangmo accompanied me as I sped to Great-Uncle Nawang's room on the third floor. Knowing how much I missed my dear great-uncle, Uncle Tülku-la had ordered the removal of the old lama's bed. In its place were a desk and books. There was nothing to remind me of him, but every-where I felt his presence. Sadly, I had to admit how much in my life had changed. I went to the room where Great-Uncle Nawang had prayed, and there, too, nothing was the same. I wept. Uncle Tülku-la and my husband comforted me with the reminder that I was now home with many of my loved ones.

That evening after dinner Lhayag came, bringing her three-year-old son, and carrying a basket of dried fruits, cake, and dried hard cheese. She had remembered how much I liked the cheese—a Khampa specialty that tasted slightly sweet.

Everyone, it seemed, wanted to see Minzu-la, but there were just too many people. Uncle Tülku-la had arranged for a small tent to be erected on the roof of the labrang for his grandnephew—along with toys. This was the same roof where we had spotted the mule's hoofprint when I was a girl.

On my fifth day in Thalung, I went home—really home, to where I was born. It was late forenoon, all the animals were out, and I enjoyed the luxury of a quiet return to my youth. The crops were in and the fieldhands now were busy with the harvest and the threshing. There was Purah, the only dog left I knew. He was very old, almost tottering, and had no teeth. When I petted him, he sniffed me and nuzzled me, jumping up on my silk dress and nearly catching my necklace.

Several days later, some thirty members of the Sakya party assembled for a tour of my home. It was a happy moment as I gathered the new friends in my life to give them something of my past. There were my collections of miniature handmade dolls and animals, Chinese cups and a teapot, a toy stove, little dishes and spoons, and other pieces of silver that had accumulated throughout my childhood. I sat by the cookstove and told how I used to poke in the ashes beneath it. Everyone laughed as they learned of my childhood adventures.

My husband was particularly attentive and interested, opening doors and looking at everything. He even asked to see the areas not ordinarily on view, including a dark room on the second floor where five stuffed yakskins were stored. The visitors were fascinated, for this custom was unique to Kham. These stuffed skins, call *kodros*, were without heads. The only opening was at the neck, which was closed by a heavy flat stone over which was placed as inverted basket.

It was customary to use the skins of favorite yaks. The kodros held a reserve supply of wheat and barley, always of top quality. In years of lean harvest, the grain was there to be used. Every two or three years, the grain was replaced. When a lama came, we would ask him to bless the kodros to bring prosperity.

At New Year's these kodros were decorated with brightly colored cloth printed with Buddhist good-luck phrases. Prayer flags also were tied around them and they were placed in an upright position.

As a girl, I never entered this room alone as I was fearful. To me, these stuffed yak were like images of demons. When I was little, my mother threatened to put me in the kodro room when I was naughty. My husband was especially amused by this.

Sometimes the kodros were victims of mice—of which we had plenty—but we didn't bother these creatures.

On the central kitchen post still hung the knucklebones I had used in so many games. My visitors saw our shrine room, too, and stayed both for lunch and dinner.

There was a sad aspect of our tour—another reminder of change. My home always had been immaculate, inside and out. It was the largest in the Thalung area and everything always had been bright and fresh. Now there was something lacking—a touch. My mother had been away much of the time and other relatives often had been in charge. Perhaps they had done their best, but my home was not up to its previous standards. The old atmosphere was gone—the family customs, the servants, and animals—all were a bit different. I felt deeply disappointed, especially since I had looked forward for so long to giving my husband an intimate glimpse of my youth. It was another reminder of the impermanence of life. With the only child in the family gone, there was less incentive to keep up the family property for the future. My family said I could take anything I wanted from our home. I wanted nothing. But my husband wanted my collection of miniatures.

10

Nomads and Monasteries

After spending two memorable months in Thalung, some of us were having a hard time saying goodbye. One of them was Wangmo, who had made a number of friends, whom she had taught western Tibetan songs and dances. While my husband had been visiting monasteries in the Thalung area, I had renewed acquaintances with all of my friends.

Uncle Tülku-la had agreed to serve as guardian lama or mentor for Minzu-la for a year while we were in the Derge area. We now began to make our way to Lhagyal Monastery, where we planned to stay about a year. Uncle, my mother, and Ani Chimi joined us at Kazang Monastery.

While at Kazang, I purchased eight prized pieces of coral from a nobleman. It seemed a once-in-a-lifetime chance, as the coral was deep red in color and of excellent quality. I was thinking of the future and how, as Sakya Dagmo, I would make a life-sized statue of the deity, Tārā, before my death. This coral would be perfect as an ornament for my Tārā, and would make good necklaces for me until the Tārā was built. The coral, said to be the largest and best in all of Tibet, formerly belonged to a wealthy Lhasa woman who was believed to have powers of witchcraft. Some people would not buy from her, but those who did were observant of her mood. If it was good, the purchase would bring the buyer good luck, it was believed.

As a down payment, the owner, a Khampa trader, asked us to have a set of the one hundred and eight volumes of the *Kanjur* made for him at the main Derge Monastery, site of the best publishing house in Tibet. "Kanjur" means "that which has become the word" (of the Buddha); it contains all of the Buddha's precepts and instructions.

Soon after the New Year of 1954, we moved on to Khana Monastery, where my husband had the honor of choosing a new name for the monastery. The monks here didn't like the name, even though it had been chosen by the monastery's founder. People often pronounced "Khana" quickly, making it sound like the word *"khanag,"* which literally translated means "black mouth," a word associated with bad omens. My husband assembled many names, then selected the new name. It was Samdub. *Sam* means "thought" or "desire." *Dub* means "to be made ready or to be finished, fulfilled, accomplished." The name was inscribed on a document to which my husband affixed the official Sakya seal. It was a high honor for a Sakya lama to name a Gelugpa monastery.

The monks were delighted and wanted us to stay longer, but since the snow was not too deep, we felt we must continue while we were still able to travel easily.

Our journey took us into a windy, cold, treeless, and flat country inhabited by nomads. There were many deer, wild yaks, and wild mules. Nomads especially hunted the wild yaks in particular, which had less fat and yielded tender meat. Some of these wild yaks, known as *dong,* were twice as large as ordinary yaks; the saying was that they were so powerful, one could kill a human with the lash of its tongue.

To get one of these beasts, the nomads would look for an area of tall grass that in winter hid a dry and frozen swamplike hole. It would often take several hunters to bring down the wild yak. The hunters would fire their rifles in the open, and then run back to the hole. A wounded animal could be very dangerous.

Being very thick and tough, wild yakskin was used for the heaviest boots. The hair was used for tent ropes. The horns of the wild yak were used to carry liquids. The top end of the horn was polished and decorated with silver for use as a snuff bottle. The heart was made into a medicine thought to be good for heart trouble. Often the heart was eaten, with the belief that it would make one brave.

Sometimes the nomads would let the domestic yaks breed with the wild ones. A calf from such a combination grew into a strong animal something like a musk ox.

The tall grasses in this area were made into sun hats, shoes for indoor wear, and rope. I had fun weaving a miniature tent with these grasses. The nomads here lived in houses built on a foundation of grass matting and yak dung, with a tent on the top. It was very cold and snowed often. We had to buy yak dung for fuel as we moved along.

Minzu-la was growing into a seasoned traveler. He was never afraid and appeared to enjoy every day. He was crawling and had four teeth. He no longer was content to ride in a box on the back of a monk or servant. Now he sat in front of me on my horse or with others who took turns to spell me. I had made him heavy winter clothing. A fox-fur hood was wrapped closely around his face. Some people wondered why we traveled with such a small boy. But he was a good lad and a hardy one. We had no fears.

Seshu Monastery was in the heart of this nomadic country. It was famous for mushrooms, a special funeral service, and—most important—monastic debating.

The wild mushrooms were dried and kept for several years. Much of the harvest was sent to China; oddly, the nomads here seldom ate them. I thought them very good, and we had thick mushroom soup with meat nearly every day here. The Seshu monks noticed how fond we were of mushrooms, and the next year they sent us a supply of fresh ones.

The unusual funeral services at Seshu were introduced by

the sixth Panchen Lama when he visited here in the 1930s. The deceased was brought by relatives to an area outside the monastery grounds, usually three days after death. When the body arrived, a gong was sounded and hundreds of monks would come from the monastery with bells and dorjes for the service. They sat in a circle around the corpse, which was wrapped in a blanket. Monks and lamas tossed rice and placed blessed sand on the head of the corpse. The purpose of the ceremony was to guide the deceased's spirit to rebirth in a higher realm. The body then was buried, burned, or given to the vultures, according to astrology or the deceased's wishes. This funeral service was available free to all, no matter how rich or poor. The family of the deceased would simply offer a token payment, such as a white scarf. To my knowledge no such democratic custom was in practice anywhere else in Kham.

In my homeland, the tradition of formal, scholarly debate was widely practiced and led to much intermonastery rivalry. Each day in mid-afternoon, Seshu's monks poured into the courtyard to begin their practice sessions. Many debates were held simultaneously, and small groups of spectators gathered around to watch avidly.

As a girl I had seen monks debating for fun at picnics, but never had I seen such a formal presentation. In the center seated in the lotus position was a learned, often older, monk, holding his prayer beads, whose duty it was to respond to the challenger, usually a younger monk. The challenger's outer robe was slipped down and tied at the waist, revealing bare arms. As he posed his question, the challenger moved around the seated monk. At each point, he stomped heavily on one foot and clapped his hands, his prayer beads swinging from his arm. The challenger spoke loudly and fast. Perspiration ran down his face as his session, sometimes lasting twenty minutes, continued. The contestants shouted in angry tones, but always the formality was maintained. The seated monk almost always won by answering the question correctly. If he did not, the challenger would toss his prayer beads around the defender's neck proudly proclaiming, *"Khorsum!"*—"You're overruled!" We were particularly amused at the little boy monks who attempted to debate in their own way. Their challenges might consist of making a third- or fourth-grade-level sentence or reciting a simple story of the Buddha.

We left Seshu with a feeling of good will, continuing our trip into nomad country. At one Nyingma monastery where we were housed overnight, the monks insisted upon giving us a set of huge rare deer antlers. The monks said the antlers were not a religious item and there was no reason to keep them, although they had possessed them for years. My husband agreed to accept the gift and take them to the museum at Sakya. Thus our traveling party took on a slightly humorous look. One monk on horseback carried the precious cargo. The monk always had to have help in loading and unloading the antlers.

The nomads in this area called Dzachuka were hardy and healthy-looking. We were several weeks in this country, during which we went without vegetables, eating only meat, cheese, yogurt, and milk, and sometimes mushroom soup. Now and then we had rice and noodles. These generous and deeply religious nomads were eager to help us set up camp and gave us yaks, horses, and food.

At Dzogchen, the largest Nyingma monastery in the Dzachuka area, our horsekeepers ran into trouble. Upon arrival at the monastery they had not taken down their hair in the traditional gesture of respect. The Dzogchen monks, some of whom were teenagers, scolded the horsekeepers for this impoliteness.

After the traditional ceremony that accompanied our arrival, about twenty of the younger monks began throwing rocks at the horsekeepers' tent in our camp about a half mile away. Dagchen Rinpoche was with Dzogchen Rinpoche, the head lama, when the trouble began, and was unaware of the incident. I became afraid, not knowing what had caused this angry display. Some older monks, who had come to my tent bringing tea and cookies, were extremely embarrassed. They

saw the youngsters and reprimanded them, taking them back
to the monastery.

I summoned Phuba Tsering who was angry about the
incident. Apparently he had argued earlier with the monks at
Dzogchen but had not informed us. He had been to hundreds
of monasteries but had never been treated like this, he complained.

We left three days later when Chagotobdan, a man known
throughout Tibet, joined our party. He was the governor of
Derge Yilhung district, the area we were entering and was
one of those who had invited my husband to Kham. He had
fought the Communist Chinese in Kham in 1949 and lost,
been imprisoned, and later released.

Chagotobdan arrived with a large group of men from Derge
to escort us to Lhagyal Monastery. After crossing Dzogchen
Pass, an area of many robbers and outlaws, we entered
Chagotobdan's home territory. Later about one hundred Lhagyal monks joined us, and soon after our party swelled to
about four hundred, as Derge representatives and citizens
joined us. So as to arrive on an auspicious day at Lhagyal, we
stopped to tent for a day and two nights in this beautiful
country.

A two-story residence at Lhagyal was to be our general
headquarters for a year, although we would be doing much
traveling in the area. After the usual welcoming ceremony,
Chagotobdan and his family came to visit us. I was preparing
to exchange gifts with them, when suddenly I discovered that
the keys to our boxes of gold, silver, jewelry, and other
valuables were missing. Usually I kept strict charge of these
keys, but this time I had asked Aunt Chacha to be their
custodian. I had been wearing my heavy headdress and necklace for our arrival at Lhagyal, and with the keys I would
simply have been too weighted down. She apparently had lost
the keys in the snow on the approach to Lhagyal. Always
superstitious, she gravely forecast that this was a bad omen
indeed. The boxes would have to be broken open so that we
could present our gifts. Aunt Chacha and many nomads

searched for the keys to no avail. A reward was offered for their return by the monastery police.

Among the visitors at Lhagyal was Lama Asang, who was known for his skill in prophecy. He was a *duthop*, meaning one who has been enlightened, who has reached perfection— a saint. As a duthop, he was free to act according to his own wishes, no longer living a regimented monastery life. There are very few recognized duthops in Tibet. Thus Lama Asang was very popular with the nomads. He let them feed him, but he never accepted offerings of money. Lama Asang looked like a beggar or some kind of clown. His hair was long and uncombed, and he wore an old monk's robe with pieces of cloth sewn or simply knotted on it. He was considered a good lama but somewhat odd. He constantly chanted "Oṃ Maṇi Padme Hūṃ" in a loud voice, imploring others to do likewise. Minzu-la was fascinated by him.

One morning Lama Asang came to visit, bringing me a small carved wooden bowl with a cover and lining of silver. Inside was tsampa mixed with butter. It didn't look at all appetizing, and I feared he would ask me to eat it. Quickly restoring the cover, I put it aside.

"You must keep this bowl with you," he implored. I promised to do so. Having just arrived here, I was anxious not to annoy anyone.

When I offered him some fancy Chinese candy, he announced indignantly, "Oh, that's just like soap. I don't want any." But he took several cookies.

He was restless and said he had no time to sit. "But maybe I'll come back again later," he said.

Noticing Aunt Chacha's sadness, he asked, "What's happened to you?" And she unfolded the story of the lost keys.

"Please tell me where they are," she begged.

Lama Asang's eyes were turned skyward. "You will find the keys four days from now to the northwest," he began, and then described an area in Lhagyal district. He then departed. We then disposed of his gift of tsampa, but I kept the bowl as an item of faith.

Four days later, a nomad found the keys in the described place. The chain was broken and the keys scattered. Aunt Chacha, quite expectedly, was very impressed with Lama Asang.

Our home, adjacent to the temple where my husband spent much of his days, was very comfortable. Many visitors came from throughout the area to see him. Nearby was a large pond where many frogs croaked endlessly each evening. During my first few weeks at Lhagyal, I spent much of my time doing chatsas and koras around the temple.

So many monasteries wanted to see my husband, it had become clear that we would have to stay in Kham much longer than two years. Many of the monasteries were far apart, and their requests for my husband's services were continually increasing.

After three months had passed and we felt better acquainted with the Lhagyal area, we made plans to travel to Dzongsar Monastery for a year's stay. Dzongsar, which had about five hundred monks, was an important seat of learning in eastern Tibet. A distinguished and very strict monks' college was located there. This was where Uncle Tülku-la had spent seven years studying. It was the finest religious training center in the Sakya school. Dzongsar also was the residence of Dzongsar Khyentse Rinpoche, Uncle Tülku-la's lama and teacher, who was known throughout Tibet. One of the main purposes of our trip to Kham was to receive teachings from him. My husband and all of the members of our family would receive the Lam-Dray and the Drupthap Kundu, the combined teachings of the Sakya school. These rites would take many months.

On the way to Dzongsar, we made a detour to the Dzing Namgyalgon to see a historical statue of Mahākāla, the wrathful aspect of Chenrezi and a special Sakya protector. Built in the twelfth century, this famous figure contained inside a walking staff, was said to belong to the Lord Buddha. The staff was the type used by all mendicant monks. On its top, the staff had a replica of a chöten from which hung three dangling rings. The rings signaled that a monk was present and asking for food. The tinkling sounds of this so-called alarm staff also possibly told harmful dogs and other animals that the monk did not wish to be disturbed. This staff had been given by an Indian king to a Chinese emperor. My husband's ancestors, the Sakya Pandita and his nephew, Chogyal Phagspa, had been given the staff by the Mongol emperor, Kublai Khan. On the way home from China to Sakya, the two had had a vision at this holy place and built the Namgyalgon Monastery.

After the temple was finished, Sakya Pandita requested a Nyingma lama to remove any evil influences and obstacles to Buddhist teaching there. As the lama was performing the ceremony, the temple turned inside out—signifying that the harmful elements had been dispelled. The lama then said, "Now do the consecration," an act believed to ensure that the temple would be forever sacred and not be destroyed by the elements. When Sakya Pandita performed the dedication, the temple then returned to its normal position, an indication of Sakya Pandita's spiritual powers.

The first time I took an offering to the statue, I felt the stories were true and that its protective power was authentic. I was touched by the awesomeness of the statue's face. During the week-long stay, I performed daily prostrations and hoped to gain much virtue. Dagchen Rinpoche and monks attended in ceremonies to remove obstacles and ensure success of the teachings he was to receive at Dzongsar.

One day was devoted to a tour of Mahākāla's holy lake, an inviting jewel reached by a walk past a canyon where jagged rocks looked almost manmade. We believed some of Padma-sambhava's hidden treasures rested in the lake, which was on a fifteen-thousand-foot-high plateau. Few visitors went here because people of the Dzingkhog area chose not to publicize the holy lake. They wanted it to remain clean and pure. The lamas performed an offering to the nagas that we believed dwelled in these waters. I helped burn incense and offer prayer flags to the local deities. Minzu-la sat speechless, staring intently at his elders.

Two miles before we arrived at the Dzongsar Monastery, Dzongsar Khyentse Rinpoche, Dilgo Khyentse Rinpoche, and hundreds of other lamas, monks, and residents greeted us on horseback. Their mounts were decorated in the finest traditional outfits, according to their rank. Our party grouped together in an open valley as the welcoming party circled us, riding counterclockwise.

This was a breathtaking scene on a beautifully sunny spring morning. I knew I would never forget this ceremony. As they approached, the sun reflected on the golden summer hats of the ranking monks and lamas who were carrying banners emblazoned with color. The two groups dismounted and exchanged scarfs.

When we actually arrived at the monastery, another three hundred monks greeted us. We settled in the eighty-room, four-story labrang, known as the Red Labrang. It was an impressive place for the thirty of us. The labrang was a square structure with a huge open courtyard. It had been a year in renovation in preparation for our arrival and was beautifully furnished with elegant china, bedding, and Oriental rugs.

Dzongsar Monastery was in a warm area where wheat, barley, and vegetables were grown. Tigers and leopards lived in the woods. It was thought to be an area where the *migös* roamed. These large, hairy demons in human form, possessing great strength, are similar to what in Nepal is known as the *yeti*, the mountain demon or abominable snowman. Domestic animals were not put out at night for fear that they might become victims of migös. We believed that a migö could lift an animal and place it atop a tree. We never saw one, but often saw what we thought were the results of their destruction.

Even though I thought I could hear the migös from our home at Dzongsar, I felt blessed and protected in the environs of Dzongsar Khyentse Rinpoche. All of my life I had heard of the virtues of this man whom Tibetans regard as a reincarnation of the Bodhisattva of Wisdom. He was the most learned Sakya lama in Tibet, and also was highly regarded among the three other major schools of Buddhism. He was the most realized teacher with whom I ever had been closely associated, and I was especially impressed with his ability. I felt his spiritual teaching and blessings were very effective.

He was an imposing figure, tall and white-haired. Minzu-la listened carefully to the words of this man and called him the "white father." Minzu-la was a favorite with Dzongsar Khyentse Rinpoche, who took the boy into the religious ceremonies in the temple at least once a day. He was determined to do something special for Minzu-la, who by now could hum and mimic his elders in prayers, picking up a bell and ringing it in his own childlike way. It was up to this lama to determine whose reincarnation Minzu-la would be. To make this determination, he went into a week-long retreat.

For a month Dzongsar Khyentse Rinpoche planned Minzu-la's first birthday celebration. The birthday arrived and we rose at three A.M. Dzongsar Khyentse Rinpoche joined us soon after the initial event, a ceremony similar to the Western baptism.

The rites involved clipping a small piece of Minzu-la's hair and offering it to the Buddha. This meant Minzu-la was following in the footsteps of the Buddha, who had his hair clipped at the age of nineteen. This was one of the first steps towards enlightenment. This ceremony also was to ensure long life. Minzu-la's hair had not been cut before this time.

The highlight of this day came in the afternoon in the courtyard of the monks' college. Minzu-la behaved admirably throughout the rites. An impressive list of gifts from Dzongsar Khyentse Rinpoche was read by a secretary. The roster included gold, silver, tea, horses, mules, religious objects, and an outfit belonging to Rinpoche's first incarnation, Jamyang Khyentse Wangpo. Among the most important of the presents, however, was a set of thirteen volumes of religious books—the collected writings and biography of Khyentse Wangpo, a nineteenth-century geographer, doctor, mathematician, and theologian. Dzongsar Khyentse Rinpoche also gave Minzu-la important religious objects that he had personally used.

Then the assemblage of several hundred persons fell quiet. A secretary-monk stepped forward and read from a sealed document, recognizing Minzu-la as the reincarnation of his paternal grandfather, the late Trichen. My husband and I had been told of this earlier in the morning. We were very proud and pleased, for the Trichen had been a popular, learned, and commendable leader of the Sakya school.

Later, for two weeks I attended instruction on the basic teachings of the Sakya school, beginning with a lecture by Dzongsar Khyentse Rinpoche. Then men and women broke into separate groups of about ten or twelve. We practiced physical exercises, performed yoga, and did breathing exercises. Although we women wore only one pantlike garment, extending from the waist to the knee, we never became cold with so many of us in the small room, all exercising.

Our teacher was a nun who was very serious and skilled in these techniques. It was an entirely new experience for me. The goal of the program, based on ancient Buddhist teachings, was to cleanse the circulatory system and to move and breathe properly, which balance functions of the body and mind.

It seemed that the teacher was always watching me from the corner of her eye. I wasn't nervous, but I wasn't taking the mental discipline associated with the exercise too seriously. I struggled to keep from giggling. We were grunting and making other funny noises as we stretched and bended. Tibetan women traditionally didn't do this exercise in a group. I tried to remind myself that this was dharma practice, but the scene was too humorous. My problem was compounded because the Khyentse Sangyum Kusho, the wife of Dzongsar Khyentse Rinpoche, also was a giggler. Together we were bad examples. Later I was to regret that I didn't take full advantage of this unique opportunity.

In the early fall of 1954, an important telegram arrived

from Lhasa via Derge Monastery. The Dalai Lama requested my husband to join a group of government officials and religious leaders in a trip to China. Each of the four major Buddhist schools in Tibet were to be represented. The agenda included talks with Mao Tse-tung. His Holiness was disappointed with the Communists' complete disregard of the interests and welfare of the Tibetan people. His Holiness hoped to persuade the Chinese leaders to carry out the promises they had made in the seventeen-point agreement of May 23, 1951, which, in fact, had been forced upon the Tibetan government. One article of that agreement, nevertheless, provided for the protection of established religious customs and institutions.

The new head of the Sakya school, Drolma Rinpoche, obviously was too young for such a trip, so my husband was selected. At first Dagchen Rinpoche wanted to decline the invitation, for it came in the middle of the Lam-Dray empowerment. Three hundred lamas and monks from throughout eastern Tibet had come here at great sacrifice. These included Dilgo Khyentse Rinpoche, Trungpa Rinpoche, Sogyal Rinpoche, Tathang Rinpoche and Tülku Kunzang—highly accomplished lamas from several of Tibet's major religious schools of Buddhism. They received the same teachings as I did. This was a major step in their careers to carry on their teaching lineage in mahāyāna Buddhism. It was awkward and inconvenient to interrupt the rites, as they could not be resumed easily at a later date.

I had feelings of uneasiness and fear about such a trip.

"Will they try to trick us again?" I thought. "Will they try to buy us, taking away our remaining freedoms?"

I envisioned them swaying Tibetans by catering to them and presenting their best face. But Dzongsar Khyentse Rinpoche convinced my husband that he shouldn't refuse the Dalai Lama, and so Dagchen Rinpoche decided to go. Some of the nobles would be bringing their wives. Did I want to go? Only a very few servants could be taken. I didn't see how

I could manage with a small child. My goal always had been to visit India, not China, so I decided to stay in Derge.

Some two weeks later a letter came from the Dalai Lama saying when he would arrive in Chamdo. My husband made arrangements to rendezvous with His Holiness at Kardze. Lam-Dray was stopped and the monks prayed for my husband's safe trip. To ensure his safe journey, we made lots of prayer flags for the monastery and for a nearby mountain. This was seen as a very important trip for the future of all Tibetans. Our freedoms were at stake.

It was the first time my husband and I would be separated for any length of time. When we said goodbye, I found myself advising him to "act with wisdom" and to "be careful of Chinese food." Many Tibetans were wary that Dagchen Rinpoche could become ill from eating unfamiliar seafoods.

Khyentse Rinpoche suggested a week's camping trip, after which I returned to study writing, spelling, and grammar. I hadn't had any writing instruction since my days at Sakya. Khyentse Rinpoche's secretary, known throughout Kham for his penmanship, was my tutor. We were also taught how to make a pen of bamboo and how to make good ink. Lessons were held in Dzongsar Khyentse Rinpoche's palace, and on warm days, outside. Our writings always were concerned with religion. For example, we might be asked to describe a deity. "What is in his hand?" the instructor would ask.

Sangyum Kusho and I became close friends. I admired her sweet nature and sense of humor. She wore no makeup and dressed conservatively. She told me of her childhood days in Kardze and we reminisced. Her nephew Sogyal Rinpoche, about six years old, was like a big brother to Minzu-la.

Both of us became very interested in a new Chinese sewing machine we had purchased at Kardze at the request of Tse-wangyal, our tailor. One day Sangyum Kusho and I went to the palace room where the machine was housed and began to sew. I knew a little about its operation because we had had a machine at Lhagyal Monastery. The next day we had a lesson from her tailor. We clearly had found an amusing pastime. I made aprons for Wangmo and Sangyum's servant, hemmed a scarf, and fixed belts.

The second day, however, we were interrupted by a visitor, Tülku Kunzang, a lama who had come to Dzongsar for Lam-Dray. He entered without knocking, bearing two porcelain bowls of dried fruits and candies. He apparently had heard of our secret interest. Seeing us at the machine, he frowned angrily. "A lama's wife is supposed to study, read, and pray," he began, disgusted that we would spend our time doing what he believed was inappropriate for our station in life.

Sangyum and I looked at each other, puzzled as to what to do.

"This is not becoming to a lama's wife," he continued. "If you don't stop this, I will tell Dzongsar Khyentse Rinpoche." The scolding continued and extended to Wangmo and Sangyum's servant.

It soon became known to many persons at the monastery that we had been scolded for "wasting our time." One monk's reported reaction was, "Good, now they won't do it again."

But that didn't stop us. We did it again and again, taking the precaution of posting Sangyum's nun outside the door. She, however, was fearful, remembering the original scolding. But Wangmo was excellent at covering up for us, telling the curious that we were studying or writing. My mother also knew about the sewing and favored it, as it meant I was learning a new skill. Of course, if my mother had objected I wouldn't have continued.

Ever after that, Tülku Kunzang's bowls reminded me of the scolding. Finally I ordered Wangmo to take mine away.

After about a month, the first letter arrived from my husband, telling of his trip and arrival in Peking. He had flown by plane from Chengtu to Sian, and had gone the remainder of the way to Peking by special train.

Time dragged for me. There were parties and some visitors that helped the hours pass. One day Khyentse Rinpoche's party and I went on an outing that included debating and athletic events. In one of these contests, a yak saddle was placed on a rock. The contestant then had to grasp the saddle and, standing on his hands, bend down and with his mouth pick up sweets, usually dried fruit, placed in a dish of yogurt. Failure resulted in falling face first into the bowl of yogurt.

Despite my best efforts to the contrary, Khyentse Rinpoche and others were beginning to spoil Minzu-la. He wanted to draw everywhere. The boy was advanced for his age and the monks were overjoyed when he amused them with his art work. His favorite subject was Durdag, a deity in the form of a skeleton who is the lord of the graveyard and who subdues human anger. Minzu-la, busy with his chalk, was too liberal with his Durdag, often drawing him on the monastery walls. But because of his position as a Sakya lama no one stopped him. Monks even blessed his art on the walls. Also Minzu-la could do a ceremony with a bell and drum that made us very proud. He watched his elders carefully.

For protection against harmful obstacles, Minzu-la wore a red leather belt set with precious jewels that was two-and-a-half inches wide and weighed about a pound. From it hung pendants of various sizes and shapes, the largest being about four inches square, made of braided silk and containing papers on which were written prayers in Sanskrit. Even before he could walk, like all babies he wore a similar amulet down his back. Our boy wore a chuba of yellow and orange, so he made a colorful picture in his robes.

Another letter arrived from Dagchen Rinpoche, saying that they had met with Mao Tse-tung and two other government leaders, Chou En-lai and Deng Xiaoping. There had been a dinner and photographs had been taken. My husband also had met a general who had fought earlier in Kardze against our friend Chagotobdan. Many Mongolians—nearly five hundred at one time—were at the sessions, Dagchen Rinpoche said, and seemed overjoyed to make his acquaintance. But, my husband said, he was virtually a prisoner in his hotel. Two bodyguards were posted outside his door, and even his servants were not permitted to enter except by request.

There was much propaganda at meetings and other events

they attended. The Chinese first showed a film of the "decadent" regime under the Kuomintang, followed by one on the "strong" Communist regime, which they claimed did not lose wars. He also had his first Russian food at a dinner at the Russian Embassy attended by the entire Tibetan party.

My husband had been meeting dignitaries from many nations, particularly, he said, at the Chinese National Day observance attended by Mao Tse-tung. Most of the Tibetans were continuing to put up a friendly front for the Chinese, being very suspicious of their hosts' intent. But some Tibetans were impressed with the factories, industry, and culture that they saw.

I was worried when I read that Dagchen Rinpoche's return trip would include a six-day trip on the Yellow River from Peking to Lunten. I had heard of flooding there from accounts in a Derge newspaper. My husband was coming back early, electing not to tour Communist China as some other leaders were doing. We didn't know why, but presumed it was because the monks still were waiting for him to complete Lam-Dray.

A telegram then arrived from Dartsedo, saying Dagchen Rinpoche would be there a week visiting Sakya monasteries and then would return home. He arrived late one morning. When I saw the sad expression on his face, I thought that perhaps the gathering in Peking had not gone well. Not until my husband finally reached our quarters and had lunch could we talk.

The reason he had not stayed longer was that he had received a telegram from his brother, Trinly Rinpoche, in Sakya, saying that their mother had died. Upon receiving this news in Peking, Dagchen Rinpoche had immediately gone to His Holiness with an offering asking him to say prayers for his beloved mother and requesting permission to return to Tibet. That was the only time the Chinese guards had given my husband freedom to move, he recalled. The Dalai Lama was comforting, saying my husband had done all that was humanly possible for his mother.

His Holiness agreed that Dagchen Rinpoche should be permitted to come home early; the important meeting had concluded and his obligations were ended. We were all deeply shocked to hear of the death of the Gyayum Kusho.

I was greatly saddened at the passing of the Gyayum Kusho, who was in her mid-fifties. She had properly fulfilled her duties as wife of the Trichen, perhaps more than many others before her. She had given birth to sixteen children, seven of them living. Through her service, she had put the Sakya family before herself. She was a powerful and respected woman.

My first thought at hearing of her passing was the memory of her words when we left Sakya as she stood in tears in the palace courtyard.

"Goodbye, take good care. I may not see you again." I had comforted her then, assuring her we would be back for a family reunion in two years. I had never resented her domineering manner and objections to my becoming her daughter-in-law. I respected her as a leader who had a job to do. She was thrilled upon hearing that we had Minzu-la to carry on the family lineage, but she never saw her grandson.

During the forty-nine-day mourning period, I gave many of my personal jewels, along with one of my prize horses and its saddle, as an offering to Dzongsar Khyentse Rinpoche, my principal lama. My husband sent money and other offerings to all Sakya monasteries in Kham and some others.

Later, the religious ceremonies that had been interrupted when my husband left for Communist China were resumed and nearly finished when another tragedy struck our party. One of the eldest members of our group, the former Sakya Shapé, who was in his early sixties, died suddenly of a stroke. His grandson Senum, the youngest member of our group, was very grieved, as were we.

It was now more than a year since we had arrived at Dzongsar, and thus it was time to return to Lhagyal. Despite the unhappiness that had struck us here we were sad to leave, for we had made many friends. For me, it was difficult to say goodbye to Sangyum Kusho. The horsekeepers had to bid a sad farewell to their newfound girlfriends who resided in the town.

Our immediate family life was about to change, too, for I left Dzongsar about two months pregnant. Minzu-la was nearly two years old.

The monks at Lhagyal Monastery were delighted to have us return. The weather was warming, and this was the first time I had seen Lhagyal without snow. The monastery indeed looked inviting, posed on a green hillside with beautiful bushes nearby. The countryside of Yilhung province was so beautiful that I turned to gardening. A plot near our residence was selected where I planted the seeds I had brought from Thalung and Lharigar—two kinds of cabbage, turnips, radishes, and peas. At last I had something of my own—something that put me in touch with the earth and made me feel less nomadic.

11

Confronting the Chinese

My husband spent two weeks at Derge Monastery where he met with the Dalai Lama, who was on his way home from China.

Later we spent a week as the guests of Chagotobdan at a summer camp several miles up the mountain from Lhagyal Monastery. Horseracing, archery, and a prayer-flag festival were the primary entertainment. There were about three hundred tents set up in a meadow filled with wildflowers, some two or three feet high. When Minzu-la walked through them, we could barely see him. Prayer flags flew and incense smoke rolled up ceremoniously. Our prayers went to a local deity, Gendzo, who by tradition must be appeased or would send disaster. It was very pleasant, even though I was pregnant. Dressed in my finery, I sat on a cushion on the grass and watched the afternoon races. By the light of the moon we played hide-and-seek in the flowers in the meadow and also magic tricks and games.

I was reminded of Sing Cham Drumo who, seven centuries ago, had also been captivated by the grandeur of this province. A reincarnation of Green Tārā, she had been so taken by the beauty of this place that she named it Yilhung, the "mind-dropping place." Two especially beautiful fields were described as this beautiful woman's bathing bowls, because of their natural depressions. Everywhere the greenery and the blaze of the wild blooms blanketing the meadows lured me to indulge my senses in the peaceful atmosphere.

During our outing, two monks came from Dzongsar Monastery with a message from Dzongsar Khyentse Rinpoche saying that he was going on a pilgrimage to Lhasa. Later we learned that the Chinese had called a meeting in Peking, saying that it was mandatory for all important monks and lamas from the Derge area to attend. Rinpoche did not want to go to a gathering that he felt would be another attempt to convert more Tibetans to the Communist cause. Traveling in the disguise of an ordinary lama, he headed west. He crossed the Derge Jamda River where Chinese troops were quartered. Many Tibetans were waiting on the other side. Dzongsar Khyentse Rinpoche blessed them, but carefully avoided any activity that would give away his identity. The Chinese officials let him through, never dreaming that it was the most famous Sakya lama in Kham who was slipping past. Dzongsar Khyentse Rinpoche's move made us realize the impending danger. How long would we be free to come and go at will here?

Sometime later a letter arrived from Rinpoche in Lhasa saying he was sorry to have missed us and that "we will see you in Lhasa." We felt strongly that his underlying meaning was "come soon."

When the Chinese soldiers made their routine inspections at Lhagyal, we hid our tigerskins, guns, and other valuables. We did this because when the Chinese saw any unusual valuables they would record them and later question us about them. We had a good warning system, our informants telling us in advance much of the time that "the Chinese are coming." But we never felt really at ease, because some of these inspections would come in the middle of the night. There were three to five hundred soldiers posted at Manikhingo, just two miles away. Chinese soldiers tried to be friendly to my husband, sometimes bringing gifts of fresh fruits and vegetables. "If there is anything you need, just ask us," they would say.

Our second son was born on the morning of September 12, 1955, just as the sun was rising over the mountains. This was a good omen—the baby would have a long life—and the birth came on an auspicious day on the Tibetan calendar. I was pleased about having another boy. It was an easy birth; once again my mother and Wangmo helped usher the baby into the world.

Monastery residents and many of the people of the Yilhung areas were thrilled that a Sakya son was born in their part of the world. Prior to Minzu-la and this infant, no Sakya son had been born in eastern Tibet. The new baby's birthday would be celebrated here by the religious community for the rest of his life.

A new permanent religious flag was placed on a thirty-foot-high standard in the courtyard of the main temple. The flag's colors signified that he was born in the Wood Sheep year. The flag and standard were similar to the ones that had been erected for Minzu-la at Jyekundo. The monks and townsfolk were elated to have this distinction for the monastery. They referred to the boy as "our precious son."

After the usual month's lapse, my husband named the baby Kunga Dorje, meaning "joyous thunderbolt." We called him Ani-la, short for Ananda, the Sanskrit for "kunga."

In many small ways we started to plan for our return to western Tibet. Some of our newly acquired things were packed for the long journey to Sakya.

Meanwhile, Uncle Kuyak passed through Lhagyal. He was going to Sakya and Lhasa, among many places, on another trading mission. It was to be Uncle Kuyak's sad mission to tell the Shapé's family of his death.

During services conducted by a prominent Nyingma lama, Dilgo Khyentse Rinpoche, we received a message from the Minyag area asking us to visit the twenty-three Sakya monasteries there. The central city of Minyag is Dartsedo, a trading center on the border between Tibet and China. At first my

husband refused. A second delegation of monks came with
another request, including a note from Chagotobdan, so that
my husband felt we couldn't say no.

By this time some members of our party were becoming
restless, as winter was approaching and the weather was
getting colder. Lhagyal winters were not pleasant, and conditions under the Chinese were worsening.

While we were planning our Minyag trip, a letter arrived
via the Jyekundo Monastery telling us of the death of Uncle
Kuyak in the Yangpachen area. En route to Sakya, he had
been kicked in the leg by a horse. He was never one to
complain and refused to see a doctor, saying it was important
to move on to Sakya. While visiting a nomad who was his
very good friend, Uncle Kuyak's leg had become very painful
and swollen. He died there at age forty-nine.

Uncle Kuyak had been like a father to me since I was five.
Deep sorrow overcame me as I looked back upon the life of
this hardworking dedicated member of our family. He had
been closer to me than to his blood-nieces and -nephews. He
had been widely trusted and respected by his friends throughout Tibet. He also was a gentleman. Prayers were said for him
at Lhagyal and at neighboring monasteries.

A grief-stricken Aunt Chacha immediately left with Ani
Chimi for Thalung in order to settle his affairs. Since the
couple had no children, Aunt Chacha planned to give the
house and nearby lands to Uncle Kuyak's mother and brother,
who had been caring for the property while we were gone.
Under the law, lamas and monks could own only monastery
properties. Thus, as the only noncleric male in the family,
Uncle Kuyak was head of the household and technically the
owner of the property during his lifetime, but he could not
sell the property because it belonged to the Gaba province
government. As a memorial, however, my aunt gave to the
poor and to monasteries much money, jewels, animals, and
furnishings from our home. I told Aunt Chacha I wanted
nothing from our family home, that I was well taken care of
at Sakya. We planned that she and my mother would make

their future home with us at Sakya, and I felt our old home would be in good hands with Uncle Kuyak's family.

Ani-la now was ten weeks old—old enough to travel. We rented two buses through the station at Manikhingo and began a four-day trip to Parlhagong Monastery. For most of us, it was our first ride in a motor-driven vehicle. Climbing aboard, I realized that I was putting my life in someone else's hands. While the seats were comfortable, I was unable to relax and clutched the rail in front of me. As soon as the motor started, Minzu-la began crying. Luckily, Ani-la was asleep in Wangmo's arms. Many in our party were suffering the same anxieties. On the road, several of us became carsick. That night I couldn't sleep well because I was still "moving."

Word of our trip had spread, and crowds gathered along the road and in front of the buses, offering khatas with outstretched hands and asking my husband, "Please name my child," "Please bless this barley," "Please make a knot in my scarf." This, of course, got to be too much for the Chinese bus drivers who, in their opinion, were stopping too frequently.

Parlhagong was a pilgrimage center that had a famous statue of the Buddha considered comparable to the Jo Rinpoche in the temple at Lhasa. This statue was a gift from the Chinese wife of Songtsen Gampo, the king who first brought Buddhism to Tibet.

Most monasteries in Tibet were constructed on a mountainside, facing east, but Parlhagong was situated in a flat area on the main road between Dartsedo and Derge. The Chinese had built the road right past one corner of the main temple, in complete disregard for the contemplative atmosphere of the monastery. The road was full of chuckholes, and at night truckloads of noisy soldiers and civilians passed, collecting deer horns and plants for medicine to be shipped to China. They in turn brought rice and other foods. One of the medicinal plants the Chinese sought was *yartsagombu*, a kind of grass whose root is believed to be good for diseases of the bladder. These rare roots were dug during the month of

November; the next month the root contracts until it resembles a worm. Many Tibetans were uneasy digging these because they felt they were taking life.

Some thirteen-hundred monks, nuns, and others came for Lam-Dray services at Parlhagong. Many Minyag citizens also were on hand. All this activity caused the Chinese officials in the area to investigate. In the middle of the ceremonies they would enter the temple, look around, walk up and down the aisles, and generally disrupt events. They would question us, saying "Is Mao Tse-tung doing good things for his people?" I would have to answer, "I don't know." Then they would recount what they thought were positive accomplishments of Mao. My answer was, "That's very good."

The Chinese particularly showed off a Tibetan lama who had been in China several times and who had become a Communist sympathizer. He wrote books and lectured in monasteries, promoting the party line. Other Tibetan leaders were forced to give lectures, but most Tibetans knew when this was the case. The monks took every opportunity to miss these talks.

At these gatherings, the Chinese also gave vaccinations for smallpox as well as other kinds of injections. Our people complied, although they didn't particularly want to. The Chinese continued their intrusive and disruptive tactics. We Tibetans guide our lives very much by astrology. Certain years in each person's life are considered inauspicious. It was late 1955 and the upcoming year was to be a bad one for me, according to the prognostication of Uncle Tülku-la. This was in addition to the major inauspicious years—the thirteenth, twenty-fifth, thirty-seventh, forty-ninth, and so on, or every twelfth year. To combat these forces, one must do something of a spiritual nature such as a pilgrimage. I chose to go on retreat at Parlhagong to worship the White Tārā.

For two months and three weeks Uncle Tülku-la came to teach me meditation in my small retreat room on the second floor. There were dietary restrictions, so during the retreat I became a vegetarian. At the beginning I missed meat and even dreamed of eating it; one was supposed to forget these worldly desires. Still, I was provided with excellent food, mainly fresh dairy products.

My room contained an altar, religious statues, two cushions for the children, and a bed. Butter lamps and incense burned round the clock.

I arose at 6:30 A.M. and spent about ten hours daily in prayer and meditation. My husband came in before he went to Lam-Dray. Sometimes he ate lunch or dinner with me, but I couldn't share his food. My visitors, including my husband, could only come at specified times, as I kept to a strict schedule. The children were taken out for my three-hour practice sessions.

Unfortunately, the atmosphere was not peaceful and quiet because Chinese trucks and jeeps roared past my window at all hours.

I lost weight during this session and became somewhat weak. Little Ani-la, now four or five months old, was not a strong boy, and all during the retreat he had a bad cold. Soon after, we came to realize the dangers that surrounded us.

While I was in retreat, in the nearby Lithang area, southwest of Minyag, Tibetans had begun to fight. Lithang Monastery had nearly five thousand monks of the Gelugpa school. One evening a small group of monks from Lithang who had been attending the Lam-Dray came to my husband and announced that they were leaving, as they had received a message saying that they must come home to defend the monastery. Tearfully, they asked for and received photos of my husband and a blessed charm. During the night, Trinley, our treasurer, gave them food and supplies and they left on foot. They were all young—the oldest not over twenty. The other monks didn't know that the group was gone until they saw their empty seats at the Lam-Dray. The sad travelers took a circuitous route for the five-day walk to their destination and apparently made it.

Later, the Chinese bombed Lithang Monastery. It would have been impossible, of course, for us to tell the Lithang monks not to go home. But it would have been equally frightening had the Chinese known the group was coming from Lam-Dray, because it would have indicated that we were sending fighting forces to Lithang.

Afterwards the Chinese kept a closer watch on the activities at Parlhagong. At night they surrounded the monastery, leaving before dawn to avoid being seen. South of the monastery there was a stand of juniper trees that the Chinese often used as a lookout. At midnight one could see the flashlights of soldiers in the woods.

Ani-la continued to have a cold, even after my retreat ended. My husband began to speed up the Lam-Dray ceremonies, as the incidents at Lithang Monastery made us realize the dangers that surrounded us in eastern Tibet.

More and more Chinese troops were on the move at night and each day we had news of the fighting. This had its effects at Parlhagong. Young monks would throw rocks at passing Chinese vehicles, or walk out in front of the trucks to make them stop. Other monks then would lift up the covers of the truck to reveal the Chinese wounded.

We interrupted the Lam-Dray for only three days for a routine Tibetan New Year's observance early in 1956. I sent two monks to Dartsedo to buy fresh fruits, vegetables, and cookies for the celebration, but our hearts were heavy. Planes continued to fly over in the direction of Lithang Monastery. When we heard them approaching, we would run upstairs to watch. The Chinese came to Parlhagong on more snooping missions. About five o'clock one morning, when it was still not light, some monks went on kora. The Chinese became suspicious and asked them many questions, telling them they "should be in bed."

Meanwhile Ani-la began to have a fever and was coughing and losing weight. He was worse at night. The Chinese had sent a team of nurses to the Parlhagong area to give smallpox vaccinations to the children. The medical team had arrived in a white jeeplike medical vehicle, staying as all Chinese travelers did in a waystation near the monastery. Nearby was a small Chinese medical station, built by Tibetans. Our monk doctor said we must let the nurses examine Ani-la. I sent a monk, fluent in Chinese, to ask if there was a physician and if they, the nurses, could treat my son. They reported that a doctor would arrive later.

When the doctor came, a Parlhagong monk observed the man and said he was indeed a remarkable doctor. My husband asked his teacher to use divination to determine if we should take Ani-la to this man. The answer was yes. This was a milestone for us. Never before had I surrendered myself or my child to Chinese medicine. But it was clear that our treatment wasn't helping Ani-la, who was breathing heavily by now.

One afternoon the doctor and two nurses, along with a Tibetan interpreter, came to examine the little patient. Ani-la was looking very pale. He was indeed seriously ill and, if he worsened, he must have treatment in a hospital—a large hospital, they said.

Lam-Dray ended with a big feast-offering celebration known as Tsog Kor. Many kinds of foods were displayed in a circle as offerings to the Buddha and protector deities in thanks for the teachings we had received. This food was then distributed to all.

A week had elapsed since the doctor first had seen Ani-la, who now ate little and was very weak. The doctor said we must take the boy to the hospital soon, the closest one being in Dartsedo. We decided to go there as a last resort. Lithang, to the south, had been taken over by the Chinese and its main temple bombed and burned. Many monks had been killed, others were hiding in the hills and fighting guerrilla style. The entire area had come under the heel of the Chinese, and the Tibetans were starting to fight back. The Tibetans wanted to burn some bridges in order to block shipments of supplies to the Chinese. But as long as we were in the area the Tibetans would not do this. They urged us to return to Lhagyal so they could get at their work.

Chagotobdan, at Lharigar, heard of our plight and sent a

jeep that could take eight of us and a driver. When we told the driver we wanted to go to Dartsedo, he objected. He had been sent, he said, to take us to Lhagyal. At the Chinese headquarters near Parlhagong Monastery the driver wired Chagotobdan, who replied that we were to go to Dartsedo as soon as possible. When the driver saw Ani-la's condition, he became grief-stricken, as he too had children.

We left the next day at about noon. Chagotobdan had informed the Chinese en route that the party would be coming. It was a six-hour trip to Dartsedo, and we had to cross two passes. Before leaving, we stopped at the medical station. I could tell from the look on the doctor's face how ill Ani-la was. Uncle Tülku-la was ill, too, from the ride. We were a sight indeed, with him vomiting from the rear of the vehicle.

Two Chinese nurses accompanied us, taking turns holding Ani-la. One looked at her watch frequently. She had a bottle containing hot water with sugar and medicine. She blew on the mixture first, took some in her mouth to test it, and then administered the concoction to Ani-la. She also checked his temperature. On the way, Ani-la slept and seemed to improve intermittently. About five-thirty that evening we arrived in Dartsedo, ahead of schedule. Every bridge was guarded here, but our Chinese vehicle bore an official banner that permitted us to pass.

We found the hospital on the east side of town. It had a wall surrounding it, with only two entrances. Inside were a separate children's unit and a soldiers' hospital. Altogether, there were about two hundred rooms. The driver, a nurse, and I waited with the baby in the emergency room for the doctor to arrive. Minzu-la, who was frightened of the Chinese in their hospital garb, stayed with Uncle Tülku-la in the jeep.

The physician told us that Ani-la must remain at the hospital for shots and other treatment. My reaction to the shots was a speedy no.

"You go ask your husband," the driver said. "Shots will help now. These are fine doctors. You must do as they say."

Reluctantly I agreed that the shots were necessary, and they were administered.

We took Ani-la to the home of Uncle Tülku-la's friend, Aja Kasang Wascha, a Dartsedo nobleman. Earlier we had been invited here by one of Aja's sons, Minyag Ripung Tülku, a high incarnate lama, while he was attending Lam-Dray at Parlhagong Monastery. We were impressed with this young and talented lama. Now we had come to Dartsedo without a recent invitation, but nonetheless we found our hosts delighted to see us. Aja and his wife were very generous to us. They advised us to cooperate with the doctors and acted as our interpreters in dealings with hospital personnel, and in general made relations between us and the Chinese more comfortable.

The next day a woman doctor and two nurses came to Aja's house and stressed that Ani-la must have hospital treatment. They said a week in the hospital would put him back in shape. We consented, and a bed was arranged for me in his hospital room. We never were told what Ani-la's ailment was, but looking back, I now believe that he had pneumonia.

I had never been in a hospital before, but I was less than impressed with this one. Part of it was built over a stream, into which the hospital sewage was emptied. The hospital complex was like a vision of hell: doctors with needles, strange noises, many wounded and ailing people. Children seemed to be crying all the time. The nurses and doctors all had their heads and faces covered and the nurses especially all looked alike to me. Ani-la's main physician appeared to be Russian, but he spoke Chinese. I continued to have my food brought from Aja's house. I couldn't sleep well at night and kept the light on. This whole atmosphere led me to think more deeply about the impermanence of human life. My distant relative, the Derge queen, was on a Chinese-requested trip to Dartsedo, and another bed was placed in the room for her. She wanted to comfort me and aid my stay there. Mother, Wangmo, and two other servants by now had arrived in Dartsedo and came to visit every day. Wangmo had never lived around Chinese for any length of time and was getting an eyeful. She was learning to read Tibetan, too. She was not a brilliant girl and learning came slowly. But what Wangmo learned, she never forgot. She always accompanied me and everyone liked her. She was a faithful servant.

We received the utmost courtesy. Apparently this was the first time this hospital had made such "concessions" to Tibetans. The Chinese appreciated the propaganda value of our family, so they were determined to do their best for our son.

It was the first time for me to live among Chinese and I observed all. There was a strict routine throughout the day with which I soon became familiar. At seven A.M. music was played and as many employees as could be spared went outside to do calisthenics. While this was going on, the queen and I said our prayers. "That is Communist praying," she said of the calisthenics. After a bell rang, the employees— carrying big mugs and plates—queued up for breakfast, which they ate sitting on the ground in the courtyard. Instead of tea they drank hot water. After breakfast, everyone washed his or her mug. One night, when I heard a dog crying, the Derge queen said it was medical students operating on dogs.

We placed charms, statues, and photos of deities around Ani-la's bed. One doctor looked at them with interest. Others on the medical team turned up their noses. The nurses acted as if these charms were poison, picking them up gingerly by the very edges. This deeply hurt me. One day Uncle Tülku-la burned incense, rang his bell, and scattered rice in purification ceremonies for Ani-la. The Chinese peeked in the door and snickered. By this time we were getting used to this insensitivity to our culture.

An elderly Chinese lady who cleaned Ani-la's room was not friendly. She became upset by the remains of fruit and other food found in our wastebasket. The Chinese considered any food used for such ceremonies as a waste. "They throw away too much," was her claim. Nor did she like butter lamps burning in the room, declaring that we were wasting butter.

Ani-la meanwhile was responding to the treatment. I could

now hold and nurse him again. One day the doctor came and talked to Aja, saying that we could go home the next day. If Ani-la did not continue to improve, the doctor said, we were to get medicine from Chinese doctors in Kham using a prescription the doctor gave us.

One of the nurses who had come with us from Minyag dropped by for a farewell visit. Obviously taken with our quiet thin boy with the big dark eyes, she kissed him and presented him with a little red jacket. It had a Mandarin-style collar and was quilted with flowers and embroidered. In return I presented her with a tin of Indian candies and an Indian towel. The nurse obviously was pleased, but she didn't want to take the gifts for fear of criticism from her superiors. She put them under her jacket, nonetheless, and took them home. I was so happy to be leaving, for these had not been pleasant days for me.

When we left the next morning, we had many spectators. Many of the Chinese touched and made much of our boy, who was dressed in a yellow chuba and a fox-fur hat. I extended our thanks to the head doctor, who had been most kind and understanding about our Buddhist practices. (He had accompanied the Dalai Lama and his party to China.) We paid our bill for the hospital care and left.

We stayed on a few days in Dartsedo and did some shopping. There was a prolonged ritual for making purchases in the big Communist stores. One had to stand in line and obtain a certification paper, for which one had to give his name, address, birthplace, and other information. This procedure was new to us but it seemed ridiculous and we couldn't take it seriously. At some of the stores, we gave false animal names. When these names were called we would burst into laughter. It was our small way of making fun of their system.

The next day we made the rounds of smaller independent stores. Truck gardens around the city were the source of many kinds of vegetables and flowers sold on the open market. This was where my late Great-Uncle Nawang got the seeds and bulbs for the flowers he grew in pots at Thalung Monastery. I

The North Sakya Monastery. The winter palace, used seasonally by the Trichen and his family, is on the right. (Photo by P. T. Takla)

The Sakya Gyayum Kusho, mother-in-law of Jamyang Sakya, in her headdress, which she wore daily. Photo taken in Gangtok, Sikkim, in the late 1940s or early 1950s.

Sakya Dagchen Jigdal Rin-
poche, husband of Jamyang
Sakya, on his motorcycle in
Lhasa, 1957.

*Jamyang Sakya at Parlhagong
Monastery in Kham, 1956.*

Dzongsar Khyen Jamyang Chökyi Lodro Rinpoche, the root lama of Sakya Dagchen Rinpoche and Jamyang Sakya. Photo taken in the 1950s in Tibet.

Minzu-la Sakya, age two and a half, at the Phuntsok Palace in 1956, after the family's return from Kham.

Ani-la Sakya, age one, at the Phuntsok Palace in 1956.

*Jamyang Sakya (left) and Mrs.
Kyime, wife of a Lhasa noble,
in Lhasa, 1957.*

*From left: Minzu-la Sakya,
Sakya Dagchen Jigdal Rin-
poche, Ani-la Sakya, and Jamyang Sakya holding Mati-la
Sakya, in Lhasa, 1959.*

*Butter torma at the Monlam
(New Year's festival) in Lhasa.
(Photo by P. T. Takla)*

*Tibetan ferry crossing the
Tsangpo River near Samye
Monastery. (Photo by P. T.
Takla)*

*Typical crossing of a bridge
with prayer flags overhead.
(Photo by P. T. Takla)*

*Three nomad women with coins
and jewelry braided into their
hair. (Photo by P. T. Takla)*

Piles of mani stones with yak horns in Tibet. (Photo by P. T. Takla)

From left: Tachung, the Sakyas' horse-keeper; Gyatso, a personal servant of Sakya Dagchen Jigdal Rinpoche; Sakya Dagchen Jigdal Rinpoche; Tengyam, a family servant; Mongtho, a personal servant of Sakya Trinly Rinpoche; Sakya Trinly Rinpoche; Japon, the chief cook; Ani-la Sakya; Jamyang Sakya, holding Mati-la Sakya.

Jamyang Sakya and His Holiness the Dalai Lama in Dharamsala, India, 1967. The Dalai Lama is showing the heads of a historic Chenrezi statue, formerly housed in the Jokhang Temple in Lhasa, which was destroyed by Chinese Communists in the Cultural Revolution. The heads had just been brought to him by Tibetan refugees. (Photo by James McDonald)

Prime Minister Indira Gandhi and
Jamyang Sakya in New Delhi, 1967.
(Photo by James McDonald)

The family of Sakya Dagchen Jigdal Rinpoche and Jamyang Sakya, Seattle, 1969. From left: Dezhung Rinpoche (known as Uncle Tulku-la), Dr. Kunsang Nyima, Jamyang Sakya, Legpa Dorje Sakya, Ani Chimi, Minzu-la Sakya, Zaya-la Sakya, Sakya Dagchen Jigdal Rinpoche, Mati-la Sakya, and Ani-la Sakya. (Photo by James McDonald)

*Minzu-La Sakya, left, studies from Buddhist texts with his great uncle Dezhung Rinpoche in Seattle. (*Seattle Times *photo by George Cardonen, 1961)*

From left: His Holiness Sakya Trizin, Dezhung Rinpoche ("Uncle Tulku-la"), and Sakya Dagchen Jigdal Rinpoche in Seattle, 1978.

From left: Sakya Dagchen Jigdal Rin-
poche, Dilgo Khyentse Rinpoche, Jam-
yang Sakya, Ösel Mukpo (son of
Chögyam Trungpa Rinpoche), Chö-
gyam Trungpa Rinpoche, and Rabjam
Rinpoche, at Rocky Mountain
Dharma Center, Colorado, in 1982.
(Photo by Adrienne Chan)

Jamyang Sakya in her family shrine
room, Seattle, 1989. (Photo by Niels
Thomsen)

*Sakya Dagchen Jigdal Rinpoche and
Jamyang Sakya, Seattle, 1989.*

recalled as a little girl how I had drawn Buddhist symbols on the pots.

The women vegetable-sellers were a pitiful sight, for some were crippled as the result of having had their feet bound. Formerly great ladies, they now hobbled about, doing manual labor under the Communist regime.

Our medical mission and shopping chores completed, we wired Chagotobdan that we were returning to Parlhagong Monastery. We also made arrangements with the Chinese officials to rent two buses to take us from Parlhagong to Lhagyal.

Hundreds of Minyag people were waiting along the road for us as our jeep passed through this territory. Trinley, our treasurer, had sent monks to many of these monasteries to pray for Ani-la's recovery.

We planned to stay only briefly at Parlhagong, as Chagotobdan was anxious to have us return to Lhagyal. Phuba Tsering, some seventy horses, and the party of horsekeepers had left Parlhagong the week before for Lhagyal. He was to proceed out of Lhagyal by a northern route and then turn west to meet us at Shigatse. Somehow the Chinese got word that after our departure from Parlhagong the Tibetans were planning to blow up the bridges in the area. So on the scheduled day, our two buses did not arrive; nor did they the next day. It was awkward, as we had everything packed and ready to go. Three monks from Parlhagong went to the nearby town of Shintujang, where there was a telegraph station, and wired Dartsedo to inquire about the delay. It gave the Chinese more time to bring troops into the area.

The Chinese at Dartsedo said that, due to an emergency, they had had to send a lot of their buses to China and that our buses would be on their way as soon as possible. It was clear that they wanted to catch the Tibetans off-guard or that they wanted to buy more time before the Tibetans attacked.

When the three monks returned from Shintujang, we were shaken by their news; however, we attempted not to arouse the monks' fears any more than was necessary. It was obvious now that if we were ever to get out of here, now was the time. I felt great sadness about what was about to happen here, but I also thought how brave these Tibetans were to strike back against such powerful enemies. Many Tibetans, however, considered themselves just as powerful and a match for the Communists. They saw their mission as preserving Buddhism.

At Parlhagong I visited a shrine that had a statue of the White Tārā and prayed for safe passage. Maybe these merciful deities will help us to get through, I thought.

Late in the fifth day of waiting for the buses, the immediate family decided to go ahead in Chagotobdan's jeep, leaving the rest of the party at Parlhagong. My husband, the two children, two servants, and myself made the drive to Drago without incident, and the next day went on to Tawu Monastery. There we took Ani-la to the nearby Chinese hospital, where he received a shot and medicine. He still had a cough and fever. They told us that if he did not improve, he should be taken to the hospital in Kardze. But the next day we passed through Kardze and went on to the Dhongthog area where my husband had agreed to spend two weeks teaching.

Dhongthog Rinpoche's monks were very annoyed when they found that the Chinese had not kept their promises and that Uncle Tülku-la and the rest of our party were still waiting in the Parlhagong Monastery. A head monk went to the Chinese officials at Kardze to complain. The Chinese there were surprised, not knowing our immediate family had been brought to Dhongthog Monastery, and the next day the two buses were on their way to Parlhagong to pick up the rest of our party. Three days later we were all together again. I wondered how, if we continued to have this much trouble with transportation, we would ever get back to Sakya.

Dhongthog Monastery was unusual for it was the first in Kham to have electric lights, which had been installed in a few of the head lama's rooms. The electricity was generated at a nearby power plant on the Dhongthog River.

While we were at Dhongthog, a Chinese gymnastic team

and circus came through on its way home from performances in Lhasa and Shigatse. The Chinese officials in Kardze invited the immediate family, but Dagchen Rinpoche was quite busy teaching. Four of us were taken by jeep to the big auditorium in Kardze. Many Chinese from the area were in attendance. Fancy buttons bearing Mao's photo were passed out to everyone; these would admit the wearer to future Chinese-sponsored events. I found this offensive and never wore mine again, but some Tibetans kept them on, treating them as merely decorative. It was a four-and-a-half-hour performance and we enjoyed all of it immensely. It was the biggest show to come to Tibet in nearly nine years. Besides gymnastics, we saw tightrope walking, a play, and many unusual types of dancing, including Russian folk dancing. The dancers were beautiful and the stage settings and curtains elaborate.

At the end of the show, I left without saying goodbye to the official or extending the usual courtesies. The next day we left for Nyarag Monastery, still in the Horkhog area. Nyarag was situated several hundred feet up a very steep hill that was nestled against a high mountain. We still were able to ride our mounts to the monastery. Once there we looked out on spectacular views of the monasteries, many villages, and the main highway through Horkhog that vehicles used on the way from Lhasa to Dartsedo. This had been used by traders for centuries. The countryside was filled with beautiful wildflowers.

But there were reminders of the era. We saw an airplane bound for somewhere and even heard shooting in the distance. The magicians and other entertainment were not of top quality here, but Minzu-la was thrilled. It was one of the last good times we were to have in eastern Tibet—one of serenity, relaxation, and freedom from cares. Undoubtedly everyone here would recall these days as a joyous interlude in the gradual stifling encroachment of the Chinese.

Our next stop was Longnak ("Black Bull") Monastery, once a very prestigious place and important to us spiritually, for this had been the home of Kyagon Cholang, a lama who was of the Sakya Khön family. He had lived here four generations earlier, at a time when frequent earthquakes plagued the area, claiming thousands of lives. Kyagon Cholang had died in the historic quake of 1800. When the tremor first struck, he had insisted that his followers leave, saying he would die for the cause of subduing the quakes. He decreed that after his death his body should remain here in a stupa, saying this would prevent future quake disasters. There had been no quakes since that time. The Longnak monks and lamas had asked my husband to perform consecration and prayers at the site.

Again we were bitterly reminded of what was happening to Kham's monasteries. For this was clearly a case of starving our religion. The Chinese preached that the monks must help produce food and that the Tibetan people were not to take food to the monks. The monks also had to attend Chinese propaganda meetings.

Thus as there were fewer monks now at Longnak, many monks were required to live at home with their families. The remaining monks made a great effort on behalf of our party, finding butter lamps and offerings. Wealthy people brought chairs, rugs, and food to make our stay comfortable. The head lama, assigned from Sakya, told us of the monastery's deterioration. Understandably, he wanted to return to Sakya.

We stayed one night and then Chagotobdan's jeep came to take the immediate family to his palace at Lharigar. In addition to his wife and two daughters, Chagotobdan's brother, Senum, lived at the palace. As we drove in, we were greeted by Chinese marching units. Many of the Tibetans meeting us had come from the surrounding areas.

Chinese soldiers occupied the first floor. There were military units all around the palace, as it was a headquarters of Yilhung province and was a Chinese station. There were always two to three hundred soldiers in the vicinity of the three-story palace, which was near the center of town. Tents housed the soldiers, a doctor, nurses, and a Chinese store. I had never lived so close to armed Chinese soldiers. Chagotobdan had impressed upon them the importance of our visit and that he would be busy entertaining us and the Chinese generally left my husband alone during the week of our stay, not asking questions as they had at Kardze.

At Lharigar the Chinese met their match in Drogetopden, one of Chagotobdan's lamas. He was a dark, tall, and heavy man about sixty; he was afraid of no one. His hair, which was beginning to gray, was seldom combed. It grew long over his shoulders, tied in the back. He dressed in sheepskins. He seldom smiled, and it appeared that all feared him, especially children. But Drogetopden was a highly respected man.

He, like Lama Asang at Lhagyal, was a drutop, or *siddha*, who Tibetans believed had achieved perfection and was possessed of magical powers. The Chinese said he was a crazy old man, but I believe they really had some measure of feeling for him too.

There was a huge prayer wheel outside the palace. Every morning Drogetopden arose at three o'clock and went out to the wheel, turning it for hours. The Chinese soldiers patrolled regularly and asked him often, "What are you doing here?" He tired of these repeated questions.

Drogetopden merely threw out his chest and said, "Shoot me. I want to go pray. Shoot me now."

After that the patrol would let him go.

He liked Minzu-la, who, with Senum, listened without fear and at length to Drogetopden's stories. He enjoyed showing them his old skullcup, drum, and bell.

We now returned to Lhagyal Monastery, which we had left some five months previously. At the same time, Aunt Chacha arrived from Thalung. She had completed her obligations after Uncle Kuyak's death and was prepared to start a new life with us.

The day after our arrival in Lhagyal, we sent for some eighteen smiths from the Derge area, seat of the great metal craftsmanship of Tibet. We planned to have these experts make dozens of musical instruments and religious implements. This project was an important part of our trip to eastern Tibet. Many of the objects were for Sakya's four main temples.

The Chinese were none too happy about the metalwork projects, but there was nothing they could do about it without arousing the ire of the local Tibetans. When the Chinese made their inspections, they mainly inquired if anyone was bothering us or if we needed any help. Still, whenever they came around we tried to conceal the major metalwork projects.

The head of the smiths was an older and highly experienced man. He was very religious, arising early to pray. While working, he often mumbled mantras. When the day's work ended, he went on kora around Lhagyal Monastery. Except for him, all of the smiths were under thirty years old. They had begun their trade while very young and often descended from generations of artisans. As artisans, they demanded special respect.

My husband and I had commissioned them to make both short and long trumpets, *chome* (containers for butter lamps), offering cups, charm boxes, and other implements. About a thousand chomes were to be made of molded silver. Most of the other objects would have a base of silver or copper, with goldplated designs over quicksilver. We were fortunate to have enough quicksilver on hand, as the Chinese strictly forbade it—along with opium and bullets—to be brought into Kham.

The smiths also were commissioned to make three elaborately decorated saddles and parts of bridles and bits. The saddles and bridles were crafted with leather and matching silver and gold Indian brocade. Traditionally the finest saddles in Tibet came from Derge, commanding top prices. All prominent families possessed them with pride.

The metals came from many sources. I had been collecting used gold, silver, and jewelry since we had arrived in Kham. We also melted down old Chinese coins and silver money. Some patrons and monks had contributed silver and gold jewelry for the project.

The Lhagyal monks helped the smiths, working nine or ten hours a day around three charcoal-fueled stoves in the courtyard. It was summer, and the courtyard was noisy with the pounding of metal. When it was too hot, tenting was erected to shade the smiths. Buttermilk was served to cool them, and they ate four meals a day. Frequently I went to the courtyard to survey progress. It was fun to observe; I learned much about this ancient craft.

The smiths first would make a design and then show it to my husband for final approval. Then the metals were melted down in small clay pots. The completed works were kept in a large room on the second floor of the palace. This storage room also was used to complete the drying of the pieces. First raw wool was placed on the floor, then blankets, and finally cotton flannel, to ensure that the handcrafted work was not damaged.

The smiths were paid monthly salaries according to their level of skill. The head smith could also designate periodic bonuses. When each major set of works was completed, we held a dinner party for the whole group, and each smith received a gift of extra food—a dried leg of lamb, big pastries, or dried fruits—that he saved to take home later. Sometimes there were also gifts of clothing. I sent to Lharigar for Chinese-made vodka, which came in barrels, for their parties, as Derge natives traditionally drank more than other Khampas. Just smelling the vodka made me woozy.

As the season wore on, we took on another worry. Khanchen, my husband's adviser and former teacher, was ill. He was about sixty-three, set in his ways, and refused to go to a Chinese doctor. I had great respect for this man, who reminded me of my great-uncle. I loved to hear Khanchen tell about the days when Dagchen Rinpoche was a boy and of early times at Sakya.

One day we were invited to attend an important dance festival at the nearby Yakzhe Monastery, in which the Nyingma monks were marking the birthday of Padmasambhava, who built the first monastery in Tibet at Samye. A highlight of this ceremony was the Snow Lion's Dance, in which several monks danced together, wearing a costume made from long white sheepskins, with a mane and tail of yak hair dyed turquoise. I had not seen a performance like this since I was a girl.

I hadn't ridden my horse, Sengerapa (Blond Lion), for some time. On the day of the performance he seemed nervous. As we crossed a road crowded with Chinese trucks and other vehicles, Sengerapa snorted and reared and appeared to be almost shaking. As we crossed a bridge over the river he reared up again; he did not want to go in the direction of Yakzhe Monastery. His strange behavior made me wonder what was wrong. The Yakzhe monks wondered why I rode such a horse, who continued to act up after we had reached the monastery. I feared the monks thought I was showing off.

Midway through the ceremonies, a monk brought a message that Khanchen was in grave condition. We left at once for Lhagyal. Crossing the bridge on the way home, Sengerapa did not rear at the trucks. He was gentle and required no leading, and seemed to be his old normal self again.

When I arrived at Lhagyal, my husband came to tell me that his teacher was gone. We realized then what Sengerapa had been trying to tell us. It was a very sorrowful and significant event for my husband and me. A figure central to our family had passed on. He was not only capable and learned but politically wise. He was widely known, having traveled in many parts of the Himalayas and India while serving the Sakya Trichen. Khanchen had been very understanding and helpful during Dagchen Rinpoche's and my courtship. And it was, I recalled, Khanchen who had given me the Kyedor Wangchen, one of the requirements of the post of Sakya Dagmo. Khanchen had been a wise and trustworthy teacher and adviser. Now my husband would have to make his own important decisions unaided.

According to Buddhists, there are three types of warning signs telling of impending death. The "outer" signs are one category. If one sticks out the tongue, for example, and does not see it, this is evidence.

There also are the "inner" signs, such as sudden personality changes—for example, a generous person might become very stingy.

The third category of "secret" signs was known only to those learned in religion. But most Tibetans knew at least some of the signs in the first two categories.

Khanchen had told us that he had seen many of these warning signs and that he felt his time had come. He had made all the proper preparations in his lifetime and had faced up to death. But travel had been hard on him.

At about the same time, my husband's brother, Trinly Rinpoche, and his sister, Tsegen-la, with four servants, arrived in Kham in a Chinese truck. The road from Lhasa to China was now finished. Trinly Rinpoche had heard of the deteriorating conditions in Kham and had been anxious to learn of our welfare. He wanted us to return to Sakya before the situation became even more dangerous.

It was my belief that the Chinese were not yet powerful enough to take over this territory. Lhagyal monks, however, were ready to fight. The unrest and intrigue continued to grow. More Tibetan guerrillas were moving into the mountains around Lhagyal, recruiting more fighters as they went along. In some areas, the Khampas were ready to fight openly with the Chinese. There had been thefts of supplies from Chinese trucks and some killings. We could not avoid being implicated because we were looked to for leadership—and hope. Hiding out near the Lhagyal Monastery were thirty or forty guerillas, led by Drebo Tayang, a woman from the Dzingkhog area. She had been in the group that had gone to China with His Holiness. In desperation, she had begun her guerrilla activities, leaving her home and placing two children in Chagotobdan's care in his palace at Lharigar. Daytimes the band would waylay Chinese trucks and kill their drivers. At night they would try to get supplies—food or whatever they needed. We were only two miles from Manikhingo, and the Chinese were strengthening their headquarters here more and more. Undoubtedly it was some of these trucks that were being raided by the guerrilla group.

One evening two of Tayang's men came to Lhagyal and asked to see my husband. She had sent some jewels for him to bless. She also asked him what move she should make next. Tayang desired revenge and was willing to fight for her country and her freedom. This posed a great danger to our party. If the Chinese found her and she were forced to divulge that she had taken orders from my husband, we would be in serious trouble.

Usually on these occasions my husband had drawn on the wisdom of Khanchen, whose counsel we missed daily. My husband went to the big temple of Lhagyal and attempted by tossing his dice to foretell the future. His advice to Tayang was to be careful, to fight skillfully, and to remember that she was outnumbered. He told her to move out of the Lhagyal hills. My husband also warned her to be leery of messages and systems of communications. Tibetans were being paid generously to spy. The two men stayed about two hours and were given tsampa, meat, and cheese. Two horses were loaded with supplies, but no arms.

Tayang, whom I had met earlier on the way to Dzongsar Monastery, had sent a message to me, along with a piece of coral, asking me to keep it and "Remember me and pray for me," which I did.

The next evening two army officers and eight Chinese soldiers came to the Lhagyal palace. They had been informed, they said, that two men had been here last night. What were they doing here and who were they, the Chinese wanted to know. I observed the Chinese questioning my husband's treasurer, Trinley, some monks, and a group of horsekeepers. The Chinese cleverly disguised their real purpose—to watch our movements—by asking, "Have any of the guerillas been bothering you? Just let us know and we'll help you. I'm sure you wouldn't be a part of such activities."

"Many Khampas come and go and we don't remember any specific ones," Trinley said.

The delegation obviously did not believe Trinley, but they left without further questions.

Meanwhile we said farewell to Uncle Tülku-la, who was returning to his duties at Thalung Monastery. He kissed Minzu-la goodbye and gave him a blessing. A big tear ran down the boy's face.

The weather was getting colder and it was also time to bid farewell to the smiths. They had finished six hundred butter lamp containers and planned to make the remaining four hundred next summer at Lhagyal. We held a three-day farewell party in their honor. The men had done a commendable job, we thought, and they were paid accordingly. Some took their pay in yaks, horses, tea, and silk material. We also gave each of them personal gifts. Monks from Lhagyal escorted the smiths back to their homes in various parts of Derge. Some of the smiths sent presents back to us, saying they had enjoyed their work and considered it a contribution that would serve religion for centuries.

It had been a sad parting. Many of the smiths felt they soon would be fighting the Chinese, and they asked my husband to pray for their protection.

12

Peril on the Road

With the metalwork finished, we began to lay serious plans for our trip home to Sakya. First, however, we visited a sacred lake in the area and, high on a steep mountain nearby, the cave of Derge Gyalse Rinpoche, the abbot of Ngor Monastery and a learned lama of whom my husband was a reincarnation. He had died in the late 1920s, having achieved a high level of spiritual power. Many deities had appeared to him, especially Vajrayoginī, the female dakini.

Gyalse Rinpoche had lived here in solitary retreat for thirteen years, his food brought to him a couple of times a month by students and other patrons. Water dripped into the three-room cave, which was above the timberline just a few steps from the snowfields. Even Minzu-la went on the dangerous climb, which in some places required the use of ropes.

Inside this cave were a tanka and Rinpoche's prayer wheel, book, and simple cooking intensils. Wildflowers grew around the cave. What a pleasant place, I thought. From here, one could look up at the snow peaks and down at a lake and greenery and deer grazing in a valley. Beautiful birds sang from their peaceful vantage points amid the bushes. We were told that deer came up to the entrance of the cave, but we didn't see any. The cave was filled with a sense of warmth. Minzu-la was so excited he couldn't eat.

The trip down the mountain was even more dangerous. We clung to ropes and clutched branches. Our clothes were dusty, dirty, rumpled, and torn. But I considered myself very fortunate to have seen this holy place, which was only accessible to tourists in summer.

While in the area, we made a kora around the lake, a three-hour walk. At one end was a Chinese installation—a large building with a red roof. As we passed by, we noticed the Chinese soldiers playing basketball. They stared back at us. Since the Chinese—many of them road-builders—had arrived here, the lake had become dirty and dark. Besides fishing here, the Chinese did their laundry in the lake. As Buddhists, we believed a rare and sacred golden fish inhabited this lake. A nomad had said that the fish was caught by a Chinese, who became frightened at his catch and tossed it back in. After this, the lake turned dark and became polluted.

On the ride back to Lhagyal, I reflected on the grandeur of the cave, but was saddened by the despoiled lake. There were many farewells, and my husband was indeed grateful for the hospitality we receive at Lhagyal. The monks were equally pleased with the religious services he performed. He thus gave a special tea ceremony called *manga*, and his photo, money, and a white scarf were distributed to each of the monks. Lhagyal monks had seen the monastery host hundreds of visitors during our stay in Kham. By custom, our quarters were kept furnished, just as though we had left only for a day's outing.

The day before our departure, there was some unhappiness. The monks said, in effect, that since there were four Sakya males in our family—my husband, our two boys, and my husband's brother, Trinly Rinpoche—one should stay at Lhagyal. We said no to their request, but explained that if conditions changed, one of the four would come back to eastern Tibet.

Chagotobdan asked us to stay on at Lhagyal. He apparently

felt that we would be safer here because of his relationship with the Chinese and that no such protection would be afforded us when the Communist takeover came to western Tibet. We declined for many reasons, but getting home to Sakya was foremost in our minds. So instead, Chagotobdan, accompanied by his family, came to arrange our transportation to Lhasa. The first leg of the journey, with several stops, would be from Manikhingo to Chamdo.

In many ways I was happy to leave, even though I had made friends here and it seemed like home. When we departed that winter morning in late 1956, many of the monks were tearful. Hundreds of them rode on horseback with us to Manikhingo, where we boarded a bus and truck. The bus was laden with white scarfs. Driving into the lake area, we had the driver stop for a last look. As we moved into the nomadic areas, people put money in the scarfs and tossed them toward the bus. Minzu-la and I gave the scarfs back—or tried to—as we passed along. The nomads were very noisy and excited.

Our first major stop was a visit of several days at Derge Monastery. We stayed at the adjacent palace of the Derge queen, who was away at Jamda. Her son, about seventeen, had joined the guerrilla fighters in the hills. The Communist Chinese were forcing her to appear at meetings in Jamda and were generally using her for propaganda work. I felt great sadness for her. Derge Gonchen Monastery reminded me of Dartsedo, as it was surrounded by mountains. Juniper trees were visible everywhere from the palace. But in the estates around the town, many foodstuffs were grown.

A year earlier we had ordered a set of religious texts from the big printing house here. Forty boxes of books had been sent to Lhagyal, to be taken home to Sakya in the care of Phuba Tsering, who had left Lhagyal about a month before us. Not all of the horses and mules were used as pack animals, but those that were carried our books, brick teas, silks, grain, and nonbreakable and nonperishable items. The books were wrapped first in cloth and then placed in wooden boxes and finally wrapped in waterproof heavy yakskin.

Some of the horses were owned by servants and horse-keepers. Horses were much cheaper in Kham and would bring a good price in Sakya. However, some planned to keep the animals for themselves.

The Chinese taxed everything that went into the Derge printing house and had closed some parts of it. Known for its accuracy in the production of religious books, it was now operated by about thirty monks. Earlier, hundreds had worked here. The paper received from the Chinese was no longer of top quality. They saw the monks as nonproductive and even took a dim view of the food taken to the monks there. Understandably, it now took longer to have orders filled, and the printing house wasn't open as many days a week.

I was impressed with the operations, nevertheless, as I watched the production lines. The printing was done with wood blocks and roller presses. Both sides of pages were used. As the pages were completed, they were placed on nearby tables to dry. For the better books, the pages were made smooth with a large conch shell. Usually the leaves were edged with red or yellow ink. Good books had a drawing of the Buddha or a bodhisattva, on the first, second, or last page. Best books had wooden covers. Titles were printed in both Sanskrit and Tibetan.

In one section of the three-story printing house, the wood blocks were stored in long, orderly lines. Half a dozen carvers were hard at work. I tried my hand at carving, which was done with two special knives.

Our anxiety rose as we prepared to leave for Jamda and Chamdo, for the Tibetan guerrillas were attempting by every means to halt Chinese activities along the twisting roads through the mountains. Our four Chinese drivers shared our concern, as many vehicles had been lost and the drivers and passengers killed. They knew the Tibetans were good shots, aiming at gas tanks and tires. Before leaving Lhagyal Monastery, we had been required to guarantee the safety of our drivers and vehicles. Now we began seriously to question our own safety. We did our best to get the word out that the Sakya party would be passing through the troubled area. When we left Derge, we placed on both of our vehicles huge yellow flags with the letter "S," for "Sakya," inscribed in vivid red. We set out, traveling southwest, crossing a bridge over the Jamda River. There had been fighting here. Chinese guards were stationed on both ends of the bridge and traffic was single file. Tibetans here said that when you crossed this bridge, you were in their territory.

This was one of the most hazardous phases of our travels in eastern Tibet. Because of the great numbers of incidents, the Chinese had stopped much of the traffic on this route. This was the first time traffic had been allowed through this area in some months. But we were in the position of going now or never, as we knew conditions would not improve.

The nervousness of our four drivers, who were assigned two to a vehicle, did nothing to calm us. Ordinarily one drove and the other rode in the back of the vehicle, but now they were both up front.

"Show your lama's robes and red and yellow garments," the drivers chorused. "If ever, this is the time to show them."

A maroon monk's robe was put on the outside of the truck to attract attention. Many members of our party were afraid. Trinley and some other monks were praying, as were my mother and Aunt Chacha. I held Ani-la, and Minzu-la was comforted by Tsegen-la. Dagchen Rinpoche was seated in the back of the truck. Our orders were not to stop unless absolutely necessary.

Then Yeshe Gyatso, our ace interpreter, heard a rumbling sound and our driver braked to a halt. Up ahead huge rocks had been rolled onto the road. The Tibetan guerrilla fighters had certainly seen our convoy and taken it to be Chinese!

"Go out," a driver scolded to the monks. "Tell your people. Your people did this."

Afraid for their lives, the drivers insisted that we all get out and display ourselves to prove that we were Tibetans. Dagchen Rinpoche was in white robes, and the Chinese literally pushed him out. A few of us walked around some rocks to a higher spot where we would be in full view. The rest of the party began to move the rocks out of the road. One of the Sakya monks insisted on standing in an open space, waving his bright orange jacket in an attempt to communicate our identity. He was slightly deaf and at times found it convenient not to hear.

We knew the guerrillas were hidden nearby, but we heard no shots. Meanwhile we were filled with frustration and fear. Apparently, however, we had been seen and identified by our countrymen. We kept trying to calm the drivers, fearing that if we were captured by the guerrillas that the drivers would try to kill themselves.

It was an hour before enough rocks were rolled away and a narrow passage was cleared for our vehicles. The drivers didn't want to tarry a moment longer. They drove like maniacs over the narrow, bumpy roads as darkness approached. Yeshe Gyatso urged them to slow down, but they pressed on. Some of these mountainsides were so steep I felt sure that if we went over the edge our bodies would never be found. Many times the road was only wide enough for one vehicle. At every curve, our drivers would honk their horns repeatedly.

Meanwhile our two boys were crying. Many of the passengers still were praying fervently. Aunt Chacha looked like a corpse, she was so terrified and carsick. We had brought tea and milk in vacuum bottles, along with dried meat and cookies. But we had neither time nor inclination to eat. We were traveling downhill much of the time now. We passed a number of Chinese road-building camps. When we stopped for gas, we stayed in our vehicles. There were no more road blocks and we arrived in Jamda at about ten-thirty, completely exhausted.

It was very dark and there were very few lights on in the town. We woke the dogs, who barked and snapped at us. Yeshe Gyatso found us lodging in a Chinese barracks. We were happily reunited with the Derge queen. Tonight she was so happy to see us that she stayed overnight in the hut, even though we slept on straw mats full of bedbugs.

It was sad to say farewell to this kind woman in the morning. Her son, who was in hiding with the guerrillas, had very much wanted to come into town to see us, but my husband advised against it. We departed, the queen hoping desperately that the Chinese would send her on a propaganda mission to Lhasa in the next year.

We set out through another strife-torn and dangerous area. It was mostly flat, though we had to cross some mountain passes. The drivers were worried, but they knew that the Tibetan people had faith in us and would not harm us intentionally. Nevertheless, they asked for an escort and eight Chinese trucks joined our group, several of them carrying Chinese troops. The guns on some of these trucks were loaded and ready for action. Our two vehicles were placed first and last in the convoy. Both still were flying the big red Sakya flag.

The Chinese undoubtedly thought this would increase their chances of safe passage. En route, we saw results of earlier fighting at the site of a chöten in the center of a canyon where three roads converged. We saw two damaged trucks, their gas tanks and tires riddled with bullets. The trucks had been part of a convoy of forty that had attempted the trip from Jamda to Chamdo a few days before we left Lhagyal Monastery. Only two trucks got through. The rest of the drivers were killed and their cargoes stolen. We had heard that six Tibetans and about one hundred sixty Chinese had died.

About an hour out of Jamda we heard shooting in the distance. Our two drivers began arguing as to which of our vehicles would go ahead, the truck or the bus. It was decided that the truck would remain in the lead.

Trinly Rinpoche was fearful and said simply: "Don't talk. Pray to the White Tārā." Aunt Chacha, always carsick, was sitting up bravely. Yeshe Gyatso and my husband's servant joked and observed that "When you are carsick, the medicine you need is Chinese and fighting." We prayed aloud together in the bus. In Minyag our drivers had complained about our prayers, but this time they urged us to continue. We learned later that the sounds we had heard were not guns at all but Chinese roadworkers blasting with dynamite.

That afternoon we stopped at a small town, again mostly inhabited by construction workers. We were sure that any Tibetans here worked for the Chinese. Once again our party was the center of attention. Admittedly, Minzu-la and Ani-la were cute in their orange lamas' robes. Some of the Chinese were amazed that we were traveling with small children in such a dangerous area. We bought charcoal and food from a Chinese restaurant and made a fire and cooked our tea outside. Two of the armed trucks were sent on ahead.

After a hard day of travel we stayed the night in another barracks in Moncom. The next morning we arose at five o'clock for an early start. That afternoon on the Tsawa Pass, we stopped for lunch at a construction workers' camp. In the camp there was a four-story lookout tower from which the Chinese could see for miles around. We saw two trucks that had been shot up by guerrillas.

While our drivers rested, Yeshe Gyatso and another monk went walking. Inside the tower they saw a number of Chinese wounded, lying on cots. Later Yeshe Gyatso learned in a conversation he overheard in a restaurant that there were many more wounded here. Apparently the men had received their wounds while riding in the two damaged trucks, which were the very same ones who had gone on ahead of us the day before. The Tibetans had found their mark while the trucks were several miles out of Tsawa Pass, and the vehicles had limped back into the town, their gas tanks leaking. This incident made my husband and me more afraid than we had been at any time since leaving Lhagyal. But our fears were needless, fortunately, for the next part of our journey was peaceful, and we saw no more of the Tibetans' destructive handiwork.

The next day we stopped for a scenic respite at the big

bridge over the Gyama Ngu River. It was built over a deep gorge, and as we gazed down on the swift waters below our minds temporarily turned from the hazards of traveling through a battle zone. The road continued along the edge of steep cliffs, where there were frequent rockslides. The drivers now maneuvered slowly. Then, Chamdo came into view and we thankfully ended a trip that we would never forget.

The Communist Chinese had been in Chamdo, a big trading center and crossroads, since 1950. Earlier the Dalai Lama's soldiers and a Tibetan government unit had been quartered here, but the facilities had long since been taken over by the Chinese Army. Despite such conditions, we had a pleasant stay. We were housed in a hotel built around a large courtyard. The hotel was operated by Chinese, with mainly Tibetan help. Dozens of tents were pitched in the courtyard, and it was noisy and teeming with people sporting an array of costumes—Chinese, Lhasan, Khampa, and nomad. Some of our party also elected to live in the tents. Food was dispensed from large metal caldrons in the center of the courtyards. A whistle blew the signal for the hotel guests to line up and squat in a circle to eat their food. Our servants brought our meals to our rooms, and some of our group ate in their tents. The day after our arrival, monks from the nearby Sakya Changra Monastery labrang brought us momos, cheese, meat, and vegetables, for which we were thankful.

That morning, as the drivers were preparing to leave for their trip back to Dartsedo, they came to my husband, asking him for the two Sakya flags that we believed had guided us safely from Lhagyal. "You don't need them," they said. "It is less dangerous if we keep them." But my husband firmly declined, stressing that the flags bore the sign of the Sakyapas. The drivers left and the flags subsequently turned up missing. We felt sure they had been stolen by the drivers. Trinly was very angry and wanted to relate the entire affair to Chinese officials, but one of the monks advised against it. "They'll punish the drivers," he said. He also pointed out that if

Khampa guerrillas caught the drivers with the flags, they would be in certain trouble.

We were in Chamdo over a week, delayed because of the arrangements for transportation. Getting two buses or trucks was not easy because we sought to charter them exclusively for our party. We were told that the delay was because of roads and bridges torn up by the Khampa skirmishes, but we knew better.

Two Chinese officials, one of whom my husband had met on his 1954 trip to China, invited the party to dinner. Making the excuse that Ani-la was ill, I didn't go. Among the guests was Lama Zhibala, the head of Chamdo Monastery, which we could see from our hotel. The monastery had come under the influence of the Chinese and there was some variance of opinion as to Zhibala's political allegiance. He had greeted us upon our arrival. He wore elaborate lama's clothes, but on his brocade sleeveless upper garment there were many Chinese pins, buttons, and insignia with Communist slogans and photos of Mao Tse-tung.

"Why is he wearing these?" I thought. I tried to avoid having doubts about lamas and monks. I was of the opinion that he was not pro-Chinese but had to cooperate with them in order to get food. Some five to six hundred monks lived in the monastery. Some of them were present at the dinner, so the Chinese seized the opportunity to expound their usual propaganda, my husband said. He was thankful that I hadn't attended.

The next evening our interest centered on the wedding of a Chinese couple, held in an auditorium on the first floor of the hotel. The bride was a schoolteacher. We surmised that much of the fanfare was designed to impress her students, about one hundred of whom attended the affair. Many of them were Tibetans. The Chinese often staged an event to entice youngsters and lead them further toward Communist activities and doctrine.

Many in the crowd could not get into the jam-packed room, so they gathered at the windows. Yeshe Gyatso lifted me up to see too. I wasn't impressed. The students were throwing rice and shouting congratulations in Chinese. It was not the usual Chinese wedding with a solemn family in attendance and fancy foods. Later a window was broken and the Chinese called a halt to the viewing by outside bystanders.

At last we were informed that we could have two trucks, which would be sent from Lhasa. I went shopping to get rid of our Chinese paper money before going to Lhasa, where the currency was different.

The night before we were to leave for Lhasa, a theft occurred. We had in our possession a total of seven pistols, which were approved on our travel permits and vouchers. One of these was a prize pistol, kept on a decorated gun belt that doubled as a money belt containing about three hundred sterling silver coins. My husband had put the pistols in the custody of Tsephel, a Minyag monk and interpreter, who placed the pistol and the belt under his pillow when he slept in his tent in the courtyard. The next morning the pistol was gone, along with the money belt. We believed the thieves were members of bands of juvenile delinquents that had emerged from Chamdo's growing population of lower-class, uneducated Tibetans, whom the Chinese had brought here from many parts of eastern Tibet. These youths were fed and clothed and taught Communist doctrine. Theft was a part of their lifestyle at this busy crossroads.

Later that morning as we prepared for departure, a number of Tibetans arrived and began to help load our belongings on the trucks. They were lugging them away enthusiastically when our cook scolded them and warned them not to touch anything. I saw no reason to be unkind to these people and told the cook "let them help."

We left about nine-thirty A.M. A lama from Derge, his niece, and servant—all of whom had been waiting three months for a truck—received my husband's permission to join us. The road to Lhasa was a better one; most of it had two lanes. However, when we started up a high pass on one rough section, one of the trucks slowed and made strange noises.

The drivers stopped and conferred. The two decreed that we were overweight because we had taken on extra riders.

"But each day our food supply will become lighter," Tsephel said. "We will give you extra pay."

Angrily the unfriendly lead driver said, "Tonight when we stop at a road camp near a hot spring, we must state our tonnage and it must not be over the limit."

I was worried because, if we truly were overloaded, they might insist we be delayed at the road camp. But Tsephel confidently assured me, saying, "All right, we will wait."

The driver intimated that it wouldn't be necessary to weigh the Sakya belongings—just the new passenger lama's party and their possessions. We continued on to the hot springs.

As it turned out, Tsephel discovered that a big box and a large bag of sugar were stored under the lead driver's seat in the truck. Tsephel pointed out to the driver the cache of goods.

"This," he said pointing to the sugar and box, "is making the truck overweight."

The driver, embarrassed and surprised that his secret was out, turned in disgust, mumbling under his breath. He lost his temper and threw a pair of pliers on the ground. The other drivers just looked at each other in disbelief.

"All right, forget it," the angry driver conceded. "Even if we are overloaded, we will take you."

Tsephel, however, argued and threatened the driver, saying, "We won't easily forget the trouble you caused us."

From this point on, all the drivers were very cooperative. They doubtless feared that we would report the incident. But we never would have done that.

When we arrived at the hot springs that night and looked for our specially crafted cooking utensils and our sterling silver teapot, they were gone. Then we recalled that I had handed that particular basket to a nomad with a shaved head who had helped us load in Chamdo. It was clear now why we had had so many offers to help at Chamdo. These helpers had been helping themselves. I apologized to the cook; he had been right all along.

We borrowed kitchen equipment from a Chinese camp and made the best of it in our barracklike lodgings. Some of the party forgot their worries and bathed in the hot springs.

Two days out of Chamdo we moved into the Kongpo area. It was forested here and the temperature was warmer. Fresh vegetables could be had year-round, as well as lots of nuts and dried fruits. The women and men here both wore pillbox-type hats, and the working people were attired in simple sheepskin clothing. Women also put makeup and markings on their foreheads and noses. The Chinese were engaged in logging here, and the lumber was sent to many parts of Tibet. The homes here resembled Western-style log cabins. Residents believed that the fitted logs would be the safest construction materials in this earthquake-prone area.

Wild monkeys were everywhere along the roads, many with their young on their backs. They chattered noisily and delighted in throwing nuts and pine cones at our trucks. Minzula begged our driver to stop so we could get a closer look.

In the town of Tamo, the Chinese officials said our guns were legal for passage but that our money was not, even though our travel permits clearly stated that we could take our Chinese silver pieces into Lhasa.

"You must change the silver for paper currency," said one Chinese official. "You can give us the silver and we will give you the proper amount in exchange when you get to Lhasa."

The silver coins had been issued under the Nationalist Chinese and the Communist were trying to get rid of them. Lhasa was using both kinds of money, although most merchants refused the Chinese paper money. We knew the silver was worth much more than the paper currency because it could be used in India, Nepal, and many parts of Tibet. When we protested, the official said, "We must discuss this with a higher official, then come back and check. If you take the coins, there is a limit on the number that each person can retain."

They didn't know we had seventeen boxes, each containing one thousand silver coins, in the trucks parked outside the installation. So they said they wanted to count our silver money. Yeshe Gyatso and Tsephel knew we were over the limit. They quickly went to work while the Chinese officials were conferring. Unbeknownst to me, they hid six of the boxes in our lodging.

When the Chinese returned and inspected the boxes, they found only eleven. "That amount is permissible," the official said.

But I was worried and stared quizzically at Tsephel. He ignored me. He knew the Chinese and could match their trickery. We were greatly relieved. After all, it was our own money.

We took the northeast approach to Lhasa, stopping near the big Ganden Monastery for lunch. We asked for water and a place to change our clothes at a nearby house, preferring to arrive in the holy city in more formal attire. On the road, we passed many Tibetans who were carting firewood into the city in horsedrawn wagons. It was sad, I thought, that these people had to eke out a living by such rugged means.

It had been four-and-a-half years since we had been here, and the changes were nearly unbelievable. New buildings were everywhere. Lhasa in effect had become ringed by new Chinese structures. There were several bridges over the Kyi River (a tributary of the Tsangpo) where none had been before, and there were guards on each. We saw new road signs and electric cables. Despite all these changes, Lhasa still had the flavor of home.

We stayed in a relative's big home in downtown Lhasa; the first floor of our building was made up of shops. Our rooms on the third floor were not adequate, so we pitched a tent on the roof. Our plan was to stay in Lhasa until we could get trucks from the Chinese to go to Shigatse.

The Dalai Lama was not in residence in the Potala, having gone to India to attend the celebration of the 2500th anniversary of the Buddha's birthday, accompanied by the Panchen Lama and Tanjiwu, the Chinese administrator in Lhasa.

Many Khampas and Lhasa residents were on hand to greet us upon our arrival. We said hurried thanks to the drivers, including the lead driver, who seemed in a great rush— probably to sell his Chamdo goods. Prices had risen as much as fourfold. Even butter and fuel were hiked in price. There was higher pay, too. Three Chinese officials and an interpreter came to pay their respects, so to speak, to my husband and our party. They said that they were glad that we had made it safely from Kham and alluded to the "treacherous" acts of the Tibetans there.

Following custom, we visited the Jokhang, the holy temple, the day we arrived. Since we were so near, I could visit it easily each day. I visited all of the important shrines in the city, taking along melted butter in quantity, for each temple contained hundreds of butter lamps. I placed a small quantity of butter in each until my supply was exhausted.

In the temples there were more butter lamps glowing now, I felt, sensing a new devoutness brought on by the occupation of the Chinese.

Many Khampas who had formerly been in Kham, for example, gave their jewels in the holy temple. There were more Khampas than Lhasa residents in the Jokhang, it seemed. On many of my visits there, I saw people we had met on our trip to eastern Tibet.

There was a Sakya monastery here, Tingeling, which I also visited, and the beautiful Potala. From the Chagpori, the medical college, I looked down on the city and thought it had become too large and overpopulated.

One saw the traditional Lhasa headdresses. Aprons worn by women as a symbol that they were married were shorter now and not multi-colored. Traditionally, there were five or more colors for aprons. There also were few silk tassels braided into the hair. Indeed, young Tibetan girls wore ribbons or simple pieces of yarn of one color in their tresses. Many women now were not wearing coral necklaces. Makeshift charm boxes, without prayers, were smaller and from India, not Tibet. Charm boxes no longer contained turquoise, but rather drab stones. I was astounded to see that many Tibetan girls had cut their hair shoulder-length, Chinese-fashion, and were wearing bright-colored ribbons atop their heads. One saw many youngsters with the red ties at their necks that Chinese schoolchildren wear.

Chinese schools, in which the children learned both Tibetan and Chinese, had been established. They had Tibetan teachers, however. Formerly there had not been public schools in my country. Youth groups also were prominent.

Propaganda was rife. Lhasa now had a newspaper published twice weekly that printed world news with a pro-Chinese slant. These papers were tacked up at street intersections. The texts and captions were in Chinese and Tibetan. Those who could read stood at the intersections and read aloud to others. I confess I became very interested in the weather forecasts.

The Chinese officials used microphones around the city, blasting out propaganda. Loudspeakers blasted forth at the corners near the Jokhang, the holiest site in Tibet. "Khampas are like Americans," was among their sayings. The Chinese used the Tibetan words "*logchodpa,*" meaning "those who have perverse conduct." Whenever there was a lecture, there were cheers for Mao Tse-tung, the Dalai and Panchen Lamas, and the Chinese people.

Our party was asked to attend a number of movies, but we went to only one. Staying home proved a particularly judicious move one evening. Some of the family had wanted to go to this particular film, but my husband said no. He was busy getting things ready for the trip home to Sakya and had no desire to go. About ten o'clock, we heard shooting at the theater, about three blocks from the Jokhang, and the next day learned of a tragedy there.

It seemed there were several guards at the entrance to the theater. A Khampa who did not have a ticket had wanted to go inside, but a guard had told him to wait. The Khampa objected and started to scuffle, and the guard fired several shots at him. Standing behind the Khampa were a woman and her son, about nine, both of whom were killed by the guard's bullets. Enraged, the Khampa shot the Chinese guard in the arm. The newspaper, of course, gave a detailed account of the Khampa's crime. He was jailed, but we never heard what happened to him.

Many nobles and some lamas now were taking salaries from the Chinese in payment for appearances at meetings which were mainly propaganda-oriented. The Chinese could see my husband's influence with Sakya followers and hoped to use him to get their views across to the people, so it was natural that they attempted to pressure him. Three days after we arrived in Lhasa, two Chinese officials came to our residence.

"What are your plans during your stay in Lhasa?" one asked politely. "Is there anything we can do to make you more comfortable?"

"I plan to be here two or three weeks, during which we expect to visit temples and monasteries and see a number of our relatives and friends," Dagchen Rinpoche said.

The Chinese replied that he must visit higher Chinese officials here to discuss what role he would have at their meetings and to actually observe some of the propaganda meetings. We were in effect back home now, they stressed. My husband balked—politely.

"I'm busy with my own religious duties, having just arrived here," Dagchen Rinpoche said, "But I will visit the officials one day."

Soon after, we went to a dinner party at the Chinese government headquarters. At the reception before dinner, my husband was surprised by one official's statement.

"We began paying you a salary for two months while you were at Lhagyal Monastery when we learned you were coming home," the official said. "It's not much compared to your qualifications, but it will be increased later."

Dagchen Rinpoche said he would not accept the funding, saying he had performed no work. But the official said the money was waiting at the home of the Sakya representative, Batsa, in Lhasa.

My reaction was, "Who gave permission for this salary? Why are you paying when we haven't done any work?"

"We knew you were returning," one official said. He appeared annoyed that a woman was making such queries. He responded but looked directly at my husband.

"All government officials, nobles, and prominent lamas are accepting salaries," he said. "You won't have to do any special work, just occasionally attend important meetings."

After the dinner, an official said they would contact us again. The next day Dagchen Rinpoche told Batsa to return the money to the Chinese. He later tried, but the Chinese would not accept it. Batsa urged us not to worry about the salary. Later we made arrangements for two trucks to take us to Shigatse. We accepted the money given Batsa to pay for the two trucks.

Two officials and their interpreter returned to our residence for a farewell appearance and again pressured my husband about the meetings.

Dagchen Rinpoche said that he had no time for appearances at later meetings, that he had too many religious duties to perform. He had been away almost five years and he had to catch up with monastery affairs, he explained.

In the back of his mind was that he wanted to finish the Lay-Rim, the equivalent of the final examination and graduation in the Sakya school of religious studies.

The Chinese again were not satisfied. Their objective was to show that respected and trusted Tibetans were taking salaries and that others would follow suit.

Even my husband's brother and officials of the Drolma Palace in Sakya were taking the salaries, the Chinese said. We had not been aware of this. That is when my husband accepted the salary money to pay for the renting of the trucks.

We chose a new route to Shigatse that took us west over high mountains and the Yangpachen country. It was a good road and the drivers were cooperative, stopping when we requested. The Chinese had built an airport just off this highway near Nam Tso.

Both Ani-la and Minzu-la were not feeling well on the eve of our departure. Ani-la was coughing and feverish; we took turns holding him. There was much to see along the way, including white rocks that lined the road for miles in some spots, put there in honor of the Dalai Lama on his way to India. These white rocks are found in many parts of my country. Nomads gathered them and placed them on both sides of the road as a sign of welcome to prominent lamas. Such rocks had been placed in honor of Dagchen Rinpoche in Kham, but the rocks usually were off the main thoroughfare near a monastery or town, not on a main highway.

Intermittently along the road we passed tents housing Chinese and Tibetan construction workers. We rented three of these tents for one overnight stay. It was very cold and windy and the tents had a sand floor. The nearest water was a mile away. The Chinese buildings nearby were a fort, a medical station, and a restaurant for the airport patrons, which we had not seen before.

The next day we left at three A.M., without breakfast, because the drivers emphasized the long day ahead. They drove fast over the bumpy roads. The boys still were not feeling well.

That afternoon we asked the drivers to stop so we could hold a special service at the spot at which Uncle Kuyak had died at the home of a nomadic family. We walked about a mile from the road to the family's big tent. Several hundred feet from here was the spot where Uncle Kuyak had been cremated. Aunt Chacha always had wanted to see the place where he passed on. Blessed mandala sand and holy water were tossed on the spot by her and several monks. She was greatly relieved when this last rite was performed, as was I. She also collected a little soil from the spot where he was cremated, to be placed at pilgrimage holy sites. This was to help the deceased attain a speedy and favorable rebirth.

The nomad family brought us warm milk, cream, cheese,

yogurt, and meat, which we shared with the drivers. Our party would have liked to spend the night here, but the drivers were fearful they would be observed by other passing vehicles. They had been instructed to stop for eating and sleeping only at recognized Chinese stations.

We had just got under way, starting up the Shogu Pass, the famous mountain pass between Lhasa and Shigatse, when one of the trucks broke down. It was very cold, with snow all around; our breath froze in the air. The ailing children were put in the other truck.

Never had I wanted tea so badly as we had had none yet that day. The dried grass under the snow was too wet to burn. Finally, we decided to use some of the woven bamboo mats that covered the bricks of tea in order to make a fire. That way we finally warmed enough water for one or two cups each.

Three hours passed and no one came. We prayed to the Buddha and White Tārā. Fortunately, we all were wearing our heavy fur-lined winter clothing.

Finally a truck appeared. Luckily it was from the same agency in Lhasa where we had rented our vehicles and the two drivers knew each other. The other driver had an extra fan belt, which was what we needed, and soon we were on our way. We felt our prayers had been answered, fortunately, for it was nearly sunset. The drivers too were amazed. We were terribly hungry, but we were so happy that we began to sing. On the summit we passed prayer flags and prayed, but did not stop. That evening we tented again in one of the Chinese stations.

The next day we crossed the Tsangpo in the identical place where nearly five years ago we had crossed in a yakskin boat. Now there was a ferry that held four trucks and was operated by a pulley. When a bell sounded, four or five men began pulling for the crossing. During the twenty-minute ride, we stood up in the truck. Once across and into the Tsedong area, we had lunch at a Chinese cafeteria-style restaurant.

Here we learned that on the way from Lhasa a number of

items had fallen off the truck. In them were more than three hundred silk scarfs, several yards of silk, a big brick of tea, and some of Aunt Chacha's clothes. Many were to be used as homecoming gifts. It was ironic, I thought, that we had specially selected most of these items in Chamdo and carried them across much of Tibet, only to lose them so close to home.

That evening we were greeted in Shigatse by my husband's second eldest sister, Kala, and many friends and other relatives. We had not seen Kala in nearly five years.

There were numerous changes here too. About half the population seemed to be Chinese. Here there didn't seem to be so much animosity between the monks and the Chinese. Oddly, I felt the city actually had a friendly attitude toward the Chinese, in great contrast to the general attitude of Tibetans in Lhasa.

Outside the city's east side, we saw the area which had been devastated by the flood in July of 1954. Tinge Lingka, the summer palace of the Panchen Lama, had been destroyed in the flood's wake. There was no zoo now. The Chinese had rebuilt the residence and had made a new bridge. We stayed here two weeks at the big home of a longtime family friend.

Then came our reunion with Phuba Tsering and his party of some twenty horsekeepers. They had arrived at the Sakya estates in Tsedong, northeast of Shigatse, about three weeks ahead of us. They too were anxious to see their loved ones at Sakya after a nearly five-year absence. They had started out a month ahead of us from Lhagyal Monastery and had made their way with the horses and mules on the northern route through Jyekundo and Nagchuka, north of Lhasa to Tsedong country. Because they had traveled through some isolated country, they had carried guns for protection. Even though they had the necessary travel permits, when they stopped at Chinese stations they frequently had been questioned.

Our three hundred yaks were to come in late fall. They would start out in summer from Kham, grazing on the way. It was not necessary to carry grain for them—they don't eat

it. Some of these beasts belonged to servants who had purchased them during their travels. Some persons had placed
orders for the animals when we left five years ago. They
would bring double their price in Sakya.

So the valuable books, silver pieces, religious works, saddles, and other items that had come this long way by truck
now were loaded on horses and mules for the trip home to
Sakya.

Minzu-la was much better now, but Ani-la was not in
perfect health. Many people were attracted to the boys and
were generous with toys. Ani-la was a cute boy, dark in
complexion, with long bangs.

We took a leisurely trip home, some seven days, during which
I got the mumps. I kept a scarf wrapped closely around my head
so my new facial shape wouldn't be so noticeable as we began the
homecoming ceremonies at the various towns. It was in Shap that
I had my first injection, given by the Tibetan monk doctor who
had come with us from Lhasa to treat the boys.

There were no Chinese in Shap, famous for its bread,
which now I didn't feel like eating. It was a glorious time,
with the townspeople dressed in their finery dancing all the
old familiar dances in our honor.

We also stopped at the Gonpagye Nunnery, where some
fifty nuns gave us what I considered their most elaborate
welcoming ceremony. They were attired in their best ceremonial hats and silver necklaces. These nuns, however, were
sad that my husband's former teacher was dead. Khanchen
often had taught there and also was generous in his support of
the nunnery. He was missed in many ways.

At Gara many officials and monks from Sakya came to greet
us. I wasn't much in the mood for greeting anyone, however.
To ride my horse was painful and when I attempted to eat I
couldn't chew. Soup was about the extent of my intake. I
would be so happy to get back home.

Gara is just on the western side of the northeast pass going
into Sakya. From here our party would ride in single file, the
monks wearing their ceremonial masks and costumes appropriate for such a homecoming.

13

Homecoming and Decision

Since I wasn't feeling well and indeed could barely stand up, I decided to make the trip into Sakya early in the morning under the cover of darkness, without official ceremonies. My husband and Minzu-la planned to arrive later with an official party of two hundred. I arose at about four o'clock and along with Ani-la, my mother, Wangmo, and a few others began the trip home down the pass. At the Drum River two men from Sakya arrived to help us. The river was dark, cold, and icy, and I couldn't see the small bridge without a flashlight. Before we finally found it, we fell through the ice and got wet. Even some of the horses went in deep and had to be pulled out.

As we approached the Phuntsok Palace, I could see lights and the soft glow of butter lamps burning in the Gold Room. Wangmo's uncle, Tsechag, the monk in charge, was expecting us. Nearing the summer palace, the recent home of my late mother-in-law and Trinly Rinpoche, I looked for her room. I felt her presence as though she were still alive. She had been such a powerful figure that life at Sakya would seem strange without her.

Tsechag had told the personal household servants, but not

the animal keepers and other palace staff, that I was coming. The personal servants met us at the door, beaming ecstatically. Mastiffs barked endlessly at the "strange" visitors, prompting an old cook to scold, "Don't bark! This is your owner!" All of the servants presented Ani-la and me with scarfs, which I politely returned. Tsechag informed them that I was not too well, which was obvious.

One of my first acts was to visit the Gong Khang, the palace protector's shrine room, in which were kept many religious items designed to ward off evil. Included was the Lhamo, a larger-than-life statue of a female deity of terrific aspect, famous for her bloody and licentious deeds, but at the same time a constant and redoubtable champion of Buddhism. I was depressed to see this sacred place in such a state of disrepair. The statue needed new garments. The ceiling covering of brocade cloth was almost falling away, possibly due to dampness. "We have to get busy immediately with renovations," I thought, and went to my room. The other palace rooms were resplendent with decorations for our homecoming. We had breakfast, and some of the happiness of previous days returned.

My husband and Minzu-la arrived at about ten o'clock, having taken a circuitous route off the pass, as it was not good luck on such an occasion to make the direct descent. By custom, we believed that direct descent on such an important day would imply an inauspicious decreased activity in one's future life. To ascend, however, signifies increased benefits and fame. Minzu-la was old enough to realize that he was home, that place he had heard so much about but had never seen. His grandfather's servant had been coaching him about life in the palace.

People began greeting the party, presenting scarfs and welcoming remarks, near the Great Temple. Monks led the way, some with masks, others with bells, trumpets, and drums. A pair of large colorful Tashi Taring, or silk welcoming-banners, hung from the palace roof down to the courtyard. Minzu-la was afraid of masks, still, so my husband held

him firmly on their horse. The boy was happy and in a
rejoicing mood.

There followed a reception in the big throne room of the
palace. All of the traveling party attended, along with some of
their families. Each one received desee, sweets, cookies, dried
fruit, and other food to take home. The party lasted about an
hour, and many of the guests had to stand up because it was
so crowded. I longed for privacy, but I thought that as it was
my last day of such formal ceremonies for a while, I must
attend. I wore my great headdress, the one that weighed at
least twenty-five pounds, but covered my neck with a scarf.
Some of the people apparently had the impression that I must
have been happy in Kham because I was getting fat, which
was considered a compliment. In our traveling group, those
who had wanted to return earlier from eastern Tibet said my
mumps were an indication of the Lhamo's anger; she too
preferred our earlier return.

Later that same day, Sakya government officials again came
to visit, bringing gifts of chang, tea, meat, and even horse
fodder. There also were greetings and gifts from the Drolma
Palace, even though the official family was not in residence at
the time.

In the next few days, however, there seemed little time to
rest. Fortunately I was improving slowly. Many people came
to ask about Kham, particularly about the encroachment of
the Chinese, who had not yet made a strong impact here in
Sakya. They had bought one residence, at which a doctor and
his attendants were stationed. But no army or government
official had been permanently assigned here at this time.

About three days after my return, I plunged into the
routine of active palace duties. I soon discovered that, even
though my mother-in-law had been living in the summer
palace and away from immediate activities before we left for
Kham, I had relied upon her advice more than I realized.
When I looked across to the summer palace, I felt a deep loss
and sadness. Something of the old tradition and solidarity of
the Sakya family was gone forever.

My mother and Aunt Chacha, however, were of great help to me. With Uncle Kuyak gone, Aunt Chacha felt at home here.

It was becoming more evident that Minzu-la indeed was the incarnation of his paternal grandfather. Many of the former Trichen's belongings were stored near the Gold Room. Without being told, Minzu-la knew exactly where these things were, saying, "These are mine," and so forth.

With the lunar New Year only about two weeks away, we were very busy. This year, all agreed, the celebration must be bigger than usual, more like the extended observances that we had seen in Kham. My husband rose early on several successive days to repair the Lhamo statue with the aid of two monks. A new set of clothes for the statue was made by Tsewangyal, our tailor, and the shrine cleaned.

I began inspecting the storerooms to see how much food was left. Everywhere I looked supplies were depleted. Barley, wheat, peas, and tsampa reserves all were low, and I worried. Workers got better food and wages. There simply were not enough reserves to keep the palace operating. At the same time we were compelled to make considerable outlays in the form of gifts in making the rounds of the temples of Sakya. The gift-giving was a form of repayment to those who had been generous to us upon our departure for Kham. Now it was our turn to give them something from eastern Tibet.

Records were kept of who got what, with silk and tea being the main gifts. I had purchased a number of bolts of silk in Chamdo, some with religious designs on them; many of these went for presents.

As for the temples, each was visited by all who had made the trip to Kham as a gesture of gratitude to the protectors for a safe arrival home. My husband led prayers in every one of the temples. Meanwhile Phuba Tsering and the rest of the horsekeepers took turns getting a little vacation, except when we visited the temples.

It was 1957 and the year of the Fire Bird was about to begin. The jewel-encrusted flowers from China were displayed, and the work of the Derge smiths was shown for the first time. Sixteen Arhat tankas, each telling the story of a learned Buddhist teacher, and all hand-embroidered and of excellent quality, were placed in the visitors' room—the scene of a party. These tankas had been purchased in Peking and had been embroidered by the great ladies of old China. The sixteen Arhats were famous elders who taught the dharma in the various mythical islands and continents of the Buddhist cosmogony. A later tradition holds that they were invited to China from India by Princess Wen-cheng Kung-chu, daughter of Emperor T'ai-tsung.

About one hundred fifty guests attended our observance, beginning at noon on New Year's Day. It was truly a joyous occasion; we had not seen many of these people for so long. For the first time we had a public-address system, which had been purchased in India by Trinly Rinpoche. Records were played, and the music was piped outdoors for all within earshot.

As the evening wore on, a number of guests had their turn at the microphone, including a thirteen-year-old monk who gave a little talk on Buddhism that some found amusing. Other guests were wary of the microphone, associating it with the Chinese.

Before I knew what was happening, guests were requesting that I make some remarks. Too shy to face them directly, I stepped inside the next room where I could not be seen. When I touched the microphone, the mouthpiece was damp with saliva because those before me had spoken too closely into the mouthpiece. I had to wipe my hands on my fancy apron.

Somehow finding courage, I spoke greetings of the season, thanked the guests for coming, and wished them long life and happiness. I then added a short Buddhist prayer. It was my first experience with a microphone.

It was one of the last happy New Years in Sakya, and long remembered by those who attended.

Several weeks later the Dalai Lama and his party returned home from India and my husband and his brother went to

Shigatse to greet them. While Dagchen Rinpoche was away, we began preparing for Torgyak, an annual religious celebration in the third month, when all monks come to the Phuntsok Palace for the reading of the *Kanjur*, the sacred one-hundred-eight volumes, plus commentaries on the *Kanjur*, bringing the total to one hundred thirty. The palace was generally refurbished. All of the curtains were replaced and the windows were cleaned to a shining brilliance.

A highlight of Torgyak was the monks' dances, for which dozens of costumes had to be made. Some complicated costumes were of lions, deer, and birds, their feet attached. Each dancer also carried symbolic hand implements that had either to be newly made or redecorated. Of the hundred-forty-six costumes used in the Torgyak, we were remaking seventy that had been in use for over fifty years and were ragged and torn.

Although I hadn't had a good rest since my homecoming, I threw myself into supervising the costumery. Tsewangyal and his staff of ten assistants worked all day and late into the evening to create outfits that by tradition dated back several generations. My late father-in-law had mentioned many times the necessity of remaking these costumes and, in fact, it had been his dream to accomplish this. He had brought back a great deal of silk from India for this project but had then taken ill.

While my husband was gone, a delegation of Chinese came to Sakya for some sort of special observance and for the general expansion of Communism in the area. There were plans for a school, and the Chinese were recruiting Tibetan children for it. A Chinese-run school had been tried earlier and failed—or in any case had closed.

Four of these men came to the palace while my husband was away, merely to pay a call on him, they said. Their interpreter was a well-dressed Tibetan woman who was the daughter of a Sakya blacksmith. She had never been inside the palace before. In central and western Tibet, the caste system was still strong. Butchers and blacksmiths were at the bottom of the caste. We did not mix with them socially. When

I greeted my visitors, the men directed the interpreter to sit down first on a high cushion. Tsechag, our treasurer, was shocked at this purposeful discourtesy. I motioned him not to make a fuss.

After the usual polite conversation, they asked, "When will your husband return?"

"Two or three weeks," I said.

"When we come back, we hope we can see Dagchen Rinpoche," one said.

Two of the four were young soldiers in uniform and were in their early twenties. Their faces seemed to say, "I was commanded to come to Tibet. I don't want to be here. And I'm homesick." I was saddened and felt sorry for them. Their farewell handshakes also reflected their unhappiness at this duty. When the group departed, they left propaganda pamphlets with photos of Mao and Stalin.

There was no question of getting to know these Chinese individually. The workings of their establishment were not well known to us. The closest real headquarters station, where troops were assigned, was at Lhatse, north of Sakya, which also had a telegraph. Groups of Chinese would come in the night to this building at Sakya, which was not far from the Great Temple, and then would leave early in the morning. Our guess was that there were about ten Chinese now assigned to the building at Sakya, but we believed most of them moved on to Mustang, a small remote realm in northwestern Nepal that once was part of Tibet and thus ethnically Tibetan. There were Sakya monasteries in Mustang.

The costumemaking had been under way about ten days when the Chinese asked to borrow one of our two sewing machines and some of our sewers. The Chinese said they were making school outfits for fifteen boys and girls of Sakya. All of us knew, however, that they were only attempting to foil our preparations for Torgyak. They could have easily obtained a sewing machine at Shigatse had they chosen to. Not wishing to anger anyone or cause trouble, especially when my husband was away, I said I would reply later.

One of our machines was not working well and I knew we would never finish so much sewing without the best machine, so I decided to decline both requests. Tsechag, who was fearful of Chinese retaliation, was sent to their headquarters with a scarf and message which said in part that there were other tailors in Sakya who might help the Chinese.

But the Chinese kept up their asking, even visiting Tsewangyal at his home and requesting him to work. The pressure eventually became so great that I gave up our good machine and five of the sewers.

Knowing that our sewing staff was depleted, about a dozen monks from the monastery came to the palace to volunteer their services. They were excellent workers, sewing by hand. They prayed and chanted while they sewed. They felt they were doing something for Buddhism in helping us. I arranged excellent meals for this crew.

Meanwhile, my husband returned and was pleased both with the progress on the costumemaking and my attempts to deal firmly with the Chinese.

The celebration began and the tailor-monks who had been assisting us worked up to the final fifth day of the event, when the dancing occurred. Some of these monks would attend the prayer services and reading of the *Kanjur*, then would rush back to help us. We barely made the deadline.

We also renovated the Gong Khang, which was adjacent to our palace. The temple housed many statues and images, including a mask of Palden Lhamo, consort of Mahākāla, a great wrathful protector of Buddhism. Palden Lhamo also is the wrathful emanation of Green Tārā and Sarasvati, Goddess of Learning—the latter for both Hindus and Buddhists. The statue had flaming red hair topped with a solid gold crown of skulls encrusted with turquoise, coral, and rubies. Some of the turquoise had belonged to my late mother-in-law and was very old and rare.

The mask was believed to have been made by a member of the Khön lineage. According to Sakya history, the Khön ancestors descended to earth from what is known as the Clear

Light Divine Abode. Three brothers settled in a pure and high land, Ngari, in western Tibet. One brother remained and my husband was a direct descendant of this distinguished emanation of Mañjushrī, the Bodhisattva of Wisdom; Avalokiteśvara, the Bodhisattva of Compassion; and Vajrapāṇi, who in his wrathful manifestation, is the chief tantric deity.

The mask was a sacred relic used only for the Torgyak dancing. The rest of the year the mask was kept in a glass case as the focal point of the Gong Khang. The ritualistic footwork was performed by an accomplished monk deemed worthy of the honor and responsibility.

The temple also contained a statue of the Lhamo seated on a red mule, her legs dangling. Attached to her saddle was the scalp of an enemy of religion.

My chores in the temple restoration involved carefully cleaning the silk clothing on the statues, making new tassels where needed, and arranging the jewelry and replacing any damaged parts.

Repairing the Palden Lhamo was particularly stressful work because it involved a wrathful deity. I wore a mask and a white apron. My hands and fingernails were clean and I could not touch anything else while working on the statue. I did not want to contaminate the Lhamo because the retinues might harm me or other devotees for improper service. My work was comparable to that of a surgeon doing an operation, I felt. The tedious work required that my mind be sincerely motivated. Despite the stress, I enjoyed the tasks of performing a service for a good cause. We all felt great accomplishment in completing this project. Among our contributions to the Torgyak ceremony at this time, besides payments to monks, was the presentation of eight silk banners for the posts in the Great Temple. These huge banners, containing embroidered decorations, were each at least thirty feet long. They were a very handsome addition to the temple.

The main Torgyak event, with the dancing, was held in the palace courtyard. It was a cold day, but my husband and I were genuinely pleased with our efforts. My husband had fulfilled his father's wish. And many of the people of Sakya expressed gratitude for the restoration.

Among my favorite performers were five small boys, all under ten, who danced in costumes that included necklaces and bracelets and hats with multicolored feathers. They were paying homage to the Buddha by twirling a drum and displaying other implements as an offering of music.

The torma, the offering made of tsampa and decorated with colored butter, was placed facing east this year because of the Chinese, for the purpose of warding off influences harmful to Buddhism. During the celebration, Chinese visitors took many photos of the audience and the dancing monks.

About a week before the Torgyak ceremonies, the Chinese had opened their school. The teachers were Tibetans. About thirty children, outfitted in their new uniforms, greeted the Chinese officials who had come from Shigatse for the occasion; from the palace I watched this ceremony as the officials filed between two lines of the youngsters.

The school was in a mansion near downtown Sakya formerly owned by a Sakya noble. The Chinese boasted that the curriculum included not only Chinese language, but reading and writing in Tibetan. Actually, through this instruction, the children were learning all about Communism. Children of our palace workers could have asked to go to the school, but none did. Some Sakya nobles' children, however, were sent.

After the Chinese school had been open for only a month, the children were sent home. It was all part of a carefully laid scheme. The Chinese had given clothes and gifts to the Tibetan children. Now a little vacation would give the youngsters time to think and want to come back to classes.

Meanwhile, feelings against the Chinese were mounting. During the Chinese New Year some monks had spat on decorations put up by the Communists at several spots in town. One Chinese official was stoned by a monk when he tried to lecture in the downtown area.

The early spring was brightened by the arrival of the Lhamo Tapkhen, a folk opera group from Lhasa who gave three days of performances at the palace, portraying events of religious and historical significance. These performances took place in the palace courtyard and were long affairs, usually lasting from about nine o'clock in the morning to six in the evening, with time out for eating. People brought their lunches, and vendors sold cookies, tea, candies, fruits, and scarfs. Our family palace paid for the performances and fed and housed the visitors.

There was a cast of about fifty men and women, of whom Shago Tashi was the main actor and director. Shago was a star performer, as was his wife, Lhapa. He also was well known by the Chinese as he had played in Peking with the troupe.

Admittance was free and monks and the citizenry of Sakya and towns around came to these events. So did some of the Chinese assigned at Sakya.

When the performance ended, people threw white scarfs with money wrapped in them up on the stage. After the final performances our gifts, including food and money, were put on display in the courtyard.

My mother lived a full and busy life in the palace. She went on kora every morning for two hours, a two-mile trip around Sakya. I knew when she and Aunt Chacha were due home and always had hot tea waiting. By Tibetan custom, old people and young children spent more time in this religious activity. As the wife of a high Sakya lama, I was no longer permitted to make such public appearances. However, I had a rigorous schedule of religious activities inside the palace.

Ani-la was eighteen months old and was walking. He was a good-looking child with such fine features that many mistook him for a girl. Our precious second son, however, was frail. He developed a cough, often after playing, and sometimes vomited. His health varied from day to day, but he lost weight and soon didn't seem to have strength enough to walk. Minzu-la and Ani-la were close brothers. Minzu-la was very active, visiting his Uncle Trinly Rinpoche and generally having a good time. Ani-la wanted to follow, but just couldn't make it. His cough seemed to be about the same as it had been when we were at Parlhagong Monastery. What was probably near-pneumonia ensued.

Many monks and lamas were invited to continue prayers in his behalf, all seemingly to no avail. Our fears about Ani-la's health multiplied: our fortuneteller said that he might not live a long life. Visitors were forbidden in my room, where Ani-la's bed was placed adjacent to mine.

Ani-la's physician was Hosho Ajom, a doctor and high-ranking Derge noble who had fled after fighting there. It was his eventual goal to go to India. He had come with his family from eastern Tibet with few belongings. Most of the medicines he used were from the storeroom of drugs in our palace.

Then, measles struck. Some said it was because the gods were angry. I didn't go out of the palace for over a month. Ajom was very busy, as he was one of only three Tibetan doctors in Sakya. The Chinese doctor warned parents not to give their children chang when the youngsters complained of thirst from fevers. They said this would make a fever rise. But some parents did anyway, as chang commonly was drunk by children in Sakya. Luckily none of the children of palace workers were stricken, but dozens of other Sakya youngsters died. The disease also hit families of animal keepers at the Drolma Palace.

Sadly, we looked out from the palace to the mountain east of Sakya and saw the smoke from bodies being cremated. I felt frightened and wondered what we could do besides pray.

After the epidemic, the Chinese doctor gave vaccinations for smallpox. My late father-in-law had brought men from Gangtok every so often to give smallpox vaccinations in the entire area, but this had been discontinued after his death.

Meanwhile I had been busy dispensing medicines from our drug room as Ajom's work intensified. The Drolma Palace also had a drug supply, which was similarly available.

I enjoyed going to the drug room even though it was dark, eerie, and dusty. It was on the second floor and we had to use flashlights and a lantern. Its two windows were small and barred. Many of the boxes of drugs were dust-covered, having

been there for years. Eerie religious masks of deities hung on
the posts and walls of the room. These masks were stored
here because they were worn only by Sakya family sons in
their religious dancing. Their menacing faces, half hidden in
the shadows, always frightened me as I entered the room.
Tibetans believe that spirits dwell within any religious figure.

I loved to savor the smells of so many leaves, roots, seeds,
and sandalwood, the latter from Sining. It reminded me of
my childhood in Thalung.

I also had to grind the drugs. This was done in three
different fashions—with a mortar and pestle, with a stone
roller on a large stone, or between two millstones.

If a doctor said a patient needed medicine, then some
member of the patient's family would come to one of the
palaces. The herbs were taken back to the doctor, who then
mixed them. Often I didn't want to accept pay for the
medicine, but on many occasions the buyer would insist.
Some believed that the medicine would not be effective for
the patient if there were no payment.

Ajom tried many medicines on Ani-la, but none seemed to
work. The boy was growing increasingly weak and now had
to be carried. After some time Ajom confessed that his
knowledge of such a case was exhausted and suggested that
we try a Chinese doctor who was a children's specialist.

My husband and I were reluctant at first to summon the
Chinese doctor, but finally agreed it was necessary. A monk
was sent to request that the Chinese doctor "Please come to
the Sakya baby."

About four-thirty P.M. that same day a tall physician,
accompanied by a nurse and interpreter, came to the palace.
The physician was called by most Tibetans "Big Doctor."
Ani-la's eyes were closed and he cried little. It was extremely
difficult for him to breath.

"Who is your doctor?" the physician asked.

Ajom replied that he was the physician and that he had
tried everything. Big Doctor then asked me, "Will you show
this patient again to the Tibetan doctor?"

I replied that I would, that he was very accessible, living in our house. Big Doctor then said firmly, "No, you must choose—either him or me."

There was a pause.

"You must choose," Big Doctor repeated.

Ajom pleaded, "Don't choose me."

I began to relate the story of our trip to Dartsedo and added that "Ani-la has been better all through the year." Big Doctor became more friendly when he learned about Ani-la's stay in the Dartsedo hospital. I promised that Ani-la would be his patient only.

Big Doctor was distressed when he learned how high the boy's fever was. "Why didn't you tell us before?" he asked. "When nothing helps, then you come to us."

Medicine was administered, after being taken from a kind of portable medicine cabinet carried by the nurse, and a shot given. The doctor again reminded us not to give Ani-la any more Tibetan medicine, saying it was to blame for his continued ailment. The doctor did not tell us the boy's ailment, saying only that his fever was extremely high and that he was critically ill. It is the Tibetan custom to ask the seriousness of a patient's condition, but not to be concerned with the official name of the illness.

"We will do what we can," he said. "But we cannot be sure whether he will live."

Blood tests were taken and the doctor said a microscope was needed to analyze results. A request was made to the Chinese clinic at Lhatse, and two Tibetans quickly rode there astride Sengerapa, my horse, and Tsering Sernya, my husband's best horse.

Ani-la appeared a bit improved. Meanwhile word came that the Chinese were sending their best pediatrician from the hospital at Shigatse. After he arrived he used an oxygen mask on Ani-la. This was frightening to us as the obvious conclusion was that there was no breath left. Even though he had been riding all day and night from Shigatse, the new doctor stayed at Ani-la's side. He even helped prepare Ani-la's food—

a cereal mixed with boiled milk—and tasted it before feeding it to Ani-la. The physician told us he was under directives from the Panchen Lama and Chinese leaders in Shigatse to save this Sakya son. He was under tremendous pressure. He was at Ani-la's bedside for two nights, eating only a light supper and drinking Chinese jasmine tea, until the crisis passed.

The next day we were told that a blood transfusion would be necessary. Some of the family objected to using blood from someone outside the family, and others were afraid. Taking blood out of one person and transferring it to another was difficult for them to comprehend. The pediatrician first had to convince the family that the transfusion was an absolute necessity. He did this by showing us a book depicting many types of healthy and diseased blood. I volunteered for the transfusion, which turned out to be two instead of one. Taking blood from me was regarded with great seriousness by the family. Servants hovered outside the bedroom door, some in tears.

Ani-la began to improve and looked better. As the days passed, the pediatrician brought toys to the boy. The doctor had two sons of his own in Peking, he said. His wife also was a physician in Shigatse.

While at the palace, in their spare moments the Chinese were taking note of guns, bullets, radios, and other items of interest to them. They also noted an embroidered scroll given to the late Trichen by some Nationalist Chinese dignitaries. They read from documents on shelves and on the walls denoting strong connections between the Sakya family and past political regimes of China. They talked among themselves, but we could tell from their expressions that they were surprised at finding these political and religious links showing the high regard the Nationalist Chinese had for the Sakya leaders.

Ani-la continued to improve and the pediatrician left for Shigatse. We had offered him a fee, but he would take nothing, saying that was forbidden, that such work was only part of his job.

Meanwhile, a long neglected debt came to light, causing tension between the Phuntsok and Drolma palaces. Before we had gone to Kham, the Sakya government had received a large loan for renovation of the Great Temple at Sakya. When the Drolma Palace took over as the ruling house, the record of this debt had passed to their hands, like all other official documents. During our five years in Kham nothing had been done about it.

Two Lhasa government officials now came to Sakya saying that the debt must be paid. The Sakya government officials said that since there were not sufficient funds in its coffers, the Phuntsok and Drolma Palaces would have to help pay. The latter stated flatly that the debt was "not our business," having been incurred during the term of my late father-in-law.

A meeting was called, during which the Lhasa visitors again insisted the loan must be paid. My husband's representative said the Phuntsok Palace was not in a position to pay anything. He stressed that the Phuntsok Palace had spent a great deal during the construction and would like to account for these expenditures face-to-face with the Dalai Lama. The Phuntsok Palace and its estates had already spent considerable sums for part of the renovation. They had fed many persons during that time and had spent extensively, as was customary, after the Trichen's death.

The officials from Lhasa realized that they had hit a snag and returned home.

The debt renewed old problems between the two Sakya palaces. Thus my husband definitely made up his mind that he would go to the Dalai Lama to discuss both the debt and the succession to the title of Trichen. Many relatives and followers urged him to try to regain the title but he declined. My husband had discussed the topic with His Holiness when they were in Peking and again upon his return. But he wanted to be sure the Dalai Lama understood the historical precedent for the succession for future generations.

Before going to Lhasa, Dagchen Rinpoche wanted to complete one last period of instruction, the Lay-Rim. He buckled down to studying for the event that would climax in the eleventh month with ceremonies, dancing, prayer, and teaching.

The issue of the costs for renovating the Great Temple remained alive. Supplies in the palace were depleted. Many horses had been sold. The supplies on the estates also were diminishing. It was a bad omen if a new wife's supplies were depleted. Some persons, with hindsight, looked upon our trip to Kham with disfavor. But others declared it wonderful, for it brought two new Sakya sons.

The rivalry between the two palaces continued, especially because of the debt, but there was an attempt to be polite. We had presented gifts to members of the Drolma Palace upon our return from Kham and they had reciprocated after their trip to India.

The fifth month came and with it Lhamo Chö, a day of offering to the patroness of the Sakya family, featuring horse racing. The ceremonies were at a pilgrimage center about two miles up the mountain south of Sakya. There was a two-mile course, with the horses racing toward the temple at the pilgrimage center. Before the starting gun, the horses and their jockeys rode three times around an incense offering to the mountain deities. This parading was partly to show off the costumes of the riders and the decorations of the horses. My husband and I didn't attend this summer's festival, which included a procession up the mountain and prayers to the Lhamo, because of Ani-la's illness and pressure about the debts. None of the Phuntsok Palace horses won in the major races.

Meanwhile, my husband finished his major studies and ceremonies for Lay-Rim, begun before we went to Kham. Thus we felt that all of the loose ends were tied, and we were ready to make our trip to Lhasa.

We planned to stay only a couple of months, leaving my mother and Aunt Chacha in charge of the palace. They were adjusting well to their life there, even though they missed Uncle Tülku-la and the rest of the family in Kham. About sixteen people were in our party, led by Phuba Tsering, on the first lap of the trip to Shigatse. We stopped in Shigatse for several reasons: we wanted to see the Panchen Lama at Tashi-lhunpo and to get X-rays for Ani-la, as recommended by the Chinese pediatrician. We also had to obtain transportation to Lhasa.

The day of our arrival in Shigatse, we had a visit from the Panchen Lama's prime minister, Tendong. Tendong was very pro-Chinese, we felt, but maintained the pretense that he still was concerned with religion. However, he was very hospitable and friendly to us.

Tendong said he would arrange for a private audience with the Panchen Lama at the summer palace in front of Tashi-lhunpo. He sent his car for us and we paid a courtesy call about ten o'clock one day. At the main gate of the palace, two Chinese guards stood by. Tendong and other officials met us at the gate and escorted us to the second floor, where we spent a half hour with the Panchen Lama. Presents were exchanged, and he gave us his blessing.

The Panchen Lama, now about twenty-two and very tall—much taller than the Dalai Lama—asked why we were going to Lhasa. My husband explained that it was on palace business. The Panchen Lama was pleased with my husband's religious work in Kham. It was plain to see, however, that the Panchen Lama could not do much without consulting the Chinese who constantly surrounded him. Tendong was really in charge, we thought.

I was impressed with the Panchen Lama. He was so friendly, talking with our boys on their level. Minzu-la chatted about one of his playmates and we all laughed reservedly. The Panchen Lama was also generous, giving toys to them, including a tricycle with a front shaped like a horse's head. I had never seen one so elaborate. This two-passenger model was clearly from China. My husband remarked that it was embarrassing that we came away with more gifts than we had offered. I had been in charge of the offerings and gifts. "You were too stingy," he scolded.

At the hospital where we were to get X-rays of Ani-la's lungs, we waited in line at an outpatient clinic. It was warm, luckily, for there were many sick persons, most of them Tibetans, waiting to be treated. Finally it was our turn and we showed the paper that we had been given by the pediatrician in Sakya.

After the X-rays were taken, Ani-la was given some medicine, and we were told to report back in three days. When we did, the doctor told us the X-rays showed a dark spot on one of Ani-la's lungs. I was questioned at length. "Did he fall down?" "What had the boy eaten before the X-ray?"

The pediatrician who had come to Sakya was called again, along with others. This mystery continued for about ten days. Coming back each day was time consuming and a strain on us. We were gravely worried.

Finally, it was determined that another X-ray would have to be taken. An army doctor was called in. When Ani-la undressed for the X-ray, the doctors at last found what had been puzzling them: Ani-la was wearing a small charm, a statue of the White Tārā, wrapped in silk and hanging from a string around his neck. The charm was compared with the spot on the X-ray, and the mystery of the "lung spot" was solved. Ani-la had been wearing the charm during the first X-ray, but we had slipped it around to his back and the Chinese apparently hadn't noticed it. Not all of the doctors found humor in this incident. We, of course, were so relieved that we could think of nothing else. We didn't care if they were angry.

On our final visit to the hospital, one of the doctors chose to give us a glimpse of the current advancements of medicine. My husband had requested that we be shown the hospital. Most of our party was taken on this tour, during which we were shown the surgery and medical instruments. It was a very new hospital, but not as complete as the one in Lhasa. We were most intrigued when we were shown jars displaying human fetuses through the nine months of gestation. According to Tibetan belief, it was three months before the baby was formed, but here was a one-month baby. This doctor also discussed the heart and diet. It was a most informative day, and I emerged from this visit willing to give the Chinese far more credit for such knowledge than I had in the past.

Midway through our stay in Shigatse, I was visited by some Chinese officials, Big Doctor, and an interpreter. They wanted me to sign a document saying that I would head a women's propaganda group called the Young Women's Group of Western Tibet upon my return to Sakya. In Shigatse a women's group promoting Chinese culture was already in existence. More than a hundred women attended programs three times a week. I wanted no part of any such group and declined, saying that I knew nothing about the customs and general culture of the Chinese. They replied, "You should know. You are a head lady of Sakya." They also said that the head lady of the Drolma Palace, the Trichen's aunt, had signed, which I doubted.

I was told that all Tibetan ladies of Shigatse and Sakya would do this or they would not remain ladies. My position was being threatened. The Chinese always used an underlying threat in their pressuring. I had seen how they used these tactics in Kham. They had implied that it was not in keeping with my station and rank to decline. They emphasized that when in the future "equality" among peoples of Tibet was achieved then those who had not cooperated with the Chinese would have no position in the Communist ranks.

I replied, "I am not like the women of Shigatse and Sakya. I am a Khampa, and I do not wish to lecture." The interpreter did not repeat exactly what I said, but instead mumbled something in polite terms. Big Doctor, however, understood some Tibetan and his face showed anger. My husband told me to be cautious and reply later.

"You do not need to begin duties now, but you should sign soon," one of them remarked, and they left.

Their objective, I perceived, was not to get my signature at this time; but for propaganda purposes they preferred to have me sign at some ceremony with many persons attending.

When I talked back to the Chinese, Wangmo was shocked at my outspokenness. I realized, after the visitors' departure, how frank and brave I had been. I also realized that I had been caught unawares.

Later I went to visit the wife of Tendong, whom we called Tendong Lhacham. She was a Khampa, and I thought she might help me to get my message across to the Chinese. But when I told her what was in my heart about my country and further explained my shyness, fear of crowds, and lack of knowledge of Chinese customs, I soon learned that she was sold on Communist doctrine. I was at her home and she closed the door, leaving us alone.

"We no longer are free," she said, urging me to sign. "Every year the Chinese become more powerful. You must learn to live with this. If not, later you will be degraded to the level of a roadworker."

In regard to the salary I would receive if I signed, she added, "Some think it is like taking poison, but it is not that way. Use their money. Later they can't throw it up to you because everyone will have taken these funds. You didn't ask for them."

I left, firmly convinced that this wasn't what I wanted at all. That evening when I told my husband the events of the day, we decided that we would leave soon for Lhasa.

Three days after my conversation with the Tendong Lhacham, we received an invitation to dinner and a program at the home of Yaputang, the top Chinese official in Shigatse. The headquarters of Yaputang was on the south side of the city. Guests at the dinner included a general, obviously of very high rank, and one of the same officials with whom I had declined to sign for the propaganda lectures. I swallowed my pride and shook hands with him.

Soon after it became known what the tenor of the conversation was to be. Yaputang began, saying, "We sent a representative to ask Mrs. Sakya to lecture and she said 'no' immediately. She thinks erroneously. It is all right with us because she is a friend. Otherwise, it would be very grave."

Obviously they were attempting to scare me into signing. I pretended I wasn't listening and continued to eat my dried melon seeds. Actually I could understand Chinese fairly well by this time, but pretended that I could not. Somewhere in this conversation, Yaputang complimented me by saying I was very frank and truthful.

My husband replied that it was courteous of the Chinese to ask me, but that they must remember that I was a Khampa.

"She states what she thinks right away," he said. "That's the way Khampas are. She doesn't want this and thus it is natural that she tell you so frankly and immediately."

To which the Chinese replied, "Oh, that is good. She didn't tell a lie—she is an honest person. She is better than some Tibetans, who are two-faced."

But the Chinese continued on their mission, which was to make me the leader of this Communist organization in western Tibet. I tried to explain that as the wife of a lama I was busy with religious and home-centered activities. A noble's wife, I said, had a different role. Yaputang led the conversation. They said I surely could take the salary now and begin the work later. But I again declined, saying that since I would be doing nothing, I would not be earning the money. I explained that we had business to attend to in Lhasa and also that we must go on a pilgrimage there because of Ani-la's illness. By this time I was becoming angry.

They said that if I took the salary now, when the "liberation" of my country was achieved, I would receive a higher salary.

In view of all this, I decided to give the Chinese a bone—something that would let them save face. I said that when I returned to Sakya, if the Chinese had started a young women's organization there by that time, I would try to be the leader.

But I firmly declined to take any salary until I began such work.

A secretary wrote down in a small notebook what I had said. The Chinese seemed to be satisfied.

We moved to another building in the compound for dinner. Yaputang served extra helpings of food with his own chopsticks, thus showing his guests a special honor. I could scarcely eat. We toasted the Dalai and Panchen Lamas and Mao Tse-tung—the latter first.

Then toasts continued around the table, each person giving one. When it was my turn, I simply said, "To all of you in this room—good health and may all our beliefs come true."

Big Doctor, seated on my right, was next. He said it was against Chinese policy to make toasts such as mine. "You are making your own personal wishes, which conflicts with Chinese law. Toasts should be made for the good of Tibet and China." Even Mao would not make such a toast, Big Doctor said. The doctor then drank to the People's Republic and to the "liberation" of Tibet.

A movie followed, after which we went home in a jeep. My husband warned that I must be careful. "You are outspoken," he said. "You embarrass me. Everyone has his own beliefs, but it is not always necessary to voice them."

Yaputang had given us a pass for some plays. These turned out to be propaganda productions emphasizing bad aspects of the old days of China, such as emperors with many wives. It was shown how the ancient Chinese had beaten children. However, there were some redeeming features in the gymnastic shows and singing. Whenever I saw Big Doctor at these events I was polite. But I remained highly suspicious of him and I no longer regarded him as being in a humanitarian role.

We hired a truck for the Lhasa trip after again notifying my mother in Sakya that the trip was of a religious and business nature. We did not mention how the Chinese had tried to push me into lecturing. Nor did we tell her the big family news—confirmed in an examination by a Chinese doctor at the hospital—that I again was pregnant. Miscarriages were common in early pregnancies. I did not want to have my mother worry, so I waited to tell her until I felt I was out of danger.

14

Lhasa Politics and Revolt

In Lhasa, we found temporary quarters in a home on the city's south side. One of Dagchen Rinpoche's first duties was to pay a courtesy call on the Dalai Lama at Norbu Lingka, the summer palace. His Holiness was preparing for important religious examinations to be held next year. He asked many questions about Kham.

Meanwhile, I stepped up the pace of my religious activities, visiting the Jokhang once and sometimes twice a day. Traditionally it was open three times daily and always was crowded. Usually Wangmo, the two children, Tenpa Sangpo, the monk, and I went. When we waited in the long line to go past the main image of the Buddha, the trip took about two hours. However, the monk who was the keeper of the temple was a friend of Dagchen Rinpoche, and when he saw us he would take us out of the line and let us pass through. When this happened, our visit would only take about half an hour.

The Jokhang basically is three stories of shrines containing important statues of the Buddha, Dalai Lamas, kings, and deities.

Inside the temple, there was the smell of incense and burning butter. It was dark except for the light of the butter lamps. There was a very devout atmosphere, with everybody keeping their heads bowed. Many had prayer beads and a few carried prayer wheels. Hats were removed, but ladies' head-dresses were required. One was not supposed to eat garlic before visiting the Jokhang to avoid emitting any offensive smell. Except for the prayers, voices were kept low.

There was a special ritual for visiting the main Buddha image. One first touched one knee of the statue, circled around, touched the other knee, stepped down and around to the front of the statue, and then said prayers. Most persons removed their shoes before they moved past the image. No short sleeves or bare arms were permitted among the laity. There were hundreds of lamps in the temple. In front of the main statue was a bowl into which money and jewels were dropped as offerings.

I always took a white scarf to put on one of the knees of the statue. Everyday I also took a butter lamp, or a container of melted butter, and incense. In front of the statue, two monks were on duty. One would pass the donated butter to the other, who poured it into some of the gold lamps in front of the statue.

The monks who poured the butter afterwards would wipe their hands on their wool robes. These robes were never washed, and some were so greasy they were like soft leather. In the street one always could tell a Jokhang monk by his robe.

Life in Lhasa was busy for us. Khampas and others came to see my husband—sometimes arriving even before he got up in the morning. The Chinese issued invitations to all nobles and dignitaries—including our family—for films, festivals, and similar programs.

Dagchen Rinpoche meanwhile had written a formal letter to the Dalai Lama's government in regard to the Trichen post. He asked why the eldest son in the Sakya family had not been granted the title, as had been the tradition for hundreds of years. He also asked that the Phuntsok Palace be relieved of responsibility for the expenses of the Great Temple of Sakya while the palace did not hold the Trichen post.

The request first would have to go before the Kashag, or Council of Ministers. We hired a man named Tseten Tashi to be our intermediary. I felt that all I had heard about the necessary bribery of many of the ministers for their services was true. Tseten Tashi went to the council many times to give gifts and money, asking merely for a response for purposes of clarifying the policy for the next generation of the Sakya Trichen. We were burdened with not only these payments to the ministers but the high costs of our big family living in Lhasa. We were given some answers that we regarded as excuses. Months passed. There was a humorous slogan about the slowness of government action, saying that "Communications are received, put in a box, and read one year later." However, there had been some improvement in the legislative process with the advent of the Chinese invasion.

When we had been in the capital city some six months, we moved to the Ponsho House, a larger residence on the north side of the city.

The owner of the house, the Ponsho Lhacham, was the widow of Ponsho Thejei, the noble who had caused us so much trouble earlier in Sakya. He had died while we were in Kham. His widow was a very kind woman, and there was no animosity between us. She had invited us to reside free in her best quarters. Astrologers had told her that a conflict between her family and the Sakya deities had caused the decline in her family fortunes and the sudden death of her husband. The lease on our temporary residence had expired, so we welcomed her gesture of good will.

Ponsho House was only a few blocks from the new Chinese hospital and weather station. A weather balloon was sent up from the station each day about four-thirty or five P.M. These balloons were much discussed by Lhasa residents as they made their rounds on kora. Sometimes the balloons broke and children would bring home pieces they had found. The Chinese newspaper explained the weather patterns. At first the forecasts were not very accurate, but the Chinese weathermen improved with the passing of time. They were anxious that the station be successful in every regard.

Many Tibetan women were now under the care of Communist Chinese doctors and were having their babies delivered at the new hospital. But there was always the problem of standing in line to get to see the doctors.

Instead, I contacted Chang U-Yen, a doctor with Nationalist Chinese sympathies who had a clinic in downtown Lhasa. He was not fully accredited under the Communist Chinese medical standards. He suggested a woman gynecologist, also of Nationalist Chinese thinking, who practiced in the same building. Both of them, of course, had to cooperate to some degree with the Communists.

One evening, as my time was nearing, the doctor and her nurse came to check my condition. The doctor declared "not yet," at about seven P.M. "If you have any trouble, we will go to the hospital," she said.

At about ten o'clock that evening, our new baby boy arrived. It was February 15, 1958, by the Western calendar. Wangmo, who was nervous, assisted me, along with my husband's sister, Chimi-la, who had accompanied us to Lhasa. I managed the delivery, with the two women just handing me the necessary items. The next morning before daylight the woman doctor and nurse came. The doctor was very angry and embarrassed that she had not been summoned. I explained by stressing the dangers of traveling after dark in Lhasa these days, although I also had not wanted to go to the Chinese hospital.

We named our new boy Lodro Dorje. In Tibetan *Lodro* means "one possessed of wise knowledge." However, within the family we called him by the Sanskrit name for Lodro, "Mati-la."

At the lunar New Year celebration, a dinner was given by the Ponsho family. I did not go to the Jokhang, even though one should view the Buddha statue on that day. It was so crowded that it would have taken hours in line.

We were able to keep in contact with relatives in Gangtok, including my husband's youngest sister and aunt, by means of the wireless radio at the Indian mission in Lhasa. Permission to use the radio came from Gangtok. We went between seven and eight A.M., when the airwaves were given over to nonbusiness and nongovernmental affairs. During my first talk on the radio I learned my first English word, "Hello."

We also had a battery-operated radio at home in Lhasa, a Russian-made model purchased in India. There was a newscast in Tibetan, broadcast from New Delhi. We also received a Thai station on which the announcer spoke in an Amdo dialect.

Meanwhile, our some three hundred head of yaks, dzo, and dzomo had arrived in Sakya on their journey from Kham. Tapar, a Lhagyal monk and head of the party herding the animals, dropped by to tell us of the trip west. The animals were distributed or sold in various places. Some of them, of course, were possessions of palace employees. Some of the animals were taken to our Phuntsok Palace estates in several parts of western Tibet.

Tensions generally were mounting in Lhasa. Chinese now would come to nobles' residences for such reasons as to bring a ticket to a movie. One never knew when they would arrive on the scene. Sometimes they stayed for tea and talked through their Tibetan interpreter.

Cartoons and films always depicted Americans as killers who should be destroyed. In contrast, everything about China was portrayed as good and impressively big. On stone walls along the streets were written—many times by monks— slogans declaring that the Chinese Communists were destroying religion. These, of course, were countered by writings about what the Chinese thought were the evils of Tibetans. In many places the Chinese had hung long red banners with yellow and white lettering. These banners said in essence that the Americans were aiding Chiang Kai-shek and that "We must eradicate Chiang."

Many new buildings continued to rise. There were a num-

ber of one-story barrack-type structures near the new hospital. The poor and homeless were allowed to sleep there.
Leftover food also was doled out to these people. Some simply
didn't want to work, but preferred to beg.

One day when I had just returned from the Jokhang and
was having lunch, three men came and announced that they
wanted to see my husband. They were Dorje Khotang, a
Tibetan interpreter newly arrived from Peking, and two Chinese officials. Dorje Khotang was a Tibetan who had become
a Communist sympathizer employed by the Chinese. Many
Tibetans knew how powerful he was and feared him.

My husband hated these visits for a variety of reasons,
obviously, but one of them was the purposeful disrespect of
the Chinese. For example, they sat on religious books, placed
their hats on statues, and sat on small tables not meant to be
sat on. I prepared to leave, as I was hungry. But Dorje
Khotang said, "Don't go. We have something important to ask
you." Tea was served and then Dorje Khotang told my husband and me that Tanjiwu had sent them. In Chamdo, Derge,
and elsewhere in Kham, the Khampas were doing despicable
acts—including stealing and killing, Dorje Khotang said.

The conversation went something like this: "Khampas like
you and respect you greatly. They know you because of your
recent visit. And, in turn, you like Khampas. Will you then
go to Chamdo to talk and reason with the Khampas? Tell
them not to fight, but to take care of their homes and families
as before."

I knew that my husband would never do this. But the
visitors continued the conversation, presenting several selling
points, painting the proposed trip as good, both for them and
us. They said that my husband could go by jeep and take his
own aides, that he would be paid, and that he would have a
Chinese guard.

The Chinese had tried many techniques in dealing with the
Khampas and none of them was working. On the bodies of
Tibetans killed by the Chinese, they had found photos of
Dagchen Rinpoche and the family in charm boxes. Pins with

a picture of Mao had the picture removed and my husband's photo inserted.

"No, never," was Dagchen Rinpoche's reply. "Please do not ask me." His excuses were many. He said he was busy with his own tasks, that the Dalai Lama's examination ceremonies were coming up. He also firmly reminded the Chinese of his difficulties in returning home from Kham.

The visitors said, "The Khampas will listen to you. Life for them will be like it was before. Otherwise the Khampas will suffer." Their anger was surfacing. "You'll be helping your people," was their last plea.

My husband made a final decline and told them not to ask again about this matter. The three left quickly, not even drinking their tea. After this refusal, the Chinese were more distant and suspicious of us.

Subsequently, Dorje Khotang asked another high religious figure, the Gyalwa Karmapa—the head of the Kagyu school, who was born in Kham—to make the trip to Chamdo. After refusing many times, he finally went, accompanied by a member of the Kashag, the noble Ngawang Jigme. Most Khampas did not blame the Karmapa, believing the Chinese had pressured him into going to Kham. It was generally thought that the Karmapa's visit was not helpful to the Communists, although the visit to Chamdo and other large towns was widely touted by the Chinese via public address systems and newspapers in Lhasa.

The Drawu-pon arrived from Kham with about fifty men in his party. We felt this group should be treated well while visiting here. The Drawu-pon's family had for generations been patrons of the Sakya religion and especially the Sakya family. There followed festive days of singing, dancing, picnicking, and good times in the parks. There were many parties. It was as though people wanted to have a last fling because of the continual stranglehold the Chinese kept on our way of life. Some of the conservative views of residents seemed to be falling apart. Sacred jewels, such as those on headdresses and other clothing, no longer were worn in the traditional manner. Yet there seemed to be a renewal of religion. Monasteries and temples were crowded. Many people were generous in making religious offerings. They also spent more, it seemed, for recreation. Perhaps many felt those opportunities soon would be diminished.

There were many jeeps, some autos from India, and many motorcycles now in the Holy City. Most of these vehicles were owned by nobles. My husband obtained a Russian motorcycle, but it did not work well. Later he bought a secondhand British cycle and hired a professional driver. I did not ride except for a few short trips as a passenger. Fearful for my husband, I continually warned him to be careful. Many Lhasa streets were very narrow. The central square particularly was crowded and dangerous, without traffic signs.

We used another mode of travel—mule- or horse-drawn wagons—for visits to Sera and Drepung monasteries and other fairly close spots. Many of these wagons were rented. These vehicles were good, unless it rained; some wealthy persons had covered models.

Drepung Monastery, with its white-walled buildings, from a distance looked like a heap of rice. That is what the name "Drepung" means. With nearly ten thousand monks, it was the largest monastery in the country. Because it was so big, it was impossible to tour all of it in one day. A relative, Dema Locho Rinpoche, kindly arranged our tour, inviting our party for lunch and a religious service. He was administrator of the Losarling college of the monastery and was in charge of hundreds of monks.

We spoke in low voices. There could be no noisy footsteps or running. We were required to remove our hats and close our umbrellas. Je Tsongkhapa, founder of the Yellow Hat school, had built the monastery four miles west of Lhasa in 1416. Like other monasteries, the place was teeming with activity. We heard the drums, cymbals, bells, and chantings as we moved from temple to temple. Khampas collected handfuls of maroon lint left from the robes of thousands of monks and lamas as they passed up and down the steps at the entrance to the temples. Khampas used this lint as part of their protective charms.

The disciplined monks, with their shaved heads and single-layer soled boots, walked peacefully to their assignments. Because their upper outer garment covered part of their heads and arms, one could see only their hands and faces. They ranged in age from six to the very elderly. Many of the old monks and lamas carried prayer beads in their hands.

I was astounded upon seeing the huge pots and pans constantly in use for making tea and soup. Two or three monks stood on elevated platforms stirring the soups in each pot. Dogs were everywhere, especially around the kitchen, waiting for handouts. Many visitors asked to be given ashes from the stoves to be used to ward off the sickness of animals and to be tossed on the fields so the harvest would not be eaten by worms.

In late summer, our family was invited to dinner at the Chinese headquarters. I thus returned to the scene of my first dinner "bout" with the Chinese. I noted that the furnishings now were somewhat better. Dorje Khotang was there. This time he approached my husband about an exhibit of prized religious and historical items he wanted assembled. The Chinese wanted these works to be shown in Lhasa first and then in Peking. The story was that if Mao liked the collection, then it would be shown in the Chinese capital. The exhibit, the Chinese said, would be a highlight of the 1959 celebration marking the tenth anniversary of the fall of the Nationalist Chinese government and the beginning of the Communist regime. The obvious goal was for the Chinese to propagandize early relationships between Tibet and China, thus justifying their intended "liberation" of my country.

My husband was assured that the Chinese would not keep these items—that they would be returned. They mentioned that they needed two knowledgeable men to assemble the collection, and that the Surkhang Shapé would be the noble member of the team. They urged my husband to be the lama team member because he was older and had more background on the subject.

Meanwhile, amid this conversation, Ani-la needed to go to the lavatory. So I swept him up and we went out the door of the reception room where we were assembled. To my utter amazement, there was Tanjiwu—the highest-ranking Chinese in Tibet—listening at the other side of the door. He wasn't dressed in dinner attire and no one else was there. Ani-la said something in Tibetan. Tanjiwu then recognized me, smiled, and looked embarrassed, as I was. He mentioned that he would see me later and left in the opposite direction. I had caught him listening to the conversation about the collection. I returned, feeling puzzled.

This plan to remove priceless items from the Great Temple was very upsetting to all of us, as some of the historical and religious items in Sakya dated from the time of the Mongol Khans. My husband said that if the Chinese wanted representative items from Sakya, those could be photographed rather than removed from Sakya. He added that the items were not his property but belonged to the Sakya government and the two palaces and that Sakya officials must give their permission for their removal, including items from the Great Temple of Sakya. The Chinese officials said they had the authority to take the items from Sakya and that the Sakya government would not refuse the request.

When dinnertime came, Tanjiwu appeared on the scene. I did not want to look at him and clearly the feeling was mutual. As the seating turned out, thankfully we didn't have to. After dinner there was a propaganda film showing the first Chinese to begin the overthrow of Chiang. We were driven home in a jeep.

I was greatly relieved when the tense evening ended. We never knew what requests the Chinese would make next. Most of their questions were impossible to answer. We tried not to talk too much about religion or personal and family concerns. To the Chinese, everything was sublimated to the Mao regime and the "liberation" of Tibet.

It was summer and on one important religious day we made a wagon trip east of Lhasa to Dra Yepa, a Nyingma monastery of about one hundred monks. The *sindum*, a huckleberrylike red berry, was ripe and people were harvesting them near the monastery. One would first lay a blanket under a sindum bush, then beat the bush with a stick. The fruit was placed in bamboo baskets and taken to Lhasa to sell.

There was a quiet, sacred atmosphere at the monastery. There was a statue here of Lhalungpador, the accomplished lama who slew the wicked anti-Buddhist king, Lang Darma, in 842 C.E. Inside one big cave there were three chötens, one of which contained the body of Lhalungpador.

Later we also visited Sera and Ganden monasteries, where ceremonies were held in connection with the Dalai Lama's elevation to the rank of *geshe*, comparable to a master of metaphysics degree.

After months of waiting, there finally came a decision about the Trichen post. We felt strongly that the cabinet ministers realized that they had erred earlier in awarding the position of Trichen to the Drolma Palace. But now there was no graceful way for them to admit their error.

The decision was that it was not possible to change the Trichen post now that it had been in effect several years. But in the future, the Trichen post would go to the eldest son of the two families. Thus we knew that Minzu-la would be the next Trichen of Sakya. The Kashag voted its decision and the Dalai Lama gave his seal to the document. However, we felt that he had not been properly informed of our side of the issue.

In connection with the decision, there was also a letter from the Kashag stating that a new attempt must be made to determine the amount of money spent by the two palaces on the repair of the Great Temple. Two nobles, one from each side of the controversy, were to go to Sakya and once again attempt to determine the expenditures.

At about this time the newspaper announced that two important Russians would visit Lhasa and that there would be a performance of Russian, Mongolian, and Tibetan dances. The performance was a propaganda move to permit the Russians to lecture us. The traveling troupe and lecturers stayed at a guest house next door, so we caught frequent glimpses of them.

There was fine dancing and acrobatic work in the first part of the show. Many Tibetans, of course, had not seen this type of footwork before and were impressed by it. Then came the propaganda show, pointing out that the fighting in Kham was worsening because of the "evil" Khampas. The characters portrayed Chinese soldiers and Khampas in action, the Khampas always initiating the aggression. In the act a girl and her mother were beaten by Khampas. The show ended, of course, with the Chinese victorious. It was disgusting to us.

As for the Russians, I had a preconceived impression that they would be bearded and "furry." I had seen photos of Lenin and Stalin. Our two visitors, however, were bald, short, heavy, and not in the least impressive.

Meanwhile we were helpless in the face of an aspect of Communism far more serious than the cultural invasion—the economic grip that threatened the foundations of our livelihood and centuries-old peaceful way of life. The harshness of the Chinese view was stark. Chinese officials traveled in our agricultural areas counting yaks, horses, sheep, and other animals, acting under the pretense that they wanted to vaccinate and prevent disease. They also counted the fields and their production, particularly the estates of wealthy land owners.

Traders—the traditional great merchants of my country—were having a difficult time, as the Chinese were controlling imports. If the traders were allowed to pass through the border, they were highly taxed. The traders were searched, even to the point of having their hats and shoes removed. Tibetans were urged to buy Chinese products and there generally was a tightening of control on the economy. One could not buy any large quantity of Chinese goods from their stores, as the Chinese were afraid the Tibetans would resell the goods and the Communists didn't want any more traders.

The Chinese had urged producers to "bring your wool, barley, and other items to us and we'll pay cash." The prices were good at first, but then became lower and lower. Payments were shifted from silver coins to Chinese paper money, which Tibetans disliked. It was a convenient way for the Communists to keep track of how much money the populace had. However, there still was plenty of food in Lhasa, in contrast to the situation in Kham.

Daily the Chinese were continuing their construction in the capital city and the Chinese population was expanding. They also were buying many homes around the central square, for which the owners were given high prices. Thus the Chinese came to the owner of our residence, the Ponsho Lhacham, offering to buy and saying, "Just tell us the price and we will pay." Nobles sympathetic to the Chinese said in effect that, "You don't need this large house," and stressed that the land should be utilized to its fullest for the good of all. In Lhasa nowadays, one often wondered about the trustworthiness of one's own servants and close friends. I always could trust Wangmo, fortunately. Chinese, however, were frequently known to bribe servants of the higher classes, including monastery aides.

A severe storm came in the fall, with heavy rain, wind, and hail. Rivers were flooded and bridges washed out, and some lives were lost. Oldtimers said they never had seen such a storm in their lifetimes. We also heard a noise something like a bomb or explosion from the mountainsides near Lhasa. All this was thought to be a bad omen.

"The mountains are crying," it was said. "Something will happen in this country."

For the third time in Tibet, it was said that a comet appeared. Some also saw small clouds shaped like bows. This was interpreted as indicating that the country would have war. When one saw this bad omen, it was customary immediately to draw a bow in the earth. This, we believed, would reduce the evils of the omen. Special prayers were said at all the monasteries.

One morning I and others in the residence were awakened by the largest fire I had ever seen, a blaze in the new hospital. Quickly we ran to the top floor of our house for a full view of the flames and smoke. Much of Lhasa's citizenry was awakened.

A number of ailing Tibetans were patients in the hospital. As a propaganda move the Chinese evacuated all of the Tibetans first so they could boast of placing their lives above those of the Chinese. Two Chinese were badly hurt in fighting the fire. The flames burned for four or five hours. Finally the Chinese enlisted the help of Tibetans. Hundreds responded, carrying water in buckets and other utensils in a brigade. The water came from wells and ponds. Others tossed on salt in an attempt to quell the blaze.

The hospital was four or five stories high and the most modern facility in the city. The roof and several stories were damaged. A later newspaper account said the blaze started in the kitchen.

When the fire was out, the Chinese told their Tibetan helpers to leave, obviously to hide the dead. The Chinese, we felt, did not want to reveal details of any aspect of their administration of this showplace health center. One Tibetan interpreter working at the hospital said six Chinese died. We thought that more than this had been killed.

When I went on kora the next morning, guards near the hospital told us to "move along," whereas before they always had been polite.

The Chinese attempted to rebuild the razed area in a hurry. It was a two-month job, and workers were summoned from all around. They received high wages and were paid in Chinese silver coins.

Soon after, the Chinese wanted to widen their sphere of propaganda and urged Tibetans to read newspapers. I still didn't know much about Europe, so I wasn't interested in that area. Egypt, Germany, Thailand, and Russia always were in the news. Little was said about India.

Although the Chinese newspaper was published twice weekly, the newspaper stories only related events in general areas of Kham and seldom dealt with specifics. The stories also were laced with propaganda, so we had no way of knowing what was happening to Uncle Tülku-la, Uncle Kunsang Nyima, and Ani Chimi. We had to rely on persons who came to Lhasa from Kham to learn actually what was happening in eastern Tibet.

The Chinese always advised my husband to tell the Khampas not to continue to fight. "You must," the officials said, adding, "they will listen to you."

It was of some relief, then, that we were paid a visit by a monk named Getrup, from Jyeku Monastery, who informed us of what had occurred in Gaba. Getrup said the Communists at first had bombed Ranyak Monastery, not far from Thalung, and that fighting had occurred at another smaller monastery, Bam Chu, in the area. The Chinese had forced the captured Bam Chu monks to wear Chinese army uniforms and put them in the front lines. If the monks turned back, they would be killed by Chinese. So they had no choice but to advance. Thus some of the Bam Chu monks had to fight their brother monks in the Ranyak battle.

When word was received of the fall of Ranyak, Getrup said, people of Thalung knew it was just a question of time before the Chinese took Thalung Monastery. Thalung had five hundred monks, half as many as at Ranyak. Thus the Thalung town and monastery were evacuated.

Uncle Tülku-la, Uncle Kunsang Nyima, and Ani Chimi had fled to an area known as the Goshang, a nomadic area in the Changthang. All of those fleeing from Ranyak and other parts of Gaba also went to the Goshang, making an encampment of more than a thousand. After the Tibetans had been a month at the Goshang, the Chinese came and opened fire on the camp. Getrup had fled in the night during the fighting, not knowing what had happened to the three members of my family. So we could only speculate about them, wondering whether they were still safe, captured by the Chinese, or—by this time even—taken to Peking or some other part of China. Getrup, who was a deeply religious man, remained optimistic and tried to encourage us.

Getrup, whom we had known well in Jyekundo, was in many ways a changed person by his ordeal. His temperament often changed abruptly. In his flight he had gone three or four days without food, having only water. Finally he had gotten some food from a nomad, he said. I wondered if I ever would see my two uncles and aunt again and if they too would be changed, their personalities altered.

The Drawu-pon, who had visited Lhasa, attempted to return to Jyekundo, Getrup said. However, when the Drawu-pon learned that Ranyak had fallen, he turned back. Luckily he had come upon his wife and family, who were escaping from Jyekundo. They too went to the Goshang, Getrup said.

Sometime after Getrup arrived in Lhasa, the Chinese broadcast that thirty guerrillas had been captured in the Changthang. We were very worried that this was the Drawu-pon's group. However, the broadcasts never mentioned captured lamas because the Chinese knew it would arouse the ire of the populace.

When we heard about the thirty captives, we sent scarfs, butter lamps, and money to the Jokhang and temples in the Lhasa area to have monks pray for the Drawu-pon and his party.

Khampas continued to arrive, often fleeing the Chinese they had fought in Kham. There were some guerrilla incidents involving Khampas at Yangpachen, northwest of Lhasa, and other areas. From these Khampas we heard many stories of the bravery of my countrymen. The Chinese would cut pieces of flesh from captured Tibetans, who wouldn't even cry out. It was felt that the Buddhist religious system was at stake. "It doesn't matter if I die," they would explain.

In the ensuing days, many more Khampas came to Lhasa, some directly to me. About fifteen arrived every few days.

They first stayed on the east side of the city. I frequently sent our cook to the Khampa encampment to see if they had any news of my family. Some said that Uncle Kunsang Nyima was not with Uncle Tülku-la, who they said was heading straight west. During the fighting in the Goshang they had been separated. I had great fear for Uncle Kunsang Nyima, although I was hopeful that Uncle Tülku-la really was on his way to safety.

One evening after we had been out for dinner, we approached the courtyard to find Uncle Kunsang Nyima and a monk coming to greet us. I was happy to see him but shocked at his appearance. Uncle Kunsang Nyima had come by truck from Nakchuka to Lhasa. His hair was long and he had lost much weight. He had snowburn in one eye and appeared weatherbeaten. Tears came to his eyes when he saw us. He went to my husband and was blessed, along with his fellow traveler, the monk.

I was so unnerved I couldn't speak. We held hands and then went inside to talk. Uncle Kunsang Nyima told how he had been separated from Uncle Tülku-la and Ani Chimi in the Goshang. The morning of the battle, Uncle Kunsang Nyima had been helping a patient about half a mile away from them. Uncle had made it out of the Goshang, and along with about five others continued by horse to Nakchuka. He waited there five days for Uncle Tülku-la but then learned from some Khampas that he was on his way west to Sakya. Uncle Kunsang Nyima had gotten a change of clothes in Nakchuka— laymen's garb.

It was hard to realize that I might never again see my hometown and loved ones in Thalung. I thought about Lhayag and her children and my other close girl friends, wondering what fate they had suffered.

Uncle Kunsang Nyima had one bit of good news: the Drawu-pon had joined some Tibetan guerrillas and was safe.

After hearing about Uncle Tülku-la, I wrote my mother and Aunt Chacha in Sakya to tell them that he was on his way. I also told them that Dagchen Rinpoche's and my plans were to stay in Lhasa until after the New Year's festival and accompanying celebration for the Dalai Lama. Then we planned to return home to the palace.

I spent my days visiting the shrines and sorting out many of the belongings we had accumulated during our time here. Some, such as the motorcycle, were sold; others were given away. A good share of my spare time was spent at my hobby—making and remodeling jewelry—something I had come to excel in since I learned this art from my husband's two eldest sisters at Sakya. Often I remodeled necklaces, charm boxes, headdresses, and earrings in the Lhasa style, which included more pearls. If I needed a certain kind or size of pearl or other gem, I would send one of the servants to buy the desired item at one of the many shops in the Barko, the central square. Most merchants knew my family so well that they would allow the servant to bring an assortment of gems back to me to make a selection. I worked from bowls of pearls, usually using only a thread, but no needle. Back home in Sakya, once started on this I disliked stopping and often worked late into the night by the light of two candles. Here at least we had electricity in the residence. Many nobles' wives learned some of the skills of this art from me; I also picked up many techniques from them.

It also was fashionable to knit, and yarn was readily available. Because I had knitted since I was six years old, a number of women took lessons from me. As the wife of a high lama, I, of course, was not supposed to be using my idle time in ventures such as knitting. But jewelry-making was permissible, since it was not menial labor and had religious connections.

At the 1959 Chinese New Year observance, which preceded ours, the Communists took advantage of the occasion to make much of the fact that it was the tenth anniversary of the takeover of China from the Nationalist government. In front of a new large theater, decorated with a huge red star on its top, were banners depicting Stalin and Mao Tse-tung.

We attended a celebration in the theater. Dances, movies,

and later in the evening lecturing and propaganda were featured. Inside the theater was a large banner that said, "Wipe
Out Imperialist Americans." The Chinese had invited many
nobles, high lamas, and public figures.

Eight Chinese teenage girls performed Tibetan dances perfectly, but did miserably when they came to Tibetan songs,
as they could not pronounce the words well. During this
celebration, movies were shown of the Chinese New Year in
Peking and of China's growing industrial power. Lectures
were given outside the theater. Even in the central square of
the city there were signs about the anniversary, the growing
strength of China, and the eventual "liberation" of Tibet.

A group of more than a hundred Chinese who had been
sympathetic to the Nationalist cause had come to Lhasa and
established a variety of concessions, including shooting galler-
ies where one could win candies, cigarettes, and other items.
One could hardly pass the area, which wasn't far from our
house, without hearing these people shouting for business.

These newcomers were uneducated and unskilled, but they
had paid their own way from China. They dressed in old-
style Chinese garb. Some of the men had acquired Tibetan
girl friends during their few months' stay here, and a few even
married Tibetans.

They had heard that Lhasa was a prosperous place and that
it would be wise economically to settle in Tibet. However, the
concessions didn't do well in Lhasa and, in fact, they barely
eked out a living. This naturally proved embarrassing for the
Communists.

One day to our astonishment, the Communists without
warning came with about a dozen trucks and rounded up the
concessionaires and shipped them back to China. The Communists explained their actions by saying that the concessionaires simply did not want to work, that there were plenty of
jobs in China. Our impression overall was that the situation
economically must be bad in China if the concessionaires had
been coming here.

The treatment of these people had a deep effect on us. We

wondered if we too someday would be sent off in such a highhanded manner. We assumed the concessionaires had been sent to labor camps. It was a pitiful sight to see them leave. They were obviously distressed and some appeared near tears. They had a helpless look. The new Tibetan wives and girl friends tearfully were left behind.

The Chinese were now requesting the Dalai Lama to come often to their functions, frequently asking him to lecture, but he was very busy.

Everyone was excited about the coming New Year ceremonies. The populations of the three main monasteries in the Lhasa area—Drepung, Sera, and Ganden—not only were swollen because of the upcoming holiday, but because of newly arrived monks from the fighting area in Kham and now from western Tibet. With many of them came refugees.

The Communists had a large installation, which included underground or cavelike facilities, near Samye in Lhokha. The main Khampa stronghold at this time also was in Lhokha, at Lhagyari. Many flags flew around the Tibetan headquarters, proclaiming that it was the site of the "Protective Army for the Buddhist Religion." Tibetans working as spies for the Chinese were caught here and punished. We heard daily by word-of-mouth of frequent guerrilla encounters in these areas. Most of the Tibetan populace did not believe the propaganda we heard on the public-address system. There was some thought of a general uprising or revolt against the Chinese, since we felt they had broken agreements in regard to the two countries' relations.

Many of the Tibetan faithful were volunteering for the army. The Khampa refugee group had a secret office in Lhasa where men went to volunteer.

Among many people there was a false feeling of security, the view that "the Dalai Lama will take care of us." It was a natural feeling, reflecting Tibetan optimism. And the Dalai Lama had said that we had truth on our side and that eventually our will would prevail.

About three days before the Tibetan New Year, a group of

about thirty-five Khampa monks came to Lhasa. Two from Thalung were among a small group who came to the Ponsho residence to visit us and to bring news of Uncle Tülka-la. They said he was presently at an estate near Reting Monastery and planned to make his way to Sakya slowly.

I sent a message back asking him to come to the capital, assuring him that it was safe here and that he should not fear being recognized from the Goshang incident. If he came to Lhasa, I said, then we all could go back to Sakya together after the holiday activities.

The city's population seemed to have swelled to about three times its normal size for the holiday season. Taxes were paid at the end of the year and many of these taxpayers stayed to see the New Year activities.

Lhasa's shops all were decorated with bunting and inside music was played. Goods in the Communist stores were rationed as usual. One had to stand in line to make purchases. There were bargains, however, available from the nomads in the city, who would sell their goods cheap before going home. But food prices soared, as people were hoarding it.

Many persons were out doing kora. I went to the Jokhang and the Ramoche Temple almost every day during the New Year month. The Dalai Lama went early in the morning to the Jokhang, but I sometimes saw him on his way home being carried by eight bearers in his glass-enclosed sedan chair. He gave generously to the monks, as this was the year of his examination. The populace also was generous in its giving.

In a building near the Jokhang were several large kettles used for feeding soup and tea to the thousands of monks who were here for the New Year. People donated food, which was carefully inspected before being accepted. Charcoal and wood were burned to keep the kettles busy twenty-four hours a day. The food was taken to the monks in the Jokhang, each monk receiving a huge wooden bowlful dispensed with a dipper from a bucket. Many of these visiting monks slept at the monks' residences, or *khamtses*, in the city, but ate at the Jokhang.

Before and during the holiday, relatives, friends, Khampas, and the religious faithful brought us gifts of food that completely filled the storage space in the Ponsho residence.

New Year's Day was pleasant, but more quiet than if we had been home in Sakya. The Chinese loudspeakers gave greetings that said in essence, "We wish you the best for the New Year." There was much music, some of which was very good. But here also were Russian and Chinese songs and frequently the Chinese national anthem. Radio and public-address-system news principally was about Russian achievements and how the Soviets were attempting to aid Communist China.

There was an air of tension on the fifteenth day of the first month, the day of the great Butter Festival. Shops were closed that day. The Chinese generally kept out of sight being aware of the potential for conflict. The fifteenth day is a celebration in honor of the magnificent miracles the Buddha performed from the first to the fifteenth of the month to impress the leaders of competing religions. The celebration had been established by Je Tsongkhapa, the founder of the Gelugpa school. This is also the day that two honored nobles are traditionally advanced in rank. They rode through the city, each costumed as an early king and trailed by eight attendants identically dressed in the old-style garb and jewels.

The Butter Festival, held in the evening, cast a spell of magic over the city. The event featured the display of carved tormas. There were over a hundred entries displayed around the central square, some of these two-stories high. The tormas depicted figures in the Buddhist pantheon. These included birds, deer, angellike figures, and elegant Buddhist deities. The tormas were of butter and were placed on wooden backing, behind which were colorful paper backgrounds. Sections of these big decorated tormas were like puppets, having moveable parts.

The monks had begun weeks earlier making tormas. The three largest monasteries were in fierce competition, sometimes having several entries in the festival, none of them the same. The butter was kneaded in buckets of cold water to make it pliable, then dyed either blue, green, yellow, or red. From these basic colors, the monks made a rainbow of hues. Certain monks became noted for their special designs.

At other times, the gifted designers saw their talents come to life in decorated colored-sand maṇḍalas placed on an elevated floor of a temple or on display tables. These maṇḍalas, or magic diagrams, represented mansions of certain celestial bodhisattvas. The sand was carefully crafted by monks who poured it through various-sized funnels. Made for special festivals and religious occasions, the artworks were blessed and then declared sacred. After the festival or event, an abbot dismantled the work. The sand then was distributed as protection against disease and other adversities. None was wasted. For example, a small amount might be sprinkled on animals, tossed on water as purification, worn in a charm box, or placed in homes.

We started out on the rounds from the Thenpa residence, the home of my husband's cousin. The children were left at home. Our party was lead by two police monks from Sera Monastery, who cleared the way for us. There were so many people that it was almost dangerous to go, we thought. But it was considered a good religious deed to make these rounds. The displays were lit by a bright moon and lanterns and butter lamps. We locked arms and walked forward in a line, not daring to turn around because it was so crowded.

The Chinese detested this beautiful spectacle for two reasons: they looked upon it as a waste of butter and they hated the religious aspect of the tormas. But they didn't say such things directly to Tibetans.

The Chinese had erected some large posters and flags in strategic spots outside the central square, angering the Tibetans. After we had made the rounds and returned to Thenpa's house, violence broke out over these displays. The Tibetans shouted for the Chinese to take down the posters and flags, but there were no Chinese out on the streets to hear their demands. Tibetans then began hurling rocks at the posters,

tearing them down and walking over them. Then they fired
shots at the remaining ones. It was a terrible marring of the
New Year. The monk police on duty, of course, didn't appre-
hend the Khampas and monks who had perpetrated the
damage. This greatly angered the Chinese.

We walked home about eleven P.M. escorted by several
monks, taking a roundabout route. Never had I been out that
late on the dark streets of Lhasa. I couldn't sleep well that
night because of the trouble about the signs and posters and
because of thoughts about the shooting.

That night there also were some skirmishes—Tibetans in
fights with Tibetans. Rocks were hurled at windows. We
learned the next day that a boy of eight and a woman of fifty
had been trampled to death at the festival, which some fifty
thousand people had attended.

Amid these mounting tensions in the city, Uncle Tülka-la
and Ani Chimi arrived from the north of Lhasa. At first when
I met Uncle Tülku-la, it seemed like a dream, and I couldn't
speak. It had been two years since we had seen each other.
He appeared dark and weatherbeaten and had lost considerable weight. Uncle Tülku-la was fearful that the Chinese would
recognize him from incidents in eastern Tibet. He used dice
in part to determine what he thought were safe routes to the
Jokhang.

Immediately I wrote my mother at Sakya, giving her details
of our intended trip home after the final Butter Festival
activities.

Then an invitation came from the Chinese for what they
said was to be a very important meeting and party in their
headquarters. We simply couldn't refuse, the hosts said, because the Dalai Lama and all of the prominent people of Lhasa
would be in attendance. There were no extra tickets for
servants.

When we arrived at the headquarters we saw many jeeps,
buses, and trucks parked nearby. I dismissed them from my
mind.

Upon entering a very large room, we were served tea. Then

very pretty Chinese girls served us fruits. Indeed many of the important people of Lhasa were there, including His Holiness' two tutors and his elder sister, Lhachom Tsering Drolma. Eventually there were more than a hundred of us in attendance.

Time wore on and there were repeated finger-food servings. Tables were brought for those who wished to play mahjongg. We paid our respects to the tutors, whom my husband knew, but whom I had not met formally.

There was an air of expectation. I became suspicious, thinking that there was some very important message forthcoming or that we might be forced to sign some paper. I then noticed the uneasiness in other guests. Our eyes met, and seemed to say "What now?" I felt trapped.

It was getting dark. A pretense of calm spread through the guests. Finally, an interpreter stepped up and announced that His Holiness would not be able to come, but that there was a special program of a movie and dancing and that we could take our choice. Then General Tanjiwu came and greeted us, but soon after quickly disappeared.

We passed into another room with an elevated stage where we were entertained by dancers and with a propaganda drama in which Chinese and Khampas were fighting. In this rendition, of course, the Khampas lost.

We, along with the tutors, were among the group that viewed the movie. After it was shown, we peeked into an adjacent room where we saw Tibetans and Chinese dancing Western ballroom style to Chinese music, something one seldom saw.

When it was time to leave, nearly everyone seemed in a hurry to depart. Strangely, the general and the other Chinese leaders had disappeared. There was no one to thank or greet going out the door. There arose a feeling of distrust, but no one said anything. We were brought home in a bus. My uncles were extremely happy that we were back safely.

The significance of all of this, we concluded, was that nothing of significance had occurred—and the Chinese had said it was to be an important event. Obviously their plans had changed or gone awry. In retrospect, the occasion seemed increasingly suspicious.

The following day the loudspeakers announced to the public that the Dalai Lama had been unable to attend the function the previous night, but that he was coming to another party slated soon. Obviously the Dalai Lama had not come for his own reasons and this was what had changed their plans.

Shortly thereafter we learned through Khampas and nomads that a great number of planes and Chinese troops had arrived a few days earlier at Damzhung airfield north of Lhasa. Our conclusion upon hearing this was that on the night of the meeting the Chinese had planned to abduct the Dalai Lama and all of Tibet's leaders at the dinner that night and take them to China via those planes. That is why, we surmised, the trucks, jeeps, and buses had been lined up waiting outside the headquarters. That also was why they had quickly substituted the mediocre movie and other unspectacular entertainment. The Tibetan people learned of this and became very wary. The Dalai Lama remained at Norbu Lingka under close guard.

About three days later, three Chinese came to the Ponsho residence and told my husband that next month they hoped to open the exhibit of Tibetan artifacts. They said my husband must take care of that office and work further with the Surkhang Shapé. They emphasized the importance of the project for the world.

My husband agreed to these orders but would not give up on one point: he said that when he was ready to return to Sakya, he would depart, that he was obliged to take his family back. The Chinese were agreeable to this. Perhaps they thought that if my husband were at Sakya, it would be even easier for them to obtain these treasured items.

Now, my husband observed, the Chinese didn't seem to be in such a hurry about the exhibit. Earlier there had been much more stress, but now the urgency was gone.

The Chinese then renewed their invitation for the Dalai

Lama to come to the Chinese headquarters to view a theatrical performance. He had agreed to come on March 10, and to the later Chinese stipulation that no Tibetan soldier was to accompany him beyond the Stone Bridge. The Chinese said that he could be accompanied by two or three bodyguards, but that they were not to be armed. This invitation was a very suspicious one in the eyes of the Dalai Lama and the idea that the trip was to be kept secret was even more preposterous, for it would have been impossible to keep any trip His Holiness made outside the palace from the people. Still, His Holiness felt that he had no alternative but to comply with the orders. Daily the relations between the government and the Chinese were worsening.

We knew nothing of this imminent trip. We knew that the Dalai Lama had been invited by the Chinese, but were aware of no date or time.

Thus the day of March 10, 1959, started out routinely for me in the Ponsho residence. I had sent Tengyam, our servant, out early on his usual shopping mission for fresh meat and vegetables. Then we heard sounds of activity in the courtyard. The big building was home to fifty to sixty persons. I heard the people saying that many people were going to the Norbu Lingka.

Tengyam returned home excited, saying that most of the shops in the central square were closed, that something of importance must be occurring. We sent him to the Norbu Lingka to find out what was going on. The Chinese loudspeakers related a short story, propaganda, and some news. No mention was made of the Dalai Lama.

It was my feeling that something was going to happen suddenly. I recalled seeing trucks filled with Chinese soldiers who had been wounded fighting outside of Lhasa. The Chinese tried to hide them, but while on kora, we could see them arriving at the hospital.

We went to the roof of the residence, where we saw many people heading towards the palace. Some people still were going to the Jokhang, but I didn't go. I was fearful and couldn't eat my breakfast.

Tengyam returned two hours later to report that there were thousands of people around the Norbu Lingka. People had learned that the Chinese were coming in the morning to pick up His Holiness, and the populace had come to beg him not to go.

There were many reasons for the people to be suspicious. A meeting of the Chinese National Assembly was to be held next month in Peking and His Holiness was invited. He had not given notice of his intent to go, but still the Chinese in Peking announced that he was coming. This angered the Tibetans greatly. The people also were acutely aware that in eastern Tibet some high lamas had been invited to Chinese functions and had never been seen again.

There was shouting and turmoil as the crowd—estimated as numbering up to thirty thousand—gathered outside the wall of the palace. One of the new cabinet ministers, Samdup Phodrang, accompanied by a Chinese official, drove up to the palace in his own automobile. The minister was not yet known to many people. Thus the Tibetans concluded that the car was a Chinese one that had come to take the Dalai Lama away. The minister showed his face clearly, hoping to be recognized, but to no avail. One stone was thrown and then came a panic reaction; the car was bombarded with stones. Samdup Phodrang was injured and taken to the Indian consulate's clinic.

The Tibetans were shouting that the Chinese must leave, that Tibet must be left for Tibetans. Then a young monastery official, Phakpala Khenchung, was stoned to death by the mob. It was well known that he had been close to the Chinese.

At about noon, the Surkhang Shapé announced on the loudspeaker that the Dalai Lama would accede to the people's wishes, that he would not go to the Chinese headquarters. Rousing cheers came from the crowd, who continued to stay at the palace, but in smaller numbers as the day wore on.

The Chinese officials, of course, were greatly angered and accused the government of secretly leading the agitation by the people against the Chinese, and charging that Tibetan officials had refused to take arms away from the Khampas. The Chinese threatened that further action would be taken.

Later that day it was announced that some seventy governmental officials, citizens, and members of the Dalai Lama's bodyguard had declared that Tibet no longer recognized any Chinese authority and had endorsed a declaration made earlier denouncing the seventeen-point agreement of 1951, which was based on the assumption that Tibet was a part of China.

That day, the loyalty lines were clearly drawn. Now if one chose to be sympathetic to the Chinese, that was his decision, but there was no sitting on the fence. Either you were a good Chinese or a good Tibetan.

Tighter security was kept by the residents at the gates of the Ponsho building.

On March 12, a meeting of Lhasa women was held in front of the Potala to protest the Chinese actions. Thousands of women of every rank gathered to tell the Chinese to get out and to proclaim that Tibet was independent.

When I received my invitation to the meeting, I went to the Ponsho Lhacham to ask what I should do. She advised against going, but suggested that we send our personal servants. In my case, that was Wangmo, who volunteered to go. If there were questions, she could answer them. She was familiar with my thinking. She had been at previous meetings. When people saw her they knew she was my representative. Also, I could trust her. The invitation said that if we didn't go, we were to send money, which I did.

The leader of this gathering was a Lhasa trader, Serong Kunsang, the mother of six children. She was aided by some nobles' wives.

While the women, including nuns, were gathered in front of the palace, the Chinese took photographs and movies of the demonstration—no doubt for future use against these people. The Chinese closed the gates and at first weren't going to let the women out, Wangmo said. Using a loudspeaker, the Chinese urged the women to halt their activities, saying that they would not be harmed. Even some Tibetan women who were in the employ of the Chinese spoke out against the demonstrators.

Some of the women then went to Dekyi Lingka, the Indian trade mission, in hopes of getting help from the Indian consul-general. There was little he could do, but he promised to talk to the Chinese.

Bravely the women demonstrated all day in the central square in front of the Potala with their anti-Chinese posters. All shops were closed and Chinese were perched on the roofs of the buildings with their guns ready. Eventually most of the women left, some of them joining with the general populace to protect the Dalai Lama at Norbu Lingka.

Meanwhile Khampas were coming every day to see my husband. Uncle Tülku-la, regretting deeply that he ever had come to Lhasa, was frightened and remained in one of the bedrooms much of the time.

The Chinese continued their threats over the public-address system, saying that they would shell the city if the Tibetans did not surrender. The Chinese tried to look calm, but they were not; we could tell by their hurried manner. They traveled rapidly and in groups. We had heard that the Chinese were going around in their vehicles, picking up their Tibetan employees and some anti-Tibetan nobles to assure their safety. For some of these people, it was kidnapping. The Jokhang was open, but people went through it more hurriedly now. It was mostly the extremely old and devout who went on kora these days.

In this frightening atmosphere, we were torn as to what action to take. There was no guard at the Ponsho residence and it was on the edge of town. But we kept close watch on who was entering and leaving the building. We had no animals for travel. Some friends and relatives urged us to go to Sera Monastery. But this would mean splitting up our family, as I could not stay within the monastery walls and would have to be housed in a tent outside. Others suggested that my husband go to the Norbu Lingka, where many leaders and important lamas were standing by with the Dalai Lama. But no women, except those in the Dalai Lama's family, were permitted here either. Still other advisers suggested we move to Sho, a guarded residential area in front of the Potala that was the home of my husband's uncle, General Muja. But my husband stood firm and said that we all would remain together in the Ponsho residence.

It became necessary for our own protection to attempt to slow the number of visitors who sought to see my husband. Other lamas and nobles also were cutting down on their visitors. It was becoming impossible to know whom to trust. Most of the people who came to see us were armed.

Thus early on the morning of March 13, when some six Khampas arrived at the residence and asked to see Dagchen Rinpoche, I said he wasn't in. They waited on the second floor. They must have sensed that my husband was home because they settled down, declaring that they wouldn't leave until they had seen him. These were mostly men who were on their way to fight. They wanted final blessings from my husband, who was in a bedroom on the third floor along with Uncle Tülku-la.

The group increased until there were about forty Khampas. The men removed their rifles from their backs and rested them on the floor. Then they removed their knives and swords from their belts and placed them on the floor. They also untied their braids from around their heads in the traditional gesture of respect.

At about eight o'clock, two boys standing watch on the roof informed us that a jeep and some Chinese soldiers had stopped outside the residence. The Chinese were on their way up, the boys said.

Six soldiers holding their rifles ready, accompanied by an interpreter, a Tibetan whom I knew well, walked directly past the group of Khampas. The Khampas then followed them to the third floor and could hear my conversation with the interpreter. The interpreter first asked for my husband. I said he had gone out to one of the temples. Then they asked for his brother. I lied again, saying he also was out.

"What are these people doing here?" the interpreter asked. I said they were waiting to visit my husband.

The interpreter obviously didn't believe my story about Dagchen Rinpoche being gone. He and the soldiers began looking around. Meanwhile the Khampas had positioned their rifles and knives and retied their hair around their heads and appeared ready for action.

With the butt of his rifle, the interpreter shoved open the door of the bedroom where my husband and Uncle Tülku-la were sitting. The interpreter looked at me with contempt. I was speechless with fear.

"Who's that?" he asked in great anger, with accusing eyes upon me.

I explained that our guest was my uncle and nothing more. The Chinese were not swallowing that. They obviously thought the Khampas were a guerrilla group and that Uncle Tülku-la was their leader.

Finally the Chinese got around to their pretended mission. There was an important meeting at ten o'clock, and they said my husband and his brother must attend. To us it was clear that the Chinese had only one thing in mind—to capture the two and imprison them or at least hold them in custody.

Dagchen Rinpoche said he hadn't finished his prayers, that he hadn't dressed, and that he couldn't make the meeting today. The Chinese insisted he come. They meanwhile had gone to his brother's room and found him, also ordering him to come to the meeting.

My husband meanwhile had cleverly led the Chinese out from his bedroom into our visitors' waiting room. There was a large glass window in the adjacent room where the Khampas were gathered. They could see everything that was going on in the visitors' waiting room.

Dagchen Rinpoche, in an attempt to calm the situation, suggested the Chinese sit down and have tea. But they refused and proposed that the two get ready to leave.

We all doubted that there was any ten o'clock meeting. The Khampas were ready to halt any attempt to remove my husband from his home and the Chinese knew it.

"I'm not coming with you now, but I will come with my brother later," Dagchen Rinpoche said.

With this, the Chinese knew they were beaten. The interpreter's eyes were cast down in defeat. They started to leave.

"Be sure to come," the interpreter said as they departed.

Our Khampa friends had saved my husband from being taken away and may have saved his life. Without them we would have been powerless.

Later we learned that the same Chinese had gone to another residence close by and had taken away the noble, his wife, and two children. The noble's parents had stood by weeping as their son was put into the jeep. He was taken to Chinese headquarters, where many nobles and their families were being held.

The events had left all of us stunned. After receiving brief blessings, the Khampas left, saying they were confident my husband would use his special spiritual powers to chart his next movements. "Please protect us," they said as they departed to join their fellow guerrillas. I presumed they understood and forgave me for attempting to conceal my husband. I felt they knew how risky it was for anyone to tell the truth during these times.

Tengyam, our servant, rushed home from the central square to report that he had heard on the Chinese loudspeakers that "the Sakya lama had forty Khampa guards at the door of his home." The message strongly condemned my husband. At last the Sakya family had joined the perverse Khampas! Earlier the Chinese had avoided singling us out.

Dagchen Rinpoche no longer felt safe in the residence. He put on monk's clothes and went to the home of a distant relative only a few blocks away. We all felt the Chinese would return that day.

I so wished we were home in Sakya. Uncle Tülku-la and

Ani Chimi too were upset and spent much of their time praying.

With this close call behind us, the Ponsho residence moved to fortify itself. The Ponsho Lhacham was terrified. Two large wooden doors formed the entrance to the compound. Boards were placed against the gate and few persons were admitted. She ordered heaps of stones placed on the roof of each corner of the residence. The idea was that if the Chinese broke down the doors, they would be stoned.

Dagchen Rinpoche, after consulting a number of people about what we should do, decided we would leave Lhasa and go temporarily to Nalanda, a Sakya monastery north of Lhasa. We told no one immediately. We sent one of our former horsekeepers to Nālandā to arrange for about twenty horses or mules. We had no idea if he could get through.

The next few days were agony. At any time I expected the Chinese to return for my husband. He slept at home each night and then would return to the relative's house early in the morning. Chinese usually came on their missions in daylight.

The Tibetan government and the Chinese were continuing to discuss their worsening relations. Many Tibetans thought their side would win if there were an uprising. Some monks came from Sera Monastery, asking if we wanted to go there. They stressed that the Chinese were not allowed at Sera. But we declined.

Many people now were leaving the city. Only a few shops were open.

The horsekeeper returned, saying that two Nālandā Monastery lamas could arrange the necessary animals. They were kept a day's trip away from Nālandā, so would have to be brought there and then to Sera, where we would pick them up. I then began packing smaller, valuable belongings.

We told only the Ponsho Lhacham that we were leaving. She was surprised at our scheme, indicating that she didn't think conditions would be that bad in Lhasa. I asked her to care for some of my jewels, money, and other prized possessions, including fur hats encrusted with gold and precious stones.

I also asked the Ponsho Lhacham to care for our family pet Gyari, a German shepherd that less than a week earlier had become the mother of six puppies. Gyari, who had been with us for six years, was very aware that we were leaving. While I was packing, she brought each puppy, one by one, in her mouth and placed it in front of me. Extremely intelligent, she didn't want to be left behind. Her actions said "Don't leave us." The servants and I took her puppies back to the bedroom and closed the door. She made soft crying noises as I did. But I knew we couldn't take them all on what would be a perilous journey.

Others at the residence were told only that the family was going to visit Sera. One never knew whom to trust.

On the evening of March 18, we learned that the Dalai Lama was no longer at Norbu Lingka. We had no idea of his whereabouts. Some people even thought he was in one of the nearby monasteries. Some thought he had been taken away by the Chinese, but we believed that the Chinese would announce immediately if they had him in custody.

15

Flight to Freedom

Early on the morning of March 19, our party of fifteen left the residence, several of us carrying white scarfs and melted butter on the pretense that they would be used for religious offerings at Sera.

The breakfast table was left set with dishes and cups filled with tea to suggest that we would be home later that day. Uncle Tülku-la started out first on the only horse in our possession. The rest of us left on foot at later intervals. It was about six-thirty when I departed, wearing one of Wangmo's chubas over my own silk one. My husband wore an ordinary monk's garment. The children each had a dark blanket wrapped around them to disguise their clothes. Our faces were partially covered with scarfs as a disguise.

As I prepared to leave, there was a sad surprise. Tsomo, a sweet girl of about eleven whom the Ponsho Lhacham had taken in after the girl's parents died, had become close to me during our stay. She sensed we were leaving.

"Take me with you," she begged. "Don't leave me."

She held my hand and cried. I was near tears myself and my heart ached. But I knew we couldn't take her along. She was the Ponsho Lhacham's servant. Her mother also had been the Ponsho Lhacham's servant. When her mother died, the Ponsho Lhacham had promised to take care of Tsomo for the rest of her life. This was considered a strong obligation that was taken very seriously and was similar to parenthood. When Tsomo reached marriage age, with the Ponsho Lhacham's permission, she could leave. If I took Tsomo, it would be like kidnapping. But I had close ties with her and did her special favors.

Uncle Kunsang Nyima was to come that evening with some of our religious treasures, a number of them hundreds of years old. A trader we knew was to return to the city with some donkeys to carry the precious objects.

My husband authorized me to carry a small pistol, along with eleven bullets, which I was to use if an emergency arose. I had never in my life fired a gun, and I doubted whether I could do it.

My husband, Minzu-la, and three monk servants were visible in the distance as we entered the main road from Lhasa to Sera. There was frost but no snow. Many people were out, but no one seemed to be talking. Sad looks prevailed. Most of the travelers were going toward Sera. Usually at this time of morning monks were coming into Lhasa, cheerfully singing and praying as they walked. But now there were no monks going into the city.

We stayed at Sera only about an hour. It was crowded and confused. Many persons were moving there and the monks were extremely busy taking care of them. These monks also were manning lookouts in the surrounding mountain area. The fourteen horses and mules were awaiting us but there were no saddles. The Nālandā monks had thought we had our own. The Sera monks finally scraped up some saddles and bridles—some of them yak saddles.

We set out again for Nālandā, this time mounted, but still spread out, avoiding traveling in a group. Besides myself, our immediate group consisted of Ani-la, Mati-la, Ani Chimi, Wangmo, and Tenpa Sangpo, Ani-la's servant. There was a Chinese power station and bridge as we began the ascent of

Phenpo Pass. The bridge was guarded on either side by men in what appeared to be Tibetan Army uniforms. We stopped here and relaxed, seated on some rocks, while watering our horses. When I asked one guard who operated the power station, he answered that it was the Poshung, meaning the Tibetan central government. I then felt more at ease, and asked him a number of other questions about the bridge and the distance to the summit. I noticed that on the other side of the bridge there was a large building with wooden shutters that looked like doors on the side of the building. I never gave this structure a second thought. The same guard continued tactfully scrutinizing our group. The other guard, about twenty feet away, watched us but said nothing. They apparently were concerned with Khampa guerrillas and other armed Tibetans who might damage the power station. But we were three women, two babies, and a young monk, so we looked like ordinary travelers.

We departed in an effort to catch up with Dagchen Rinpoche's group, now out of view. Just before reaching the summit, we met up with them at a rest house. They had begun to worry, wondering what had taken us so long. We told them about our conversation with the power station guard. They asked, "What guard?" saying they had crossed the bridge in single file but had seen no guards on duty there.

We arrived on the summit of Phenpo Pass about four o'clock. From here we could look back upon a beautiful sight— the gold roof of the Potala in Lhasa and the Jokhang. It was nearly eleven P.M. before we arrived in Nālandā. Some Nālandā monks had come to the pass to meet us, but apparently we had missed them.

After we were served dinner, I thought at last we were safe. The Chinese probably wouldn't come here, I thought. Nālandā was off the main road and the Chinese had come here only a few times.

Early the next morning, with the arrival of Uncle Kunsang Nyima, we were told what we feared most—that the revolt had begun in Lhasa and that fighting had broken out. Uncle Kunsang Nyima had heard shelling from the Phenpo Pass.

That same day we learned how lucky we were to have even reached Nālandā. A horsekeeper newly arrived from the pass gasped when we told him that we had crossed the bridge near the power plant. The Chinese, housed in the large building we had noticed, had shot some travelers after we had gone through. Two women had been killed. Thinking back to our conversation at the power plant, I recalled that another nearby guard had said nothing. I now concluded that the guard had been a Chinese who could not speak Tibetan.

How had we escaped the wrath of the Chinese? The guards obviously had thought we were ordinary people traveling with our children. It had been a windy and dusty day, I recalled, adding to our disheveled appearances. We—thankfully—had apparently looked very ordinary indeed. We now realized we could no longer stay here.

On the second day at Nālandā, we began looking for horses or mules to buy or rent. We had turned our pack animals over to the monastery when we arrived. Uncle Kunsang Nyima's rented donkeys also were no longer available. Meanwhile we attempted to make the best of a bad situation. We visited the temples of Nālandā; my husband was busy with religious duties with the monks.

We were further alarmed when the two head lamas of the labrangs here said they were planning to leave for the Changthang. If the Chinese came, the lamas surely would be punished, they said. They feared retaliation because many Khampa guerrilla leaders had been stationed at the monastery. And the two lamas had given advice to the guerrillas. On top of all this, the lamas had played host to us. Some Chinese had referred to Nālandā as the "thieves' nest." This was because the Drawu-pon and his party of about thirty guerrilla fighters had stayed at the monastery for some time. The monastery still had some of the party's belongings, including fighting equipment. The Drawu-pon now was on his way to Lhokha.

The two lamas had many patrons to the north, they said.

They dared not tell the general Nālandā religious community they were going to leave, for fear the word would leak to the Chinese. Chinese always blamed the leaders. The monks would understand. They wanted their precious lamas saved. In some places, monks actually had asked the monastery leaders to escape.

This latest plan further confirmed that we couldn't stay here. If the Communists came, they certainly would take their anger out on us.

The next morning Wangmo washed the bright orange robes of the children and hung them outside on the roof of our labrang. It was a sunny day. Suddenly a Chinese plane, silver with a big red star on it, came across the pass. We could see it clearly. Quickly, I rushed upstairs to take the children's clothes off the line. The Chinese, I thought, might recognize them and come for us.

The plane returned about fifteen minutes later, circling the monastery several times and shooting at us. Then it turned off toward the Phenpo area, where there was fighting between Chinese and Khampas.

Little Mati-la and I stood closely together in a doorway during the strafing. Servants had the other children. It was my first experience with warfare. Empty shells were found later inside the monastery grounds and in a nearby stream. No one was killed or injured.

On our fourth day at Nālandā a former Sera Monastery monk came from Lhasa about midnight with the news that the Tibetans had won the revolt in Lhasa. My husband and Uncle Tülku-la received the news with some reservations as they felt that it was too good to be true. This good news spread quickly through the monastery. I rejoiced and immediately began planning our trip back to Lhasa, even thinking of several chores I must take care of there.

Early the next morning six or seven monks arrived from Sera. Some were barefoot, having escaped hurriedly from the monastery. They told of the defeat of the Tibetans in Lhasa and how the Chinese had fired on Sera. Even Sera's main temple was damaged, they said. Thus it was clear that the self-proclaimed ex-Sera monk, who had brought us the news of the victory, had been a spy. He had been served dinner at Nālandā, stayed two or three hours, and then had disappeared, saying he had to deliver the good news to other places.

On our radio we heard a broadcast from India announcing that the Dalai Lama was not in Norbu Lingka, and that his whereabouts still were not known. We were relieved, for again we knew that if the Chinese had captured His Holiness they would have announced it immediately. The Sera monks also knew that the Dalai Lama had fled, but they too had no idea where he was.

A few days later, another plane strafed the monastery area. This time some horses were killed. We hastened our plans to depart. The two heads of the Nālandā labrangs had left one midnight, having told us to take any of their belongings that we might need. We took a couple of tents, saddles, and some cooking utensils. They had asked us to go with them to the north, but after much consideration, we declined. They thought eventually we could get to Sakya that way.

A good share of our servants now wanted to go to Sakya, declaring that if the Chinese stopped us we could at least say we were going home. We also saw Sakya as our eventual goal, but we had no idea how we would get there, as many of the main routes now were held by the Chinese.

About thirty of us left Nālandā on the morning of our sixth day there. Our immediate party had some fourteen horses and mules. It was a poor group of horses we were able to obtain. Some were mares, some too young, and some too old and without teeth. Others had been injured in guerrilla fighting. Nevertheless we considered ourselves lucky to have them. Most of us were on foot. My husband was riding a mare—I was sure for the first time in his life, as mares are not regularly used for long-distance trips. I was reminded of an old Tibetan saying, "One may have great wealth, but it is not wealth if it is unusable when needed." We had about two hundred fine horses and mules at home in Sakya, but here, in a time of great need, we were without adequate transportation.

Members of the party were divided over which way to head. When we got out on the main road, two ravens circled our group. In my country, ravens are said to be a sign of foreboding. The omen is drawn from the bird's varied cries. We could interpret the raven's sounds in many ways. We believed we could determine from the raven's sounds what they sought to tell us. We regarded the ravens as spiritual messengers of our protector, Mahākāla. We had relied upon ravens in the past, especially when traveling. Tibetans had been using this method for centuries, because it is part of Tibetan Buddhist teachings.

This time the ravens clearly revealed that they had an urgent message and were showing us protection. So my husband and Uncle Tülku-la summoned the circling birds with prayers, asking which route we should take. When the ravens responded by flying directly east, my husband decreed that would be the direction we would take. Some in our party protested this was a terrible mistake, saying we would have to cross a main Chinese-held route connecting China with Lhasa. But my husband held firm, and eventually all of the skeptics followed him. This meant we would go east through the Phenpo grain-growing area, head south to cross the Kyi River and the main Chamdo-to-Lhasa highway, then we would skirt Ganden Monastery to eventually reach Samye Monastery. From there we hoped somehow to circle around to Sakya.

Many townspeople had been crying as we left. Here and along the way the people were greatly distressed for many reasons, including that their precious lamas were leaving. "The Buddha will protect you," they called to us. As we passed through the towns, people brought us buttermilk and chang.

Along the way we continued attempts to get horses. When we were lucky enough to buy an animal, we then had to find a saddle.

When we were too tired to continue, we stopped for the

night at the estate of a Lhasa noble where we obtained food for the animals, fuel, and water. People here knew that many of the nobles had left with the Dalai Lama and felt that the Chinese might soon be confiscating all their supplies. So they were generous to us.

As we moved along, our party grew to about fifty. Many of these refugees had brought large, heavy boxes and other belongings. The donkeys became so tired that the just lay down. Families had continually to throw away their possessions to lighten the burden.

We continued to another estate, some people sleeping in barns when they didn't have tents. At about three the next morning, the estate owners received a letter brought by a courier from the Chinese in Lhasa.

In essence the message said that many of the Tibetans were leaving and that the exodus must stop. "Return to your homes and you will not be punished" was the promise. The offer was discussed and turned down by the party. A few felt we should return to our homes or at least stay in one place. They held that there was no way we could get through to Sakya now. But most of us were of the opinion that we had to keep on the move. For if we were ever caught, we would be punished.

We departed early that morning and about a half-mile from the estate we came upon some Phenpo people and several Nālandā monks. The latter told us that the Chinese had come to Nālandā the night of the day we left. The Communists had arrived about midnight and the monastery had surrendered the next morning. So the Chinese were not far behind us, we felt.

Some of the refugees thought it advisable to heed the Chinese warning, fearing they would be caught and suffer reprisals. So they returned to their homes, afraid and tired. It was terrible for those families who couldn't agree among themselves what course to pursue, and who thus separated. I can still see them sorting out the few possessions they were carrying, too hurried to think clearly, frightened and uncertain about their choices. The road was crowded and confused. As I witnessed the remaining high lamas, abbots, and all the rest of our party walking wearily toward a place of refuge— no one really knowing where—I felt for the first time the grimness of our situation.

In this area we met a couple of monks from Samye. They informed us that the road to Ganden was held by the Chinese, so again we had to change plans. We learned that the Chinese, in an attempt to halt the exodus of refugees, were sending out planes to strafe them, particularly guerrilla fighters. We elected to continue east, heading into the Medo Gongkar area. The children slept in our arms. I carried Mati-la, my husband had Ani-la, and Minzu-la was tied on his horse. Others took turns helping us.

The next morning when we were proceeding single file on the north side of the Kyi River in the Medo Gongkar area, a Chinese plane flew over several times and then started firing. We thought we were the target, but the plane was aiming at a group of Khampa guerrillas about four miles away who were on their way to Lhokha. It was flat, open territory with no woods anywhere for us to take cover. When we spotted a small house several hundred feet from the road, Dagchen Rinpoche ordered us to dismount. Uncle Tülku-la said he was not afraid and called the names of Buddhist deities and lamas. We helped him dismount and then headed for the house.

A woman and her children lived in the dwelling. When we burst in, she asked, "What do you want?" The woman was displeased with her sudden guests and ordered us to get out. She apparently didn't know about the revolt.

The plane passed over again, low enough for us to see plainly the big red star marker. I was too afraid even to speak. But Minzu-la, now five, was very brave, going inside a barn attached to the house and taking off his charm box, holding it in his hand and calling to the small statues, "Please help us Lord Buddha and White Father," a reference to Dzongsar Khyentse Rinpoche.

The owner continued her orders: "Get out," she cried. "I

haven't seen a plane over our house until now. You are probably bad people." She let loose her big mastiff who barked but luckily didn't bite. He was confused by the excitement and noise. We stayed about a half-hour until we thought it was safe. All the rest of the day I worried abut the possibility of more planes.

We stopped at a Lhasa noble's estate for a late lunch. There we learned that there had been fighting at Medo Gongkar Monastery, only a few miles away, and that the Chinese had taken it over. So again we hurried on. We reached the Kyi River and found a wide and shallow spot where the river branched into several streams. But there was a rough, rocky bed and the water was swift and perilous. Some of the horses had to make several trips to carry us across.

As I crossed slowly on horseback, the water rose up to my knees. Suddenly I looked back and there was Wangmo, who held Ani-la, on a horse that wanted to lie down or sit down in the water. Wangmo screamed but Ani-la remained calm. There were more than a dozen old and precious charms on his belt. These included tiny statutes, relics of his ancestors and other famous lamas, and many paper prayers. These prayers were designed to protect Ani-la from any danger, such as water. One of the men who was helping me went to Wangmo's aid, pulling and pushing their stubborn beast forward.

Once safely on the other side, Wangmo was certain the charms had helped significantly. "Maybe if I had gone alone I wouldn't have made it," she declared.

After the crossing we went some two miles on the main Chamdo-Lhasa highway, parts of which had been heavily damaged by Tibetan guerrillas. We had to pick our way avoiding the holes and big rocks blocking our path. It was slow moving. Swinging east, we moved through the Jyamo country, ordinarily a peaceful farming area. Now we passed many refugees, some of them monks and soldiers who had lost in fighting at Sera and Drepung monasteries. There were sad sights, such as monks in women's boots, or boots that were not mates. Some of these poor people were hungry and deeply in want. There was some looting and robbing in the area. Some people, depressed and downhearted, just wanted to talk to anyone.

One day as we were heading toward the Jyamo and Samye GoGa Passes we noticed a group of about thirty-five men in Khampa dress across a stream from us. At first we were cautious, knowing the Chinese frequently disguised themselves in Tibetan clothes. Then we heard the Khampa chants of bravery and pride. As we caught up with them, they suddenly recognized my husband and the children.

It was a group from Jyekundo and Thalung monasteries! These men had fought the previous day at the defeated Medo Gongkar Monastery and now were on their way to Lhokha, the Tibetan military headquarters. I was so happy that I immediately thought, "Now we are saved." In the group were my girlfriend Lhayag's husband and father and some monks with whom we had become well acquainted during our months in Jyekundo. After receiving blessings from my husband, some of the men approached my horse. Their faces reflected joy and sadness. A few grasped my feet tenderly, tearful and speechless. Many of these men's families were still in Kham, but a few had some of the family's jewels, gold, silver, and money with them. They used these valuables to buy food when needed.

Our two groups exchanged stories, our group telling of our experience at the woman's house and the Khampas relating how at Medo Gongkar the previous day an airplane had strafed the monastery area. They were much distressed to see my husband on such a poor horse. They immediately shared their horses with our party, insisting on giving us five. It was particularly fortunate that we should meet our Khampa friends just in time for them to help us over the passes. The Jyamo Pass was not ordinarily open as the route to Samye, our next immediate destination. Samye was west of the Tibetan military headquarters at Lhokha. The passes were not used this time of year, but now many refugees had no choice but to take the rugged snowy route.

That evening as we camped part way up the mountain, we prayed for cloudy weather so that we would not be visible to Chinese airplanes. That night we divided up our paper money, thinking that if we should be separated all of us would have currency. The money was wrapped in cloth and tied at the waist, inside our chubas.

Arising at four the next morning, we found our weather prayers had been answered. It was dark and ominous with signs of possible snow. We reached the summit in the early afternoon. The snow was two feet deep in places. The cold wind blew dry snow in swirls about us, but it was not actually snowing. The animals were pushed up some of the steep sections until they were exhausted and foaming at the mouths. We had hired two men from the town of Jyamoda to guide us but they were baffled about the route because of the swirling snow. Whenever the trail was located, it soon was lost.

Everyone was walking except the children, who were carried. Uncle Tülku-la was supported on each arm by monks as he made his way through the pass. The Khampas ended up cutting a swath through the thick snow, which came to the horses' necks. The entire way was strewn with huge rocks which had to be gone around. Sometimes we would rest behind a rock for a few minutes to clear our faces of snow and ice and to wait for the others to catch up. We were two to three hours at least in the summit area, enduring these horrible conditions.

I had a huge blanket around me as we moved along the winding route. Our breath froze on our necks and head scarfs. The children had been given tea earlier in the morning, so when we got to the summit and rested briefly there was nothing to drink in our vacuum bottles.

The descent also was treacherous with melting snow and generally poor weather. We stopped to feed grain to the horses. All of us were famished, having had no hot food since early morning. But there was no chance to make a fire. We just mixed buttered tsampa with snow and made the best of it. The mixture was so cold we scarcely could bite into it.

Finally we reached a flat area. We saw nomads in the distance and felt we were back in civilization. We bade farewell to our Khampa friends, who now turned southeast towards the Lhokha battle area. Our plans were uncertain, we told them, as indeed they were, for we didn't know what conditions we would find after Samye. That night we stayed in a forested area and had to make a fire to keep away leopards and other wild animals. Our family and our precious horses were in constant danger.

The next evening, at about nine-thirty, we arrived at Samye, whose monks had been informed of our imminent arrival by two of our men who had gone on ahead. Trumpets and drums were sounded and the head monks of the monastery came out for the greeting. They had flashlights and lanterns, but we could hardly see our hosts in the night.

Samye, the oldest monastery in Tibet, had close ties to Sakya. The abbot there had studied with Uncle Tülku-la at Sakya and had been a student of my husband's father. We were warmly received.

During our three-day stay at Samye we learned from the Tibetan guerrillas' headquarters here that the Dalai Lama had passed through Lhokha and that he was safe, although we still didn't know his whereabouts.

It was necessary to spend a brief time here to chart the next stage of our journey and to get a travel permit from the guerrilla leader to move further into Lhokha and to cross the Tsangpo River at Dorjedrag. The freedom fighters at Samye informed us that it was not safe to go to Sakya via Gyantse, so that left us in the position of heading toward Gongkar Monastery still further south and west. The monastery was a Sakya monastery not related to Medo Gongkar Monastery. Gongkar Monastery was in a less accessible area and had many Khampas in its ranks.

Some of our servants wanted us to stay here at Samye, believing it to be a safe refuge. Even some of the monks declared that we could seek safety in the ancient, holy caves in the nearby hills. The caves had been occupied in the eighth century by Padmasambhava, the founder of Samye Monastery. But we still hoped to get back to Sakya somehow. We were the last group of refugees fleeing in this area.

At Samye we left some tents, cooking utensils, and part of our heavier belongings. But my husband insisted that we keep the important religious books.

Departing one morning, our group of twenty followed the Tsangpo along its sandy banks. Our guides were a man named Losang, a Khampa guerrilla leader, and his assistant, both of whom were familiar with the area. The hot sand blew in our eyes, stinging our faces. Often we had to shake it off our hats and scarfs or spit it out of our mouths. This was very irritating for the children. For me, it was a reminder of my pilgrim days in this area. But now we were fleeing for our lives. The horses, their footing unsure, frequently fell in the sand. We found traveling in the sand almost worse than trudging through snow.

In late afternoon, the Tsangpo was muddy, dark yellow, and dirty, partly from melting snow. There was no drinking water along the way, so we pressed forward, dry-mouthed in the heat. That night we stayed at the town of Drag at the estate of a Lhasa noble family. The caretakers of the estate were very sympathetic to the Chinese. The estate keeper at first wasn't going to allow us to stay, even though we assured him we would pay.

"The Chinese keep watch from the mountain," he said. "It is dangerous—you shouldn't stay. If you do, the Chinese will be here tomorrow."

That evening we asked to buy firewood and other supplies from him.

"I had some," the man said sharply, "but the Khampas took it." Then he called Khampas offensive names. He didn't trust Losang and his assistant. Several families lived nearby, so we bought food for the horses and other supplies from them.

All that evening we were terrified. The Chinese were just a

few air miles away. Khampa soldiers stationed at Drag went to a nearby hill to scout for any Chinese, but there were none. The estate man had lied or had sought to frighten us.

When we left the next morning, several in our group, however, said they had heard gunfire from the north side of the mountain. After traveling about a mile, we came upon several Tibetans trying to escape, en route from Gongkar Monastery to Samye. They too had heard the guns, which they said were from Gongkar Monastery, our intended destination. They said there had been several days of hostilities at Gongkar and that they expected the monastery to fall that day. The next objective for the Chinese, the travelers felt, would be Dorjedrag, where we planned to cross the Tsangpo.

When we heard this terrible news, everyone stopped. The majority of our group wanted to return to Samye, but Dagchen Rinpoche didn't think it wise. Again Uncle Tülku-la rolled the dice and the message was that we were to continue, in accordance with my husband's decision. We could hear the gunfire now but we felt we had no alternative but to go on to Dorjedrag. There, with Dordrag Rinpoche as our host, we had a hearty lunch, every now and then hearing the guns in the distance.

We crossed the Tsangpo in four small yakskin boats. A number of Khampa refugees were in line here waiting to cross, but most of our group was taken across before nightfall. Our plan now was to circle to the south, following the shore of the big Yamdrok Lake, and try to get to Sakya that way.

That evening we stopped at Kyidechokar Monastery, on the main road from Lhasa to Tsedong, the primary headquarters of the guerrilla fighters in Lhokha. The servants were so frightened they didn't want to stop at all. But we were exhausted from the crossing and other hardships of travel. That evening we received a written message from a man named Namseling, a distinguished Lhasa noble and a representative of the Dalai Lama's government for Tibetan guerrillas in Lhokha. He urged us not to stay here any longer. We should leave tonight, he said, since the Chinese were approaching from Gongkar Monastery. "Don't think about your possessions," he said. "Try for your lives." But we simply could not move on—we were just too tired. And part of our party, along with some of our possessions, still was on the other side of the Tsangpo.

At about midnight, I was awakened by the tinkling of bells and hoofbeats, signaling the arrival of some Khampas from Gongkar. It was a group led by Amdo Leshe, a well-known businessman and trader in Tibet. The group had retreated from Gongkar but left soldiers stationed at several points between there and Kyidechokar. I didn't sleep a wink the rest of the night, but stayed up sorting more belongings. We left perhaps half of our things here, carefully labeled and sealed for the time when we would come back to claim them.

The Kyidechokar monks prayed that night, saying that they had "precious elements"—a reference to the Sakya family—in their monastery. But the monks too were very fearful and most stayed awake through the night, plotting ways to get us safe passage.

The previous evening we had received a message that the rest of our group, still on the other side of the Tsangpo, would arrive at Kyidechokar about noon. So the next morning some of us left without them. Since we were traveling more slowly with the children, we knew they would catch up with us. I gave Wangmo some of my good clothing to wear because it was of better quality than hers. We dressed in layers, constantly having to make choices about what we could carry.

The next day as we pressed along, we crossed a pass, and from the summit we looked out at beautiful Yamdrok Lake, framed by majestic mountains. When we saw the lake, we took off our hats and made a religious gesture of respect to this famous holy lake and said prayers.

Uncle Tülku-la, who was not feeling well, was in the group that brought up the rear. At each place we stopped we left a message for his group and asked people to help him when he passed through. I thought of him constantly.

As we continued our travels, we did not generally tell people that we were members of the Sakya family, unless they recognized us, or that we were going to a Sakya monastery. We listened to people we met along the way, hoping for some guidance, but we often didn't trust the conflicting reports we heard. When in doubt, we resorted to divination.

Close to Yamdrok Lake, we came to Karmoling, a temporary marketplace and nomadic area. Karmoling is known for its specially dried meat. Whenever Karmoling's dried beef and lamb was put on sale in Lhasa, it was sold out immediately. We did not have much time to cook en route, so I bought five large leather bags of this dried meat. Many persons here gave us cheese, buttermilk, and yogurt. The area also had lots of hay, a treat for the animals. But it was not safe to remain here and we moved toward Dowa Dzong, where we planned to stay a few days to allow Uncle Tülku-la's group to catch up. We hoped by that time to be temporarily out of immediate danger of the Chinese.

Our battery-operated radio was still working well, and we listened each evening to the news from New Delhi. But the broadcast in Tibetan only said that the Chinese had not located the Dalai Lama. The "news" in Chinese from a station in Lhasa was propaganda.

From persons en route from Gyantse, we learned that the Tibetan government had called for volunteers to fight. Many men from the Yamdrok area answered the call of their country. We met about a hundred, all going to fight in the area of Gyantse. Most of these men were inexperienced in warfare, but a good share of them were young and patriotic and had faith that they would drive the Chinese out of their country. They had no rifles or ammunition, but some had swords and long sticks as weapons. They had many yaks as pack animals.

After crossing another high mountain pass, we were very tired when we finally arrived at Dowa Dzong. Our clothes, after four days of steady traveling, were covered with dust and grime. The horses were tired, their food in short supply. Many persons had passed through this area earlier, seeking permits to go to Bhutan. The dzong, the building that housed the government's representatives, was atop a hill. A noble and a monk were the administrators of the dzong. There also were some thirty soldiers here, none of whom we knew. Dagchen Rinpoche didn't particularly want to stay in the government building for fear of possible bombing, but arrangements had already been made by Losang.

Uncle Tülku-la's group of about seven arrived the next day. Fortunately he was improving but still he was not in good health. The group had had to stop intermittently to allow him to rest. If he remained too long on his horse, he would become dizzy and lose his balance. For at least six months he had been on the road, first fleeing his monastery, then enduring the trauma of the Goshang and now escaping with us. Uncle Kunsang Nyima had diagnosed his condition as exhaustion.

It was at Dowa Dzong that we were forced to conclude that it would be impossible to get to Sakya. The Chinese were now in the area of Ralung, northwest of Dowa Dzong, only a day-and-a-half away by horse. Khampas had sent messages each day from Ralung to Dowa Dzong about traveling conditions. Ralung had been our last hope. All routes to home were blocked.

Thus, if we were to continue, our only course was to go to Bhutan. This meant crossing the Monla Kachung, a mountain in the Himalayas that was 24,740 feet high at its summit. The pass we selected was normally open only in summer, but already many fleeing Tibetans had made the arduous trip. My husband and his brother had talked about this route before Uncle Tülku-la joined us. He was not opposed, so we decided to take our chances, which were very poor, especially with little children.

Our hopes of remaining here for a few days to give ourselves and our animals a rest soon were shattered. One evening while Dagchen Rinpoche and his brother were praying in a sacred temple at the dzong, the monk administrator arrived and presented an envelope and white scarf in the traditional gesture of respect, placing it at my husband's prayer table. The monk then left. Some three hours later, when my husband returned to our quarters, he opened the envelope. Enclosed was a permit to allow our group to cross into Bhutan. A note said that we could take any supplies at the dzong that we might need. He also asked Dagchen Rinpoche to pray for him. The next morning after breakfast, my husband sent his servant, Tengyam, to thank the administrator for the permit and to discuss with him our travel plans. But there was no one in the administrative office. The administrator and two of his personal servants were gone. His treasurer said he had left in the night without disclosing where he was going. The treasurer politely told us that the administrator had received several messages that he was being sought by the Chinese.

Now we knew it was imperative that we leave. Dowa Dzong was a headquarters for the Tibetan army. If the Chinese came, they would focus on capturing us. The further we fled in Tibet, the more the suspicion of us as opponents of Communism would increase. We no longer had an option to stay in our homeland.

That evening our group met to discuss the possibility of sending messengers, who would travel in the hills off the beaten path, to tell our relatives in Sakya that we were heading into exile in Bhutan. Three servants volunteered to carry the message to my mother, Aunt Chacha, and my husband's sisters, and to help them escape to Sikkim or India via another route. Again my husband went to the temple using divination to consult Palden Lhamo. The answer was not to dispatch any messengers at this time.

At this stage, we came to grips with some of the hard facts: a home that was no longer attainable, a venture across a treacherous mountain, and finally an uncertain future in Bhutan. But we thought our stay there would be temporary, that political conditions would change and we could return to Tibet. That gave us courage, but no one really wanted to leave Tibet. It was a wrenching decision.

We left at sunup the next day. Our horses were still not rested, but we were in a farm area where horse fodder, at least, would be inexpensive. During lunch in a small village, several Tibetan soldiers arrived on their way to Dowa Dzong. They were retreating from Ralung, which had fallen from both an aerial and ground attack by Chinese troops. Leaving quickly, we headed south up the Druk Pass, staying that night on the ascent route. Large rocks were strewn on the bleak terrain. Tents were placed over two circular walls of stone that formed a kind of dugout. There was no firewood and the yak dung was wet. We went to gather some bushes and roots, but they also were damp. Nothing burned well, so we put butter on the fire to make enough flames to heat water for tea.

We sat up, hunched together, trying to sleep under the two tents. Because of the strong winds, bags of horse fodder were placed at their edges to keep them down. One tent was held down by several blankets laid flat. That night it snowed lightly and then froze. When it was time to leave the next day, it was impossible to fold the blankets. The tent poles were broken and used for firewood. It was one of the worst nights of my life.

Before leaving that morning, we held a tea-offering cere- mony. Our group prayed and chanted, asking protection on our journey from our special Sakya protectors and the local mountain deities we believed dwelled here. The first serving of our breakfast tea was offered to these deities by tossing it in all directions.

We soon overtook many other refugees who were moving along this road with their yaks, horses, and mules. At times we thought it was hopeless, that we would never make it over this winding Druk Pass and that the Chinese soon would be after us. The temperature remained cold, but the sun came out as we continued to climb. With this warmth, we believed the deities had answered our prayers. The horses were so overloaded with the frozen tents and other heavy items that I wondered if we would make it this time. Near the summit, we had to navigate a very narrow section of road. Some of the other refugees lost their animals when they failed to keep their footing going over this treacherous place. The poor beasts plummeted far down over the mountainside. "Watch out," we heard others warn when animals anywhere near us fell. Our horses were so weak that at times we had to push them on.

On the descent, conditions improved and we passed the sacred Druptso Pemaling, the revered lake that I had visited on pilgrimage en route to Sakya years ago. I remembered how quiet we had been in the presence of this lake, as it was said that singing or boisterous behavior would cause an avalanche here. Centuries before an earthquake had caused the lake to flood the towns below it. This time, too, I didn't want to make noise. Others said we had no time to be concerned. After having been at the tail of the refugee column for days, we now passed many other refugees, some so tired that they no longer cared. They just wanted to rest.

The next day we came to Mila Sekarguthog, the nine-story structure that was said to have been built by Milarepa, the poet-saint. Again I remembered my girlhood pilgrimage here, when a monk had circumambulated the top story for me because I was too small. Now I felt somewhat like a guide to my husband and could tell him what was coming next on our journey. However, I felt strange, for we were traveling the wrong way on the pilgrimage route. In Tibetan Buddhism, the operation of prayer wheels and other rituals is conducted clockwise; we were traveling counterclockwise on the pilgrimage route.

About an hour after our arrival at Sekarguthog Monastery, the monks served us an unforgettable nourishing hot lunch. Soon after, a group of soldiers who had fought at Dowa Dzong came. They had fought one night and the next day, they said, against the enemy. The Chinese troops came at first in earth-colored camouflage uniforms that blended with the countryside. Thus, the Tibetans couldn't spot them until they were very close. Eventually some five hundred Chinese had come. Some of the Tibetans escaped by jumping out of the windows of the dzong when the Chinese set fire to it. Only seven of the thirty Tibetans at the dzong survived to make their way to Sekarguthog Monastery.

When we heard this news, we decided to leave the same day, but Uncle Tülku-la would have none of it. He had never been in this sacred area, and he wanted to visit a labrang here noted for having been built by Marpa the Translator, founder of the Kagyü school.

"I don't care if the Chinese come and kill me," he said. "This is a good place to die."

He said he had studied about Marpa, the eleventh-century teacher who is one of the saints of Tibetan Buddhism.

"I always wished to visit here to pay my respects and to make offerings to this great teacher," Uncle Tülku-la said.

The home of Marpa was preserved here and was considered a holy sanctuary. The sanctuary was on a hillside southwest of Sekarguthog Monastery. Uncle Tülku-la also had visited the retreat cave and birthplace of Milarepa elsewhere in western Tibet. Milarepa was Marpa's student and religious lineage holder, the man who became Tibet's most famous poet.

I gave up trying to change Uncle Tülku-la's mind, but extracted a promise from him.

"Please," I implored, "after you have done what you wish to do, will you follow us as soon as possible?"

I was worried that he would stay too long, that he would be unable to catch up to us. He traveled slowly, having to stop frequently to rest.

"I promise," he said.

So our party again split.

Dowa Dzong had long been a potential target both because it was a government outpost and was a Khampa stronghold. There was much food stored here and many soldiers were away fighting at Ralung. I wondered if someone had informed the Chinese that the Sakya family was attempting to escape. The nights were horrible, as I always feared that "tonight will be the night they come." They had, after all, come to Dowa Dzong at night. I kept my pistol on my person day and night. I had decided that I would not fire it unless the Chinese attempted to snatch my children from my arms.

That evening our smaller party, now of about fifteen, left

the main roads and stopped at a home that appeared to be empty. Outside there were many sheep and goats. Presently a teenage boy came upon the scene, saying that his family had left for Bhutan and that he was caring for the animals. There was plenty of horse food here and the boy told us to help ourselves for free, but we paid for the hay and grain. We felt that the parents were hiding somewhere close by and keeping watch. This was a remote area. People here had never met any Chinese and rather regarded them as devils.

The following day we came upon the last house we were to see as we passed out of Tibet. It was a beautiful place nestled in a valley with many grazing yaks, large meadows, and an atmosphere of gentleness. I could clearly see and hear water rushing over the rocks in a stream that passed near the house. Learning that we could not buy tsampa in Bhutan, we purchased two bags of it here, along with some horse fodder. We really needed five or six bags of tsampa, but other refugees also were making purchases from the owner. It was the last time for us to use paper money in our homeland.

That night we camped near the snowline on the ascent of the Monla Kachung. On the summit of the pass of this great mountain, we would cross into Bhutanese territory. Since there was no water at the campsite, someone went up to the snowline to get ice to melt for tea. It tasted strange, I thought. We ate dried meat that we had obtained from Yamdrok, which made us very thirsty. It was so cold that the tea seemed to cool off in seconds. Dagchen Rinpoche and the two eldest boys wore a kind of knitted hood that exposed only their eyes and mouth. I covered my face and head with a long, wide, embroidered silk scarf. When I breathed, ice formed on the scarf and I had to shake it off. Mati-la and Ani-la wore fur-lined garments, their long sleeves tied tightly to keep them warm.

Our tent was erected in a lopsided fashion against a cave. It was so cold that it was nearly impossible to sleep. That night Minzu-la, a tired little boy with big eyes, prayed with all his heart. A charm box was near his head. The three boys slept between my husband and me. Other refugees camped around our tent.

At the first break of dawn, we started out on what was to be the highest and most arduous climb of my life. For the beginning of the climb, I was on horseback, with Ani-la in front of me. We were tied together with a long, raw-silk-fringed shawl knotted at my back. As we prepared to depart, I dropped a precious personal possession out of my chuba pocket. It was a cherished string of prayer beads with counters of solid gold, decorated with precious jewels. Its greatest value was that it had been blessed by many lamas and that I had used it for saying thousands of mantras. I had carried the prayer beads daily for years. But there was no time to unfasten myself from the animal, dismount, and pick up the prayer beads. In these hours we were thinking about our lives and nothing else. I looked around for help, but no one nearby was on foot. As we continued the ascent, the incident remained constantly in my mind. I reasoned that the prayer beads' protective function would prevent our enemies from pursuing us beyond the point where they had been dropped. These thoughts eased my loss a little. I thought this incident had removed part of the dangerous obstacles before us.

There was no defined road up the first third of the mountain. Then the route narrowed to a trail, which we followed on foot in single file. The trail was dry snow, and very slippery. In some places the snow was three to four feet deep. Sometimes the horses were so fearful they just stood and shook, not wanting to continue. Some persons suffered from the lack of oxygen in the high altitude, but most of our family had traveled in mountainous areas and had no problem. Usually Tibetans carry turnips as an antidote for altitude sickness, both for themselves and their animals. But in this crisis, turnips had been the farthest thing from our minds.

Often it was rocky, making our way doubly perilous. The whistling sound of the wind cut through the silence that surrounded travelers so tired, doubt-filled, and fearful that conversation seemed pointless. As the morning progressed, the sun again became our enemy. Our eyes burned from the glare. I took some strands of my long hair and wound them around my head to form a kind of eyeshade. In the long lines of refugees that stretched in front and behind us some people were cutting off hair from the tails of their yaks for shades. Because the glare from the snow was so intense, I tore up my pink and turquoise embroidered silk scarf and gave pieces of it to some so they could wipe the tears from their eyes which in some cases had begun to bleed. Their hands were rough and nearly frozen stiff. Their sleeves were dusty and far too coarse to use on their eyes and cheeks.

At this low point in my morale, we came upon some seven Tibetans who had crossed the Monla Kachung, had made it to the border point of Druk Tshamba, and now were returning. They said Bhutanese soldiers were preventing anyone from crossing the border bridge into Bhutan. These people had been at the border some six days. They warned that we would starve to death at Druk Tshamba when our food ran out. This dreary tale startled everyone. But none of our group wanted to go back into the hands of the Chinese. We would take our chances with the Bhutanese. Other groups paid heed to us and, when we decided to go on, they did too.

It was dangerous having these homeward-bound people pass us. We had to lean way out into the snow to make room for them. Sometimes we heard snowslides in the distance that sounded like bombs. Snow glare, exhaustion, bad news from the returning Tibetans, and now this.

Minzu-la remarked that surely we were safe, for the Chinese would not go through such agony as we had to come and get us here. All of the boys' faces and ears were chapped and sore. Our only first aid for them and us was a little butter. Mati-la, about thirteen months old, probably was the most uncomfortable of all. We had only a few diapers and they had to be used over and over. Often he went long hours wet. In hopes that the soiled diapers would dry out, we tied them to the horses to catch any breeze. Sometimes the diapers just froze. At night they were placed under my blanket with the idea that the heat of my body might dry them some. Whenever a fire was built, some of us would hold the diapers around the flames. During the perilous traveling in recent days, we had difficulty just getting Mati-la changed. Often it meant stepping behind a rock to get out of the wind and cold for a few minutes. Still nursing, Mati-la was an understandably fussy and unhappy baby. Occasionally I let him sip a little tea and water from a vacuum bottle. On the mountain I saw no one else with a child this young.

As we approached the summit we saw large white rocks stacked so that they almost looked like humans. There also was the usual huge mound of maṇi stones and prayer flags, which we circumambulated once. All of us prayed here, even though it was so cold one could barely move against the wind, which felt like needles or darts on our faces. Dagchen Rinpoche prayed and placed a scarf on the maṇi-stone mounds. I just wanted to look back at my country. That summit was the highest spot on earth that I had ever been or am likely to be. There was an awe-inspiring view of the Himalayan range, a panorama of green Bhutan to the south, and the land of my birth to the north. The huge white rocks looked like sentinels before which the range's many pinnacles stood out. Above the floating clouds, the sunlight drenched the snowy peaks.

Strangely, I thought that now I would be losing all my familiar mountain deities. Bhutan surely would have different mountain deities to worship. These were lingering moments I would savor all of my life. The last of the old and familiar was being left behind to begin a new chapter in an unfamiliar land—if we succeeded in crossing the border. I left this scene with great reluctance.

The descent was much easier. We slid down the rough areas and walked around some treacherous points. The air was warmer, and the ground was slippery, muddy, and wet. In the distance, the scene was bright and uplifting. Our horses were very thin and weak, but we didn't lose any on the way down. There had not been any forage for them for nearly three days.

We hurried out of the snow, hoping to find a flat campsite for the night. The children were thirsty and hungry, as were all of us. We stopped at the first stream to let humans and animals drink. Just before dark we reached a flat area, not green, but where there was a stream. We stopped and rested. When we looked back at the mountain, the groups of yaks, horses, and humans looked like an army of bugs descending.

That night we camped on the edge of a pine forest where the animals could graze. Again we set up our tents, with their poles of different lengths. There was dry wood and dry yak dung here. When we made the first fire for tea, agony swept most of the group. The smoke brought tears and intense pain to our snowburned eyes. It felt as though hot pepper was being poured into our eyes. Ani Chimi's eyes were particularly bloodshot and swollen. (Her eyes were scarred internally for the rest of her life.) Wangmo, who had deep-set eyes, had escaped injury and did much of the work for us that night. Our first postsummit feast was soup, rice, and tsampa. But the steam from the soup hitting our eyes was almost unbearable.

The ears of some in our party were so severely frozen that pieces of them snapped off. Many had sore and infected feet. My husband's horse was ailing and could no longer go on; it collapsed in exhaustion. Dagchen Rinpoche prayed for his recovery. A man was left here to care for the animal until he recovered. Unguarded, the horse would be prey to wild animals and vultures.

The next day we arrived at Druk Tshamba in a border area where there were no homes. It was a trading area where bargains had been struck and friends had met under conditions of less strife. Bhutanese nomads lived here in summer. Although there were flowers and green grass, it still seemed cold to us. Bhutanese soldiers had moved here about a week earlier. Bhutan was opposed to letting Tibetan refugees pass through its borders, fearing that the Chinese might come after them. There were some two hundred refugees when we arrived here, but there were many more farther up on the mountain where they could hunt for food.

The Bhutanese soldiers were camped in tents about a mile from us near the bridge over the Manas River, our gate to freedom. About an hour after we arrived, some twenty soldiers approached, and asked why we had come here. When we explained that we had fled the Chinese, the Bhutanese asked why we hadn't escaped by another route to India. They said that we Tibetans must return and that, if we didn't leave tomorrow, we would be forced back. But having dealt with the Chinese, we weren't afraid, even though our direct request for passage had been refused.

The next morning more soldiers arrived, first telling a group of nobles to leave. When it was made known that my husband and his brother were in the group, the Bhutanese changed their attitude somewhat. They were impressed that the brothers were descendants of the Sakya Pandita, the thirteenth-century religious leader of Tibet, who was well known to Bhutanese Buddhists. The Bhutanese began to refer to them as "Sakya Pandita," giving scarfs and food to the two. Later in the evening they returned secretly with gifts of rice and eggs for my husband and his brother. The soldiers were under orders not to sell or give food to refugees.

Nonetheless, our food was dwindling and so we rationed it. All of the refugees were now eating nettles, which were young and tender; thus our delicacy became nettle soup. Back home this would have been poor peoples' food. But here it became our staple. We boiled it with tsampa and our tasty dried meat from Yamdrok. Ani-la, who could have had anything his heart desired at home, came to relish this dish. One day, when he was hungry and anxious for lunch, he called out to our chief cook.

"Yes, little Precious One," the cook answered.

"When can we have our nettle soup?" Ani-la asked enthusiastically.

"Little Precious One, I will bring it right now for you," the cook replied.

A cheered Ani-la said, "Oh, good. What about Chö-la?" referring to Minzu-la.

Some of us, including the cook, were moved to tears by this incident. Usually, back home, he had to coax the boys to eat, resorting to stories about how good the food was.

One of our daytime chores was to wash clothes in a nearby stream. The children, who obviously didn't realize the seriousness of our predicament, amused themselves by throwing rocks into the stream. For the adults, the days were long and tiresome.

Two days after our arrival Uncle Tülka-la's group joined us. He was exhausted, and had barely made it over the Monla Kachung. In some parts of the descent, monks had taken turns carrying him.

On our radio one evening we learned that the Dalai Lama and his family had made it safely through into India. A massive sense of relief swept through the camp, ending weeks of anxiety and fear for His Holiness' safety. With the most precious Tibetan free again to lead us, there was renewed hope among us all. It was the first good news we had heard since leaving Lhasa. Messengers were sent to relay the announcement to other refugees camped higher up on the slopes. This news was also a great boost to our morale, for we felt that His Holiness would appeal to the Bhutanese king to let us pass through Bhutan. An estimated seventeen hundred refugees were now on this side of the Monla Kachung, and many were very low on food.

The Chinese meanwhile sent two Tibetans, who were Chinese sympathizers, to the Bhutanese side of the mountain with the message that all of the refugees must return. If the refugees didn't comply, they would be punished when the Chinese did catch up with them, the two said. The message was delivered to some three hundred Khampa soldiers among the refugees. The Khampas captured the two Chinese sympathizers and refused to permit them to return over the Monla Kachung. A few days later the Chinese sent two more men with the same message.

The Bhutanese, who were now sympathetic to our cause, were all the more convinced that the Chinese would come and take over the border bridge. We now knew the Chinese forces to be at least as close as Mila Sekarguthog, and they may have been closer.

In an attempt to make things homey and to make the best of a bad situation, we set up our portable shrines. Butter-lamp offerings were made daily. Dagchen Rinpoche held special services for anyone who was ill. One of the Bhutanese head officers invited my husband and his brother to the Bhutanese military headquarters to conduct a long-life initiation ceremony. Then more soldiers visited us. Despite their orders, they secretly offered us money or food.

"I don't want any money," my husband assured them, "just food."

The Bhutanese had become disturbed by the killing of musk deer and mountain goats by the refugees farther up the mountain. It was the refugees' food supply, but the Bhutanese didn't want their stocks of wildlife depleted.

Some of the Khampa soldiers were becoming restless and impatient. They went to Army Chief Commander Kung-sangtse, a noble who was among the refugees, and told him of a plan to overrun and enter the Bhutanese border guard station. They said they had been very patient up to this time, but they were convinced that Bhutan never would admit the refugees and that the only way to freedom was to storm the border station. The Bhutanese soldiers would be outnumbered and it would be a simple maneuver, the Khampas reasoned.

Commander Kungsangtse was horrified at their plan and told my husband. Dagchen Rinpoche talked to the Khampas, warning them of the dangers of such an operation. Finally, I too talked to one group of the men, some of whom I knew from Jyeku. Reluctantly the would-be rebels cancelled their plans. Most of us thought that if there were any border violations, our chances of being admitted would be greatly diminished.

During one evening newscast from New Delhi, we learned that the Dalai Lama had conferred for hours with Indian Prime Minister Jawharlal Nehru and they had discussed the Druk Tshamba crisis. It was mentioned that about seventeen hundred refugees were here, including my husband, and that some were near starvation. Nehru agreed to talk with the Bhutanese king. Word spread rapidly throughout the camp. We were so happy that night that we ate more food than usual. We learned later that two monks had died from illness and lack of food in the refugee camp. Some seven of our animals also had died, including the horse we had left farther up the mountain.

The Druk Tshamba area contained a variety of wild rhododendrons, some of which were poisonous. Tibetans generally were not familiar with these varieties and only learned to avoid the harmful plants after it was too late to save many of the foraging animals. Now we were worried that even though we might be admitted to freedom, we would be unable to carry our valuable religious possessions with us. Four of our horses were dead, the others were in very weak condition.

The next night's newscast said the Bhutanese king was sending his brother-in-law, Prime Minister Jigme Dorje, to Druk Tshamba. His was a name familiar to many Tibetans. When he arrived the next day, Jigme Dorje stepped up on a big rock and talked to some six hundred refugees. At first his message was a scolding one. He thought it best, he said, for many of the Tibetans to return home. In our opinion he had to say this to save face with the Chinese. For others—soldiers who had fought, persons without homes, and indeed those with relatives and associates in India—there was a reason to pass through Bhutan, he continued. At some length he pointed out India's overpopulation, the scarcity of food and jobs, the nation's generally hard life and hot climate. He stressed that once we crossed into Bhutan, it would be difficult to return to Tibet. The refugees merely sat quietly on rocks and on the meadow ground. Clearly no one wanted to return to life under Chinese Communism.

Then he opened a briefcase and read the official letter saying His Holiness had requested that the refugees, including the Sakya Phuntsok Palace lamas, be permitted to pass through Bhutan. That request to the Bhutanese king was granted, the prime minister said. At this everyone jumped up, bowed in a gesture of respect, and thanked him and cheered.

But the Dowa Dzong noble administrator, who had been assigned for two terms at Dowa Dzong, could not pass the border upon orders of the Bhutanese king, the prime minister said. The administrator had been the central figure of an earlier trade conflict over the sale of Tibetan salt and other goods to Bhutan. He had imposed an embargo on salt sales that lasted a year, causing great hardship. He had been the lay partner of the monk administrator at Dowa Dzong who had given us a permit to go to Bhutan. I was confused about the king's ruling because I knew nothing about the salt incident. Then, urging calmness, the prime minister announced the regulations for passage through Bhutan.

Tomorrow, he continued, the first group would be permitted through—women and children and monks without food. Children were to be separated from their parents and taken by the prime minister and a group of nurses to India by a special shortcut. Then groups of two hundred would be admitted every other day—a necessity because the roads were so narrow. Wealthy Bhutanese had established feeding stations along the passage route, he said. After the talk, his aides distributed pork, shortening, popped rice, powdered milk, tea, and sugar to the hungry. We didn't queue up because we still had some food.

That evening, he added, we must surrender our firearms, knives, or other weapons we possessed, for it was ruled that they could not be taken into Bhutan. This was a great sacrifice for many of the Khampas, for whom a gun is their most treasured possession. I gave up my pistol, which had been with me day and night since I left Lhasa and which, although never used, had become a familiar friend.

That night I scarcely slept, for I was opposed to the prime

minister's ruling that children would travel separately. I was still nursing Mati-la and didn't want to be parted from any of our children. The next morning I pleaded with Jigme Dorje and he relented, letting nursing mothers embark as a group. Thus after twelve uncertain days in the Druk Tshamba, Ani Chimi, Wangmo, the children, and I crossed the bridge to freedom. Bhutanese bearers helped with the children. Dagchen Rinpoche and the rest of the family were to come two days later.

Our destination was Gangtok, Sikkim. Dagchen Rinpoche had an aunt, the Densapa Lhacham, there, and we knew she could help us. I had no idea what a refugee's life in India would be like. But I was convinced that there we would be free, with opportunities to practice our religion without harassment and to continue our unique culture.

16

Life in India

Less than twenty persons were in our group of mothers, children, and nurses, headed by the prime minister, who set out the next day. I was unhappy to leave Dagchen Rinpoche and the rest of our Sakya party because I felt the border area was unsafe. After our ordeal of crossing the Himalayas, I never trusted the Chinese. Even though the Druk Tshamba was Bhutanese territory, I worried that the Chinese might try to take the refugees back into Tibet or shoot from a distance in an effort to get refugees to return. We did not know it, but the world was focusing its attention on our part of the globe and the plight of the refugees and the Dalai Lama. In contrast, Dagchen Rinpoche was greatly relieved that at least his wife and sons, along with Ani Chimi, were safe. Our immediate destination was Bumthang, a small town that had a summer palace owned by the Bhutanese king.

Our group had four horses carrying supplies and clothing. The road was too narrow to ride except when crossing streams. We crossed a bridge and then began the long walk on the narrow roadway that soon brought us under a canopy of bamboo trees. The foliage was thick in spots; every time Ani-la lost sight of me he would cry. He missed his personal servant, Tenpa Sangpo, who was left behind. The boys were carried by Bhutanese bearers, who bowed and otherwise showed great respect for them. The bearers were mostly barefoot and wore a long-sleeved garment that fell to their knees made of striped, tightly woven material, tied at the waist. It was new to me to see so many laypeople with short hair. The hair of the Bhutanese women we glimpsed along the way reminded me of the nuns around Sakya, who had bangs and short hair, and wore jewelry.

The road was moist in some areas, especially near streams. We were warned that if we sat down in these moist places, leeches would attack us. We stopped and stared at first at the perfectly formed, big trunks of bamboo. I now realized the source of our unique Tibetan butter tea churns, which were made from these stately trees. Along the way we also saw people weaving mats and baskets from smaller bamboo shoots. They worked their magic right at the trees so that the bamboo remained moist and pliable.

It was April, the season when wildflowers of many varieties bloomed near the rushing streams. The sun glistened on beautiful waterfalls. The hillsides were covered with colorful wild rhododendrons. We walked single file, savoring the warmth of the sun and the natural splendor about us. I had traveled widely in Tibet and had seen some of these shrubs in bloom. Others were seeing them for the first time, stopping and staring in amazement.

Ani-la was three and frequently asked for his father. Minzu-la, five, was taking his adventure with less trepidation and tried to comfort Ani-la in a loving brotherly fashion. The bearers were amused by Minzu-la, and intrigued by his childish questions, even though they sometimes had difficulty understanding his accent. In small villages along the way, Bhutanese citizens watched our small band of refugees, their faces reflecting our sorrow. The bearers told their countrymen that the boys were Sakya sons. Some gave our boys fruits, boiled eggs, and popped rice. Many times Minzu-la would reach out and bless them. Often the Bhutanese would touch their heads against the boys'.

The journey to Bumthang took several days because we had to proceed very slowly with the children and mothers. The prime minister had arranged lodging at guest houses along the way. At Bumthang we were housed in bungalows near the courtyard of the palace. One of my neighbors there was Rinchen Drolma Taring, known as Taring Lhacham, a member of a prominent Tibetan noble family, whom I had seen at social events in Lhasa. She was greatly concerned about her husband, Jigme Taring, a member of the Dalai Lama's party, who had remained behind taking photos of what the Chinese had done. I told her that we had learned from other refugees that he had fled, disguised in women's clothes. She was greatly relieved. She believed my message, even though she had heard different stories about the fate of her husband and was confused.

We became close friends, living under the same roof. We had much in common, in part because of our rank and education. We even helped each other braid our hair, something that never would have happened in Tibet. At home, each of us had our own hairdresser and a personal servant who cared for our tresses. Also women of high rank wore varying hairdos that were related to our different styles of headdresses. We had many mutual acquaintances, even though there was a considerable difference in our ages. We learned a great deal about each other and shared our grief at family left behind. She helped me through the lonely hours while we waited here with little to do. The Bhutanese government furnished and served our food. We washed our clothes in a nearby river and hung them on rocks to dry. At Bumthang, a wealthy Bhutanese cabinet official presented new outfits to each of the boys. These were lighter than the fur-lined clothes they had worn since we left Lhasa. He wanted to keep the boys' old clothes as a blessing and protection. We were delighted to have these new outfits, but it took the boys awhile to get used to them.

About a week later, Dagchen Rinpoche and Trinly Rinpoche arrived with another group of about two hundred refugees. Most of the refugees were out on the nearby plain, some without tents. The Bhutanese government had to decide which refugees would go in what direction to India depending on their health and age. Although the weather here was very comfortable, the next part of the journey was a hot, humid, and dangerous passage through wild-animal country.

Trinly Rinpoche kindly agreed to lead the rest of our Sakya party, carrying our belongings, heading southeast through Buxa on a roundabout way to India. The remainder of us would head south on a shorter route to Gyagong. We agreed to rendezvous in Gangtok, Sikkim. There were less than sixty in our group, including Rinchen Taring.

We began our trip of about two weeks to Gyagong. Walking and riding, we sometimes stayed in tents, other times in Bhutanese homes. The group of twelve Lhasa nobles, also refugees, always went ahead, making reservations for accommodations for Dagchen Rinpoche. We were always last to arrive at a station because the Bhutanese asked my husband for blessings. Also we had to stop to feed and rest the children.

One day Uncle Tülku-la asked the boys if they were tired. Minzu-la answered, "Of course! The sun is burning on my back and the Bhutanese bearers are burning on my front!"

Many Bhutanese continued to line up as we passed to receive blessings. Our bearers told them proudly who they were carrying. We were well fed. There were many fresh fruits we'd never seen before, including bananas and persimmons. The bananas were growing wild everywhere en route. But there was one thing we couldn't eat—the hot red peppers fried in oil, mixed with rice, and eaten by the Bhutanese with their fingers. We used red peppers at home, but always in small amounts and mixed with other foods. Minzu-la watched in amazement while the Bhutanese ate this dish. We shared our plentiful food supply with the bearers and other Tibetan refugees on the way. What a change from the Druk Tshamba, where we had to eat nettle soup! And that had been in short supply.

Dagchen Rinpoche visited several monasteries on the way, including the famous Taktsang (Tiger Nest) Monastery, built into a rocky hillside.

One aspect of our journey was the danger of wild animals. At times our guides told us to travel closely together to avoid elephants and tigers. We saw only the footprints of elephants just before we reached the border of India. We were wary of tigers through most of Bhutan. Once I saw a rattlesnake twisted around the trunk of a tree; thankfully I was on horseback. I warned the others who were on foot. As we passed one hillside we were cautioned that this was porcupine country. If angered, they would form a ball, roll toward you, and possibly injure you badly with their quills. Most were black and white.

We had to change our drinking habits. We could not drink the water without boiling it because our bodies were not used to the bacteria. Our horses could drink only from the large rivers that rushed through the territory.

When we arrived at the Indian border in the Gyagong area, we had to contend with brief customs paperwork. Now we were in Indian government hands. Our bearers had long since become part of our party, but it was time to say goodbye. We all thanked them for their help. There were many tears at our parting. As our lives took a new course the bearers requested blessings from Dagchen Rinpoche and Uncle Tülku-la.

Minzu-la wondered what was ahead, asking us, "Who's going to help now?" We were on our own with only two servants.

Government workers took us to a large two-story brick building that looked as if it had been unoccupied for decades. The pathway and steps to the building were overgrown with grasses. Inside, the building was spacious and quiet, but because the windows were not working, the temperature was often over one hundred degrees. At night the building was cooler, luring in insects, including ants, mosquitoes, and flies.

At nightfall we could hear the crickets. There were no other sounds, since the train station and main town were about a mile-and-a-half away and there were few passersby. In the dark we watched the beautiful fireflies, reminding me of peaceful shooting stars. We first had seen them in Bhutan, where they would come into our tents. At first my eyes followed them in amazement because we did not see their bodies, only their lights changing colors, which ranged from light blue to pinkish.

I had always wanted to go to India because I had heard so many good things about it. It was the home of Lord Buddha, the place where he had formed his teachings and purified and blessed the land. In winter many Tibetans went to India on pilgrimages to the holy places. I looked forward to meeting people who were kind and friendly. But I found this section of India much different than I had imagined.

Townspeople came in the morning and evening to get water from the river near our building. Groups of women, clad in colorful *saris*, came carrying water jugs on their heads. When we tried to question them about our needs, they turned their faces away, covered their heads with the saris, and quickly departed. The people were very dark-skinned and slim and seldom smiled. Children were a little more sociable, following us but making fun of us at the same time.

We stayed much of the day at the river, where we had company from the many water buffalo which lay in the water to beat the heat. If we came too close, they shook their heads and stared menacingly, advancing toward us. I was gravely disappointed at how the residents shunned us, and now even the animals apparently disliked us.

But we learned that no travelers stopped here in Gyagong and that these Indians had never seen such a variety of odd-looking people. Understandably, they were wary. Passing before them were lamas, monks, nuns, laymen, women, and children, all in varied states of attire and disarray. Many of the Indians probably didn't even know why we were here.

We were in Gyagong at least a week before our special

government train arrived. An Indian interpreter notified us a day in advance that finally the train accommodations were available. We boarded one afternoon, mixing with other passengers on very crowded cars. Uncle Tülku-la took a seat next to an Indian woman and continued saying his mantra loudly. Frightened, the woman screamed as though he were going to hurt her. She pulled away, attracting the attention of many other passengers and the conductor. The conductor investigated and then apologized to Uncle Tülku-la, saying the woman had never seen any people like us and had never sat next to a strange man before. Women traditionally get preferred seats on Indian trains. The conductor then moved her to a different seat.

For most of us, it was the first train ride. We had done so much walking in our earlier days of struggle that I felt comfortable and at ease during the ride. But Ani-la was frightened by the noise and strangers and moved frequently from lap to lap.

The most difficult chore for us was using the restrooms while the train was moving. So at stops we would get off and go to the bathroom at the station. We had to search for one and we couldn't read Hindi. Several times we nearly missed the train. At every station, we could buy tea and pastries. Food also was sold on board, but we didn't have much appetite on the train, which traveled day and night. The train motor and whistle disturbed our sleep during the several nights of travel.

During the day we passed rice fields tended by workers and their water buffalo. Sometimes these animals lay in the water, unfazed by the locomotive's noise. This contrasted with the yaks in my own country, which would startle and bolt away at many noises, even whistling or the sound of a slingshot.

I saw hundreds of people who appeared to live at the train stations, earning their livelihood from the tourists. At every stop, vendors reached up to our open windows hoping to sell snacks and knicknacks. There were beggars of every age with their hands out. I thought "Is this the real India? Are we too going to spend our lives in an environment like this?" Many questions arose in my mind about our future. I knew we wouldn't live in poverty, but I was greatly disturbed to see so many people hungry. Many were in poor health and disabled. I had never seen so many skinny people. The boys were fascinated by these scenes of bustling humanity and were overjoyed when the trains stopped at the stations.

After several days, we reached our destination at Siligiri. There we were met by members of the Densapa family from Gangtok, Sikkim. We were guests at a reception given by Tibetan friends and disciples, who had come from Kalimpong to greet us. It was such a relief to see our countrymen again. At our other train stops, we had had to watch every single piece of luggage to make sure it was safe. We sat in an air-conditioned guest house, devouring our first real meal in days.

The Densapas' two jeeps headed for Kalimpong, with the Tibetans who had given us a reception following as an escort. Our luggage was routinely searched for weapons and contraband, but we were so happy that we didn't worry abut it. We were driven to a rented house in Kalimpong, the Dromo Bogsa, where we occupied the third floor. Our upbeat mood did not last long. Shortly after the arrival, we were informed that Dzongsar Khyentse Rinpoche had passed away in the royal palace temple in Gangtok. This shocked and saddened all of us, particularly Dagchen Rinpoche. This was his root lama, with whom he had planned a reunion. Dagchen and Uncle Tülku-la departed immediately for the memorial ceremony in the palace. They were gone about two weeks, during which they also visited with the Densapa family.

Although we were in mourning, we settled comfortably in the rented quarters. We had lots of friends and faithful Tibetan visitors who brought us food and clothing. They all gave a singular message: "You are saved and in freedom." At last, I thought, we had a home—at least until Tibet regains its freedom.

Trinly Rinpoche and his party arrived safely from Buxa and my husband and uncle returned. So our family was together.

I tried to find news of Sakya, especially of my mother, Aunt Chacha, and Dagchen Rinpoche's four sisters. We learned that Chinese authorities in Sakya were uncertain whether we were still in Tibet or in exile, so they had left our palace undisturbed, but kept the family members and palace under close watch. We decided to send Tengyam, Dagchen Rinpoche's trusted servant, and Palden Dorje, a Khampa who volunteered to go to Sakya and try to bring out family members and any sacred Buddhist items. They went on foot, posing as ordinary travelers.

Meanwhile, our Kalimpong landlord, a Tibetan who had immigrated to India after years as a trader, appeared to be pleasant. He never complained about the many visitors or noise of the children. His young daughter, a Buddhist nun, often offered pastries and hot milk to the lamas and sweets to the children. But just after we thought we were comfortably settled, our friends warned us that the landlord was a Communist spy. At first, I thought, "This can't be. Everywhere we go, we are dogged by the Chinese." But some of our close friends investigated and learned that the landlord went to secret meetings every midnight and came home hours later.

Some high-ranking Tibetans like Dorje Phagmo, a prominent abbess of a nunnery at Samling in the Lhoka area, had fled with us through Bhutan. She and her family had settled at Kalimpong too, and I had visited her. But suddenly she and her relatives disappeared from Kalimpong. The Kalimpong news media reported that she was kidnapped by Communist spies and forced to return to Tibet. That incident convinced us that we had to move out of Kalimpong. But we could not reveal our plans. Meanwhile, faithful followers warned us to be very careful about who we invited to our residence and where we visited. We too could be kidnapped, they said.

The family met privately and decided to move to Darjeeling. But we told the landlord only that we were leaving for a week's visit with a friend of Trinly Rinpoche. We left in one jeep, taking only the bare necessities. At Darjeeling, we were housed at the residence of Lhakpa Tsering, a Sherpa who warmly welcomed us. His home was a three-story brick building where we had the entire third floor and an adjacent kitchen. The building had its own shrine room. The shrine room was typical of those in wealthy Tibetan homes, with ornately carved shelves and many antique Buddhist images. Sterling offering cups and butter lamps were in use daily. The lodging was comfortable for the servants and us. Lhakpa Tsering and his wife and family invited us to stay as long as we wanted.

I felt safe in this clean, beautiful city, where I could gaze at the splendors of the Himalayas. I visited the gardens and viewing areas where one could sit and look at the mountain glories. Darjeeling had so much British influence that I found myself learning two new cultures. Many of the shops near us were British owned: a bakery, tea parlors, and photo studios. With so many blond, blue-eyed people, I finally stopped staring at these Europeans. In a few days, we sent servants to pick up our belongings and move us permanently from Kalimpong to Darjeeling. We sent the Kalimpong landlord a note explaining that it was more convenient for our family to stay here.

Our home on Tenzing Norgay road was much more private and our quarters more quiet than in Kalimpong. Also the residence was not accessible by car. Tourists did not come here, except those occasionally seen on horseback or those visiting a giant prayer wheel nearby that was about fifteen feet high, built by Lhakpa Tsering's father. Sometimes we went twice a day to turn the millions of Buddhist prayers. Tibetans called it "Mani Dungkhor," which means the "Billion-Mani Prayer Wheel." On special religious days, we took butter lamps and incense.

Every day I waited for news from Sakya and prayed for the travelers' safe journey under risky conditions. One sunny morning while I was sitting with Wangmo and the children, relaxing on the flat roof of our home, I saw the Densapas' jeep driver hurrying toward the house. Pasam came often with supplies, but this time I had a sense that he was bringing us some special news. I greeted him with enthusiasm as he approached the house.

As usual, he bowed and greeted me formally. I asked politely about the Densapa family, and he nodded positively. He blurted out that Tengyam and Palden Dorje had arrived last night in Gangtok at the Densapas'. "Then what . . . ," I urged, eager for the next words. None of the rest of the family made it out of Tibet, he said, almost apologetically. The two men would be coming to Darjeeling in a few days, he said. He had no other details, except that the family members in Sakya were safe. I did not question him further. I was deeply saddened and confused as to why the rest of the family did not escape. In tears, I remained upstairs on the roof. A little later Dagchen Rinpoche called me down to tell me of Pasam's news, which I already knew.

Four or five days later Tengyam and Palden Dorje arrived in Darjeeling with the details. When they had reached our nomad estate about five miles southwest of Sakya, Palden Dorje remained hidden in a tent. Any unfamiliar person in Sakya would be questioned, especially a Khampa. But Tengyam and the estate owner's son went in late evening under cover of darkness to the palace. Chinese were away attending a propaganda movie in the main part of Sakya about a mile away. Tengyam met my mother and Aunt Chacha and told them that we all had safely arrived in India. They were overjoyed, because they had heard rumors that the Phuntsok Palace family had been kidnapped and taken from Lhasa to China. Others told them we had just disappeared from Lhasa.

Tengyam told them to get ready to leave, but Aunt Chacha was convinced that it was her responsibility to remain at the palace. She wanted to see what might happen to our property and precious possessions. My mother, who was the younger of the two sisters, thought they should depart now that they had the opportunity. She stressed that we had given them permission to leave the palace. Again Aunt Chacha refused but said that if my mother wanted to leave, it was her choice.

The two were very close and had lived together for most of their lives. Finally, my mother said she would not leave without Aunt Chacha. My mother pointed out that no outsiders were aware that Tengyam had contacted them. If my mother were to leave, she said, Aunt Chacha would be questioned and possibly severely punished by the Chinese, especially if they learned about her contact with us through Tengyam. While the discussion was in progress, Tengyam said, the movie ended and the guards and residents returned to the palace area. Tengyam had to leave hurriedly without contacting other members of the family. Earlier Aunt Chacha had directed him to a servant family who lived adjacent to the palace. Several thousand silver Chinese coins were hidden in their home. She told him to take as many as he could, which he did at great risk. The servant's family was fearful of being seen and caught, so they threw boxes of coins from a window to an area behind the building. Tengyam and the nomad's son gathered them. Our nomad on the estate then provided Tengyam and Palden Dorje with several horses and safe arrangements for lodging on the trip back to Gangtok.

Dagchen Rinpoche then wrote a letter to the Dalai Lama in Mussoorie, at the headquarters of the Tibetan government in exile, asking his recommendations and advice for our family's future. The letter listed all the names of Sakya family members who had safely reached India and asked what we should do from now on. I was very surprised when his reply came within a month. It was a very thorough and sympathetic response that indicated he had given it considerable thought. His Holiness' advice was that Dagchen Rinpoche must take charge as the representative of the Sakya school with headquarters in Mussoorie. As the head lama, he was to travel widely in India. Trinly Rinpoche and Uncle Tülku-la and their monk servants should return to Buxa, where monks and lamas were resettling.

Our two older boys, Minzu-la and Ani-la, were to be among a select group of children to go to Switzerland for from five to eight years. Our youngest, Mati-la, was to move to Mussoorie, where he could be placed in a Tibetan children's nursery. I should assist Lacham Tsering Drolma, who was the nursery director. The rest of our servants were to remain in the Tibetan Self-Help Center in Darjeeling that was directed by His Holiness' sister-in-law, Mrs. Gyelo Thondup.

I was moved by the prompt response, and my faith and devotion to His Holiness grew. I asked Dagchen Rinpoche why, when we were in Tibet, our letters to the Dalai Lama took months and months to get a response, and those answers were never precise. Dagchen Rinpoche said that many of our letters may never have reached His Holiness and instead might have been filed away and forgotten. Dagchen Rinpoche was convinced that if the Dalai Lama had received our earlier letters, he would have responded to them.

We had a family meeting to discuss the letter. Dagchen Rinpoche called his aunt, Mrs. Densapa, who was something like a mother to him. She and her husband both came from Gangtok to the family conference. The more we discussed and thought about the recommendations, the more we were convinced they would not work for our family. The Densapas thought His Holiness' advice was sound, except that they wanted Trinly Rinpoche and his personal servants to come to Gangtok to live there. Mrs. Densapa always had been very close to Trinly Rinpoche.

Dagchen Rinpoche said he would assume the responsibility for representing the Sakya school. But the other recommendations, he said, were not the best for the family. After all we had endured in escaping together to reach freedom, he thought it was unwise to scatter the family. There was no way I could give up my children, even for a week. They were still very young. I wanted them to be tutored by Uncle Tülku-la and to stay in Darjeeling, where we liked the climate and living conditions. Nor could I abandon our faithful servants. After all, they had left their own families back in Tibet in order to serve us. If they found better jobs and wanted to leave us, I would not stop them. I often told them that as long as they wanted to stay with us and as long as we had a cupful of rice, we would be together. The servants were very upset too, especially at the idea of sending the children to a different country. Our cook observed that when Tibet was soon freed and we could go home it would be difficult to get the boys back from Switzerland. They were very close to the children and regarded them with love and respect.

None of us agreed to the separation plan. With the exception of Dagchen Rinpoche, we would stay in Darjeeling. He first went to Mussoorie, headquarters of the exiled government, for a religious conference. He then began his duties as representative of the Sakya school, traveling through many parts of West Bengal and meeting with exiled Buddhist leaders.

Then in Kalimpong, he met two British educators, Professor A. W. MacDonald, and his French wife, Siane. They were great scholars and very much interested in Tibetan studies. Later both came to Darjeeling, where they visited us often. We helped Professor MacDonald with his research on Tibetan history and language. In return, he would take the whole family to movies or out to dinner. Sometimes he also gave us financial help. He was well aware that we had no income and that we had many expenses.

Professor MacDonald was a reserved man, honest and compassionate. We became very close. It was easy to communicate with him because he spoke Tibetan fluently, as well as Nepalese and some Hindi. One of the important lessons he taught us was the significance in Western culture of being on time. In Tibet, we did not live by exact timetables and did not know the exact hour of the day. I was among those, for example, who wore a wristwatch primarily as a piece of jewelry. But under his tutoring, we learned how to be prompt. One day he invited our family to the University of Paris to assist in research on Tibetan civilization under a three-year research grant. The invitation was only for Dagchen Rinpoche, the three boys, and myself. But going to France did not appeal to me. Nor was I interested in going to any other country in the Western world. Already, I reasoned, we were too far from home. I did not want to leave the rest of the family and our servants. MacDonald continued to work with Dagchen Rinpoche in Kalimpong and Darjeeling.

At the end of 1959, ten members of the family decided to go on a two-month pilgrimage to many of the Buddhist holy places in India. Dagchen Rinpoche could not go. This year the Indian government provided much of the train transportation for Tibetans who wanted to visit these holy sites. We went to eight of the thirty-six sites considered holy places in the Buddhist world. The places on our journey included Lumbini, the site of the Lord Buddha's birth in Nepal; Benares, where he first preached his holy doctrine; Magadha Resort or Vulture Hill, the Buddha's resort where he taught the Sutra of Transcendental Wisdom; Bodhgaya, the site of the Buddha's enlightenment and the holiest place in the Buddhist world; and Kushinagara, where the Buddha drew his last breath.

It was a strenuous trip, with crowded Indian trains, heat, searches for accommodations every night, and arguments with *kulis* who helped us with our luggage. But these hardships accumulated merit and removed bad karma. We felt we had gained something very valuable in our lives. When we returned from the pilgrimage, Uncle Tülku-la and Minzu-la had gone to live in a former palace two miles outside of the city with several of their immediate servants. Uncle was to give Minzu-la religious instruction. Uncle Tülku-la, who was used to the monastic life, also was in a quieter, more private atmosphere. When I visited them, I loved to watch the winding train, the women workers picking tea leaves on the terraced tea plantations, and the foot travelers and cars going to and from Darjeeling.

After we had settled into the routine of life in Darjeeling, Professor MacDonald brought an American scholar, Dr. Turrell V. Wylie, to meet us. Dr. Wylie asked us if we were interested in going to America to collaborate in research. I did not know geography very well, thinking that the United States was part of Europe. We said we would think about it.

Dr. Wylie, from the University of Washington in Seattle, said he was traveling among Tibetans and would be back later. Before he came, we did have second thoughts about accepting the invitation to France if Professor MacDonald would take Uncle Tülku-la and Trinly Rinpoche. Dagchen Rinpoche pointed out that we were merely waiting here and not accomplishing anything. Every other week Mrs. Densapa was sending out one hundred pounds of rice, along with fruit. But we knew we would have to repay her for those gifts. Mr. Tenzing Norgay and his devoted wife brought us fruit, fuel for cooking, and other items. Often he would stop on the way from his home, which we could see from our home, to visit with Dagchen Rinpoche. He always said that if we needed anything to let him know. His wife came often and asked for blessings and religious teachings. She also would bring other Sherpas to visit the lamas.

Professor MacDonald introduced us to many Westerners, including British tea planters. They would take photos of us, then take us to dinner at British hotels in Darjeeling. We learned a great deal about Western ways on those excursions. The British influence here remained very strong. Merchants catered to British and Indians and Europeans who vacationed here at this hill town with its unique mix of East-West culture and religion. I was impressed by an unusual crowded little train that climbed the steep, winding path into the Himalayan foothills, carrying passengers between Darjeeling and Siligiri. I was astonished to see passengers gripping the outside of the cars as the train climbed snakelike through the steep terrain.

During these times I never felt this was my permanent home. We remained optimistic that soon Tibet would be free and we could go home. But meanwhile, I learned a tremendous amount about budgeting for our big family. In Tibet, I never worried or even thought about being poor. For generations we had had wealth, property, and power. Throughout our family's history, these had been earned by good leadership and spiritual teaching. But now we faced the idea of no steady income, and what we had we tried to stretch in many ways.

Now I could only window shop for things I had liked and taken for granted before. My closest friends came to me in tears and asked how we were going to survive with a big family. I was pleased by their concern, but their remarks never depressed me. I always reminded them the Lord Buddha was with us. We were free, and even though we did not have much, we were together. And we did have good health. I had faith that something good would come our way.

Some of my friends and relatives even suggested we dismiss our servants. You have done enough, you have brought them to safety, and now they should be placed in jobs in camps and settlements, they said. But I objected, feeling a deep responsibility for these long-time employees.

During these Darjeeling days, I learned who our true followers and friends were. These people came to our house with gifts and sympathy for our cause. We met many new friends. Others, even relatives whom we felt sure we could rely on, fell short of our expectations. For example, traders to whom we had given business opportunities at Sakya and who now had far more than we did failed to pay us back or show their appreciation when we desperately needed it. These financial problems, plus the fact that the political situation in Tibet was not improving, convinced me that we ought to at least consider any offers to go to another part of the world.

While we were pondering the possibilities, I became a very close friend of Mrs. Gyelo Thondup, sister-in-law of the Dalai Lama and founder of the Tibetan Self-Help Center for Tibetan Refugees in Darjeeling. I called her by her title, Lhacham Kusho. She helped me in many ways, both financially and in her encouragement and advice in personal matters. She was honest, frank, and compassionate. She had accomplished much for Tibetan refugees, especially children newly arrived from Tibet, even though she was not Tibetan and had never visited Tibet. Born and educated in China, she had lived in Darjeeling many years. She spoke Tibetan fluently, as well as English. I was a frequent guest in her home, where she served me my then-favorite food—fresh-roasted sweet corn on the cob and hot milk. I never refused the roast corn, which we did not have in Tibet. Her house was about a half-mile from our residence. Often she would call to me to join her on walks. We shared many common interests, but not religion.

For example, while on our routine walk past the Ghoom Monastery, I often would enter the temple to offer money or to buy candles and incense. She waited outside. When I rejoined her, she would admonish me with a smile, saying, "You're no longer in your country and living the palace life. You have many mouths to feed." I always answered politely, "Yes, that is true." But her words never stopped my offerings. Sometimes she would slip an envelope in my chuba and then say, "Don't refuse this little thing." When I opened the envelope, it would contain several hundred rupees and a note that directed me, "Please use this money only for the needs of yourself or your children."

Shortly after Dr. Wylie's visit, a patron and former leader in Amdo, Trochu-pon Dorje, brought a message that an official from Taiwan was at a hotel in Darjeeling and wanted to meet privately with Dagchen Rinpoche. My husband sent Uncle Kunsang Nyima to report that my husband was busy at the moment and to please send any message back with him. The Taiwan official said he was sent by the Chiang Kai-shek government, which had learned that the Sakya lama and his family had fled from Tibet with the loss of nearly all their possessions. His government offered to help in any way, even with our resettlement in Taiwan. We could keep our entire group together and there would be no obligation.

Now we had three invitations to leave India. Some of our party thought going to Taiwan would be a better choice because we would not be separated. I went to my friend and trusted advisor, Mrs. Thondup, for an opinion on the Taiwanese offer. She said that to go to Taiwan was not wise for political reasons. She suggested we accept the offer of financial help, but not to make it publically known. The exiled Tibetan government did not want to offend India because of its great humanitarian role in admitting the refugees. At the time, relations between the Indian government and Taiwan were sensitive. Most Tibetans considered the Chinese people to be one, no matter which government prevailed. Both Chinese governments frequently had attempted to subjugate the Tibetan people. She commented that she knew many other Tibetans who were receiving funds from the Free China government, even though they did not need it desperately. At that time, the Taiwan official did arrange for many Tibetan guerilla leaders and some high lamas to resettle on the island. Earlier news reports said that any financial funding from outside governments for Tibetan refugees must be cleared through the Indian government or the Dalai Lama's government.

Dagchen Rinpoche then sent Trochu-pon Dorje and Uncle Nyima, who politely informed the Taiwan official, with profound thanks, that at the moment we did not need their help. If we did in the future, we would let them know.

17

Path to the West

It was early 1960 when Dr. Wylie and Professor MacDonald sought an answer to their offers. After much family discussion, Dagchen Rinpoche had weighed the two offers carefully. We knew very little about either France or the United States. We were close to Professor MacDonald, whom we affectionately called Sup Micdo, meaning Sir MacDonald. The name MacDonald was difficult for us to pronounce.

But using divination, Dagchen Rinpoche decided that the move to the United States was best for us. This also was the preference of the Densapas. Both my husband and his brother respected the advice of T. D. Densapa, a chief administrator for Sikkim's King Tashi Namgyal. Although we had decided to go to America, we still had to work out details on how many family members could go. No servants would be permitted to accompany us under the Rockefeller Foundation grant.

MacDonald said he was sorry he could not act as educational host to the Sakya family. But he agreed that the offer to go to the University of Washington was best for us because he could not take the whole family to France.

Dagchen Rinpoche said the first step was to get permission

from the Dalai Lama to leave for three years. But Wylie said that was not necessary yet, as he had to return to the University of Washington to determine if our request for eight people would be acceptable. But I was apprehensive. I asked Wylie whether, if Tibet became free before the end of three years, we could leave Seattle and come back to our homeland. Wylie laughed at my childish and naïve question and said no, that this was a three-year contract.

We gave Wylie all of the background on our family of four adults and four children. The fourth child would be my husband's youngest sister, Kunyang-la, who was about fifteen. The paperwork would take about three months, Wylie said. Wylie left some Rockefeller monies with us. This bound us to the arrangement and made me feel more secure. We kept this information within our immediate family and servants. If we went to Seattle, we would have to make arrangements for Ani Chimi and Uncle Kunsang Nyima and the servants. We met with the servants and told them what their future might be in the next three years. Most were pleased that our family would stay together, even though they would be left behind. We said we would do our utmost to see that they were settled and secure before we left.

Meanwhile, we were to study English with more diligence. MacDonald would help us. At first I studied alone from a textbook that had Tibetan, English, and Hindi words. While I was practicing the English grammar sounds aloud, some of our servants were not pleased. Our cook especially thought I was wasting time studying English. He said it would be far better for me to sharpen my skills in Hindi so that I would be fluent when I went on pilgrimages in the future. Because of these comments, I was uneasy practicing English at home. So Trinly Rinpoche and I took instruction from a British man at his home in Darjeeling twice a week. I learned the alphabet and some simple phrases, such as "good morning," "thank you," and other basics. I found English more difficult than Hindi because some of the sounds were hard for me to pronounce. The Tibetan language has four major tone levels, whereas English is without tones. The letters "v," "f," and "th" were especially difficult.

Meanwhile, I was growing more confident that the Rockefeller contract would work out and quietly started making future arrangements for our servants. Mrs. Thondup promised that she could place some of the servants in the Tibetan Self-Help Center, where they would have various jobs. She knew our servants to be reliable and trustworthy, and most of them were young. This took a great load off my shoulders. Earlier she had turned down such requests from several noble families and the Sakya Drolma Palace.

Every day I listened to the radio news or to the reports from newly arrived refugees about conditions in Tibet. The reports were discouraging. Now Indians did not want to exchange the Tibetan paper money we had brought out. For generations Indians and Tibetan traders had engaged in monetary exchange. Now no country wanted Tibetan currency. When we had fled Tibet, each of us carried paper money wrapped in cloth and tied at our waists along with our charm boxes. When we reached India, we could have exchanged those funds for rupees. Because the exchange rate was so low, I urged that we wait until the value rose. We had pooled our money in India and placed it in a huge wooden box in our bedroom. Every time I looked at the box, I realized there was nobody but me to blame for this mistake. If we had exchanged the money, we could have lived comfortably for a while. I had been the one who had held back in my decision about going as an exile to still another country. Now I blamed myself for having too much hope that we would take back our country. I could not bring myself to believe that my homeland was lost forever. But now I realized we would have to take chances to support ourselves in some way.

We began extra prayers and ceremonies for the fulfillment of our new project in America and for the removal of any obstacles to its success. These prayers had been made for generations and we had no doubt they would be answered to our benefit. We especially supplicated the Sakya protectors.

The sounds of chanting and instruments attracted passing Sherpas and other Tibetans who observed and gave offerings too. However, they did not know that we were going to the West. This meant that we were much busier with extra visitors who brought fruit, fresh milk and other dairy products, sweets, and money. This helped somewhat with our expenses and, of course, was of benefit to the donors. I often was busy managing these extra meals and hospitality, but sometimes I joined in the ceremonies themselves. Our landlord and his family were very devoted to the dharma and also helped prepare the meals, even though they were not participating in the ceremonies in the shrine room.

Although we had lost everything, we had not lost the freedom of religious practice, which we had fought for. I felt more secure during these months and grateful for the opportunity to benefit all sentient beings and the Tibetan cause. I felt a more personal sense of accomplishment during these times.

Every day we wondered when we would hear from Professor Wylie. One day in mid-summer, he and Professor MacDonald walked up the steps to our home. My heart was beating with excitement. I was optimistic that the grant provisions had been approved. We gathered in Dagchen Rinpoche's room, where Wylie told us that all eight of us were approved for the project if we passed the medical tests by the U. S. Department of Immigration and Naturalization. Wylie said he would begin making arrangements for the check-ups. But in my mind, I saw a huge hurdle. I was again pregnant. I thought that the University of Washington would say I could not come with the other members of the family, but would have to wait until after the birth. Should I tell Wylie about the expected newcomer? Dagchen Rinpoche said that I must.

I then went to MacDonald's hotel to tell him my problem. I felt I could confide in him. I wanted him to tell Wylie very politely about the pregnancy. MacDonald did not see any problem. Only if the medical checks were delayed until just before the birth or if there were complications in the pregnancy would there be a delay, he thought. I was greatly relieved. For weeks I had thought that we were no longer eight people but nine, fearing that this might harm the whole project. MacDonald smiled and congratulated me. He explained that the University of Washington was inviting us to work on research and that it would not intrude on our personal affairs. This encouraged me because I felt the university was not only concerned about the working men in the project, but was concerned with the entire family. MacDonald told Wylie, who said if there were no complications, everything would be okay.

Wylie arranged for appointments for the entire family with two of the best physicians in Darjeeling. Both were educated in England. One of them spoke Tibetan, and one was a woman. When we arrived at their joint offices, we were the center of attention and were welcomed as special guests. The first visit involved mostly paperwork. But at later visits we were very uneasy. For example, Uncle Tülku-la and Trinly Rinpoche had been celibate monks all of their lives and had never had their bodies examined. Their bodies also had never been touched by a woman. We were told that these examinations had to be very thorough—from head to toe—because we were the first Tibetan family to enter the United States. We had come out of the Himalayan country, spent time in a refugee camp, and finally lived in India. We also had gone on pilgrimage in India, on which we were exposed to many combinations of health problems.

Most of us had never had an injection in our lives. The older persons were the most afraid, spending the night before worrying what was going to happen to them. On the other hand, the children cried briefly, but soon forgot about the shots. The lamas in mahāyāna Buddhism, having received certain high teachings and initiations, consider their bodies a maṇḍalalike sacred temple that is not to be disturbed. They experienced not so much a fear of the needles hurting them physically, but mental anguish over this invasion of privacy. I had given blood when Ani-la was seriously ill in Sakya, so I was a better patient.

We went to these appointments together with a contingent of servants following. Some curious Tibetans in Darjeeling wondered now if we were going to another country. So we answered, "We are thinking about it."

After X-rays, shots, and blood tests, we passed the examination. One of the things the doctors looked for was tuberculosis, because thousands of Tibetans had died of this communicable disease during their first year in the resettlement camps in Assam. After we had successfully completed our medical tests, Dagchen Rinpoche said that it was time for him to approach His Holiness for permission to leave. But Wylie said that it would not be necessary for him to go to the Dalai Lama on a separate trip. Wylie said we all would leave together in about two weeks and fly to Calcutta where there would be more exams and paperwork at the American embassy. During the completion of this paperwork, Dagchen Rinpoche and Trinly Rinpoche could go to Mussoorie. Dagchen Rinpoche rejected Wylie's idea of a written notification of our trip, saying that was not respectful.

Meanwhile, I had made resettlement arrangements for those to be left behind. Our landlord kindly allowed us to continue to use many rooms for Uncle Kunsang Nyima, Ani Chimi, and some of our monk servants, at a very low rent. Mr. and Mrs. Densapa agreed to temporarily pay for the rent, a loan that we were later to pay back. Wangmo, my personal servant, and several other servants wanted to be assigned to the Self-Help Center. Mrs. Thondup kindly gave each one of them jobs.

The day we left Darjeeling was both joyous and sad. During our year's stay there, we had made many friends and gained many followers, particularly among the Sherpas. They wanted to give us a proper and respectful sendoff from our home to the station, a distance of about a mile over a paved, winding road. I believed that after three years I would return. I would miss my relatives and servants, but I regarded this as an adventure that would end in three years. Some of my friends whispered that they would see me back home in Tibet. I thought, "Oh no, they will get there before I do."

Five rickshaws and wagons arrived one beautiful September mid-morning. Usually we had clouds in the morning, but this day was sunny and magnificent. The rickshaws were ceremoniously decorated with silk cushions, draped white scarfs, and leis of marigolds. I felt deep affection for these Sherpas, who had supported us in many ways. Tenzing Norgay himself came to our rickshaws to say goodbye and present a white scarf.

I rode in a rickshaw seated between Ani-la and Mati-la. Professor Wylie was in a rickshaw too. Along the route, hundreds of people crowded the side of the road, including some Tibetans and Sherpas hoping for a last blessing from the three lamas. Tourists in profusion snapped pictures. At the station, Professor MacDonald was among the well-wishers and organizers. Many people, including myself, shed tears as we left. It was very difficult saying goodbye to Ani Chimi and Uncle Kunsang Nyima.

We never envisioned that in this life, we could travel to the other side of the world. As a child, I never dreamed of the possibility of going there. Now, I thought, "Everything is possible."

For all of our lives we had concentrated and prayed to send influences harmful to Buddhism and all sentient beings to the other side of the ocean. These evil influences then never could return to harm again, we believed. But now, we were going in that direction. It was an entirely different feeling of separation that we had not experienced before—a curious distance of mind, not time.

We headed towards Siligiri. We stopped twice en route, once at Ghoom Monastery, about eight miles from Darjeeling, where the monks had arranged the usual farewell ceremonies for the lamas. Our other stop was Sonada, another big town where we were asked to bless a Tibetan official's home. We were served lunch there.

But we could not tarry, and left for the airport. We were joined here by two other Tibetans, Nawang Nornang, a monk, and his niece, Lhadon Karsip, who also were going to the University of Washington for research collaboration. We had to wait several hours for the only flight of the day to Calcutta. Again our devoted followers said their last goodbyes in the airport. For most of us, it was our first flight. I was frightened and sensed that I could be airsick, which was correct.

We arrived in Calcutta to be housed in the Pondho Mile, a low-cost hotel in a part of the city that was in an Asian settlement that included Tibetans. We were served three meals a day with touches of Tibetan style, because the owners were of Tibetan background. The bathrooms and showers were shared. Our worst problem was adjusting to the intense heat and waiting in line for cold showers at least twice a day. I learned to tolerate the many salamanders crawling on the bathroom walls. Some other guests on the lower floors complained about mice in their rooms. We had none in our rooms, but I wouldn't have minded them nearly as much as salamanders.

As soon as we had gotten comfortable in the hotel, Dagchen Rinpoche impressed upon Professor Wylie the urgency of going to visit the Dalai Lama to inform him of our intent to be away for three years. But each time Wylie said there would be time later. Right now we were scheduled for medical tests and completion of paperwork at least every other day. Many times we went by rickshaw or taxi to the American embassy for those chores. The American doctors used a Tibetan woman interpreter to carry out their very thorough examinations of our bodies. The two monk lamas were very uneasy about exposing their bodies to both the doctors and the interpreter.

While we waited in Calcutta, we eased the boring hours with tours of the zoo and the underground New Market shopping area, where one could buy nearly everything India sells. It was the boys' first time to visit a big zoo. We saw thousands of bats sleeping in trees in the daytime and animals I had never seen before, including gorillas.

Now was the time to resolve the problem of my husband's planned visit to Mussoorie to make a final appearance before the Dalai Lama. But one afternoon Professor Wylie hurriedly informed us that the paperwork was complete and that we had to depart for America in three days.

I was relieved as were some others that the ten months of waiting was ending at last. Dagchen Rinpoche was adamant about the visit to His Holiness. Wylie said nothing could alter our plans now. The reservations were made for ten people and could not be changed. The university was waiting and we had to keep to our schedules.

Dagchen Rinpoche was very disappointed. Finally, Wylie realized how much this meant to him. Wylie seemed to calm down and explained nicely that he would immediately send a telegram to His Holiness and write a special-delivery letter explaining the situation. Wylie said he would take the blame for Dagchen Rinpoche not visiting His Holiness personally before we left. Wylie departed and the two later went to send the telegram. But Dagchen Rinpoche was still unhappy. Usually I went along with Dagchen Rinpoche and he was almost always right. But I did not want any conflicts between these two. After all, we would be together for the next three years and I didn't want us to get started on the wrong foot.

I reasoned, saying that His Holiness no doubt would understand because Dagchen Rinpoche had done all he possibly could. He had written from Darjeeling announcing his resignation as a representative of the Sakya school. And as soon as we had arrived in Calcutta, he had written to His Holiness and the Kashag that he was going on the Rockefeller project and that he would come to visit His Holiness to receive his blessing and advice. I said that in the past my husband always had shown deep respect for the Dalai Lama and the Tibetan government and had carried out government orders to the letter. Sometimes he had even put government matters before his family. I suggested we put Wylie at ease and accept what had happened.

While in Calcutta, we had made many friends, including our landlord's mother. Her servant had helped us with laundry and other chores while we had stayed at the hotel. She worried that we wouldn't survive for three years in America with three small children and no servants. She was in tears. But I was not fearful. We had survived the flight from Tibet across the Himalayas. We had learned to live as refugees in a strange country. We had endured the heat of Calcutta. I thought that as long as we were together we could make it through. Now everybody had a place. The servants were taken care of, as were Uncle Kunsang Nyima and Ani Chimi. We had our freedom and also were free to practice Buddhism. The upcoming lack of servants in America seemed unimportant.

Professor Wylie had advised us to take enough Tibetan clothes to last for three years. We had many garments made by a Tibetan tailor in Kalimpong. I certainly did not envision wearing Western clothes. We had packed our most important religious items. Rimshi Surkhang, a Lhasa noble who had been to America earlier, informed me not to worry. "Machines will do everything for you," he said. "A machine will keep your food cold and fresh. A machine will cook for you. A machine will wash and dry your clothes. A machine will clean the floors of your house. And wherever you go in buildings and stores, a machine will take you up and down so that you don't have to walk steps." I was anxious to see if this kind of life he had described was really true.

Early one October morning, we prepared to board a Pan American jetliner at Calcutta airport. We didn't have to worry about a thing, but Professor Wylie bore the responsibility for ten of us for everything from seating to luggage and even directing us to washrooms. Our loyal Tibetan friends were in the farewell party for the first Tibetan group to go to America on a research assignment. Hundreds of Indians were among the spectators, along with photographers and news reporters covering the event.

As for me, I felt relieved to be finished with the seemingly endless paperwork and red tape. In the airplane, I glanced over at Wylie and saw that his face, too, reflected relief. In the airport, dozens of Tibetans had rushed up to him with thanks, saying "Please take good care of our lama." My memory is vivid of the airport scene where short Tibetans tried to reach up to the tall Wylie to place offering scarfs over his head and onto his shoulders. Once seated in the plane, he unloaded a great number of the scarfs. Starch from them lay like dust on his new suit jacket.

We were on our way to adventure in the West.

Epilogue

The white scarfs that had signaled farewell to the travelers in India were replaced by welcome leis in Hawaii and intense media attention as the Tibetans stepped off a jetliner in Seattle. The arrival of what was believed to be the first Tibetan family to come to the United States—under the mantle of scholarly research about their homeland—attracted wide attention.

As the family settled down to life on the rim of academia, they had assistance in adjusting to American culture from graduate student Gene Smith, who lived in their home. Smith, who was majoring in Tibetan studies, got first-hand information and even sometimes shock waves. One day he brought home expensive steak for an intended feast, only to find that the Tibetans later had sliced the choice cuts into minute pieces for stirfry with vegetables!

The birth of the Sakyas' fourth son in January, 1961, was historic. Gyalway Dorje Sakya ("Victorious Thunderbolt") was the first Tibetan child to be born in America.

The new mother, who had delivered her other children in Tibet herself, now was under the round-the-clock care of doctors and nurses in a research hospital carrying out the latest obstetrical techniques.

"It was shocking to see the doctor shake and spank a fragile infant," she recalls, now with good humor.

One year later a photograph of the baby seated before a birthday cake in a fox-fur-trimmed hat and other baby lama's attire was distributed internationally by a wire service. Even the arrival of a pet Lhasa Apso was news.

Jamyang Sakya became accustomed to seeing the three lamas depart for work on the University of Washington campus with briefcases. She found a true friend and mentor in Edna Georgeson, a former teacher, who instructed her in English and gave other tips invaluable to her adjustment in America. When they made an appearance at the exclusive Women's University Club, Jamyang learned a new word. "What means charming?" she asked Georgeson after the talk, having heard the reaction of some in her audience.

The fifth and last son, Legpa Dorje Sakya, ("Unerring Thunderbolt"), was born in September, 1962.

When the Rockefeller Foundation grant was over, the family realized that Tibet still was not free and they could not go home. Not wishing to return to India, they sought to become permanent residents of the United States.

Meanwhile, Jamyang, with Smith's help, began what became a career at the Puget Sound Blood Center, as a laboratory technician. Several years earlier, she, with great trepidation, had given blood when little Ani-la was gravely ill in Sakya. Now she learned firsthand about blood groups, such things as the Rh factor, and other vital components of blood.

Permanent-residency status was granted the family members in 1966, guaranteeing their future in America. But they never gave up the hope that Tibet would be freed from its Chinese domination and that someday they would be back in their homeland. Their case opened the door to easier immigration for other Tibetans. They learned that Americans were very generous, as they were given furniture, toys and household items that cushioned their lifestyles in the postgrant period. They became United States citizens in 1974.

Still there was a great void in their lives. They had a family shrine room in their home, but there was no monastery or Buddhist center. In 1974, after great struggle, a center, the Sakya Tegchen Chöling, was founded. Soon after, it was robbed twice, but the religious images, books, and offering cups were untouched. The center since has moved twice and now is a permanent monastery in northwest Seattle.

Jamyang and her youngest son, Legpa Dorje, known as Sadu-la, visited Tibet in 1986, viewing the sites of the now-destroyed Phuntsok and Drolma Palaces and the centuries-old temples of the North Sakya Monastery and its winter palace. She knew that her mother and Aunt Chacha had died in a Chinese prison in Lhasa, but her attempts to learn more details of their deaths were unsuccessful. Chinese officials repeatedly refused to cooperate. But they said that during the Chinese Cultural Revolution, tens of thousands of Tibetans were killed and buried in common graves. Since then, military camps, hospitals, and factories had been built on those grave sites.

After seeing the devastation and domination of her homeland, she realized that the United States was her true home. Before she had referred to it as her second home.

In recent years, she has traveled widely in Europe, Taiwan, India, Nepal, and Canada.

Julie Emery